WOMAN IN INDIA

WOMAN IN INDIA

BY

MARY FRANCES BILLINGTON.

WITH INTRODUCTION

BY THE

MARCHIONESS OF DUFFERIN AND AVA, C.I.

FRONTISPIECE BY REGINALD CLEAVER:
ILLUSTRATIONS BY HERBERT JOHNSON AND FROM
ORIGINAL PHOTOGRAPHS.

GYAN

Published by

GYAN

Gyan Publishing House
5, Ansari Road
Daryaganj, New Delhi-110002
Phone: 011-47034999, 9811692060
E-mail: books@gyanbooks.com

Distribution Network
gyanbooks.com
India, USA, Canada, UK, Australia, France

ISBN : 978-81-212-2414-7 (PB)
First Published, 1895

2nd Impression 2021

Printed at: Gyan Press, Delhi.

Woman in India
Author: Mary Frances Billington

WOMAN IN INDIA

BY

MARY FRANCES BILLINGTON.

WITH INTRODUCTION

BY THE

MARCHIONESS OF DUFFERIN AND AVA, C.I.

FRONTISPIECE BY REGINALD CLEAVER:
ILLUSTRATIONS BY HERBERT JOHNSON AND FROM
ORIGINAL PHOTOGRAPHS.

LONDON: CHAPMAN & HALL, LD.

1895.

MARY FRANCES BILLINGTON.

TO

HER ROYAL HIGHNESS

THE DUCHESS OF CONNAUGHT,

WHOSE SISTERLY SYMPATHY WITH THE WOMEN OF INDIA,

AND DEEP INTEREST IN EVERY EFFORT FOR THEIR WELFARE,

HAVE WON FOR HER

THE SWEET RECOMPENSE OF THEIR LASTING GRATITUDE AND AFFECTION,

THIS BOOK

IS, WITH GRACIOUS PERMISSION,

DEDICATED

BY

HER ROYAL HIGHNESS'S

MOST OBEDIENT, HUMBLE SERVANT,

MARY FRANCES BILLINGTON.

"Respect, kind treatment, and everything that is agreeable, should all be given to the maiden whose hand is taken in marriage. Her sire and brothers and father-in-law and husband's brothers should show her every respect, and adorn her with ornaments, if they be desirous of reaping benefits, for such conduct on their part always leads to considerable happiness and advantage. Women, O King, should always be worshipped and treated with affection. There, where women are treated with respect, the very deities are said to be filled with joy. There, where women are not worshipped, all acts become fruitless. . . . Women deserve to be honoured. Do ye men show them honour! The righteousness of men depends upon women. All pleasures and enjoyments also completely depend upon them. Do ye serve and worship them. Do ye bend your wills before them. The begetting of offspring, the nursing of children already born, and the accomplishment of all acts necessary for the needs of society, behold all these have women for their cause. By honouring women ye are sure to attain to the fruition of all objects!"—*Mahabharata—Anucasanika Parva.* Prose rendering by PRETAPA CHANDRA RÂY, C.I.E.

INTRODUCTION.

INFORMATION upon the subject of this book is very often sought for, and it is very difficult to find.

Missionary magazines give glimpses here and there of the thoughts and feelings and homes of the "Women of India;" persons interested in their education tell us of the schools that exist or do not exist for them; those devoted to the hospital question dilate upon the errors of native medicine, and the want of proper attendance and accommodation for women in sickness; while people of taste, and with a love of art, tell us of the beautiful dresses, the Oriental colouring, and, alas! of the corruption of native taste by European models.

Some books give us lives of distinguished Indian women, and show us how talent will make its way through every obstacle; others appeal to our sympathy with tales of woe; we weep with the writers over the unhappy child-widow, or grieve at the strict rules of the purdah; but it requires time and patience to find and to look through all the tracts, magazines, and publications that deal with these subjects separately, and it is a satisfaction to find one volume in which an attempt is made to trace the career of Indian women from the cradle to the grave, and to give some account of their customs, their occupations, their pleasures, their religion, and their dress.

Specialists and academical students of Indian lore will not expect to find in so small a compass all the data they require; they must naturally dig deeper, and make more profound researches into dictionaries and encyclopædias for the knowledge which they seek. A work of this kind does not pretend to exhaust the subject with which it deals, or to settle the many questions referred to in its pages, and the writer of this one would probably be the first to admit that there are nooks and crannies in the vast continent of India which she has been unable to explore, curious customs which she has not discovered, mines of information which she has not reached. Even so, the labour of collecting the material for this book must have been immense, and it is bewildering even to think of a stranger setting foot in India for the first time, with such a task before her; new languages, different populations, varied religions, multifarious customs, meeting her at every turn; information, true and false, offered her with equal readiness; partisans, fanatics, faddists, and legitimate enthusiasts all airing their pet theories for her benefit. What courage, what industry, what quick perception and calmness of judgment, must have been needed to carry her over so many obstacles! That she has surmounted them is proved by this charmingly written book, full of carefully sifted facts and of fresh observation. Every chapter of it shows what pains have been taken to obtain trustworthy information, to investigate every question, and to approach each one of them with an open mind and in an impartial spirit. Indeed, the judicial character of the author's remarks may cause the advocates of particular views, and especially those who interest themselves in religious or philanthropic questions in India, to be conscious of a certain want of enthusiasm in her appreciation of their work; nor can they be expected to endorse all her opinions, or to accept, without demur, her rapidly drawn conclusions upon matters which are to them of vital import. It is not, however, entirely without advantage that the cold judgment of a strange inquirer should occasionally be brought to bear upon such efforts. Criticism is a great stimulus to improvement, and if, in this case, a momentary feeling of discouragement be engendered in the hearts of some ardent workers by the severely candid observations of the author, it will surely be succeeded by a reaction in favour of renewed hopefulness and more determined effort.

The facilities of travel, and the quick transmission of news, have brought India very near to us, and every day greater and more intelligent interest is taken in her affairs and in her people; while the social condition and the "rights" of women all over the world occupy the attention of many thoughtful minds. This book will therefore be welcome to a large number of readers, who will not demand from it either finality or infallibility, but who will be grateful to the author for providing them with so much varied and useful information in so succinct and agreeable a form, and who will rise from its perusal with stimulated interest in the great Empire of India, with increased sympathy for its people, and some of them, perhaps, with a new-born desire and a real intention to aid, to the best of their ability, those many efforts which are being made to promote the moral and physical welfare of the women of India.

HARIOT DUFFERIN AND AVA.

AUTHOR'S PREFACE.

It has been my privilege to have been a member of the staff of the *Daily Graphic* since its foundation, and in that capacity I have frequently been permitted to offer suggestions for editorial consideration upon matters of feminine interest. Early in 1893 it occurred to me that very little effort had been made to show in succinct form to English newspaper readers what had been accomplished and was being attempted by the various religious, educational, medical, and social agencies at work among the women of India; and when I laid the idea, in all diffidence, I admit, before the Editor of the *Graphic* and *Daily Graphic*, he quite concurred in my own view that a wide field of indisputable importance had been practically untouched. I, however, had but a bare skeleton to submit to him. This he elaborated and worked out in detail; and while planning on my behalf a thoroughly comprehensive tour, which should enable me to see as many representative phases of the country as possible, allowed me at the same time a pleasant freedom as to the range of my travels, and complete liberty as to the choice of subjects for my letters. Of these, I contributed some twenty-eight, which dealt with many divers aspects and conditions of female life in India, to the columns of the *Daily Graphic*.

India in many respects has been written upon exhaustively; yet, on the other hand, it is so vast an area, its problems are of such supreme Imperial moment, and its population presents such wide racial variations, that it seems well-nigh impossible for the final word to be said concerning it. Of its women especially, in their inner life and thought, only the most superficial knowledge exists. Few, very few, of the thousands of English women who go to the East have cared or tried to penetrate the mysteries which lie beyond the *purdah.* Few of the very few who have done so have seen it without prejudice. In this, perhaps, my newspaper training stood me in good stead, as it enabled me to grasp facts first and draw conclusions afterwards.

I do not profess to offer a sensational book, nor have I a record of cruelty, misery, oppression, or intrigue, with which to fill my pages. In spite of countless speeches, agitations, and missionary reports, woman in the social economy of the East by no means—

> ". . . fades from view,
> A cypher of man's changeless sum
> Of lust past, present, and to come;"

and life as I saw it in the zenanas was simply rather dull, rather prosaic, with few distinctive features of romance, hardship, or heroism about it. Yet it would be unfair to classify it as wholly colourless, as absolutely unspiritualized. Family affection enters strongly into it, and even as with ourselves blood brotherhood is a binding tie among Hindus and Mahommedans, Non-Aryans and Parsees. After all, the primal elements of human nature do not greatly vary the world over. And so I have merely tried to tell the truth, and to describe the life as it really is, with its domestic interests, its social customs, and perhaps sometimes unreasoning prejudices. The longer I was away from home the more fully did I appreciate the spirit of that line :—

> "What should they know of England who only England know ?"

And if I can only convince some of those who vote away blithely, in a confidence profound as their ignorance, upon matters which are grave as issues of life and death to our Eastern fellow-subjects of the Crown, that Indian women are not altogether in such pitiful plight as some of their so-called friends come and tell us, my inquiries will not have been made in vain.

I would here take the opportunity of expressing my sincere thanks to the Proprietors and Editor of the *Graphic* and *Daily Graphic*, who have not only waived all copyright claims alike upon my literary contributions and illustrations, but concerning the latter have lent every possible assistance towards their reproduction here. To the Editor of the *Gentlewoman* also I am much indebted for the use of a number of pictures from my own photographs, which appeared to illustrate some articles on my travels for girls' reading which I contributed by permission to his pages. Mr. Syed A. M. Shah, barrister-at-law, Lincoln's Inn, claims, too, a word of recognition for the trouble he took to transcribe on my behalf certain Muslim statutes concerning the legal rights of Mahommedan women. To Sir George Birdwood, K.C.I.E., and other gentlemen at the India Office my warm gratitude for many acts of more than official courtesy is due; and, finally, I would like to testify how deep are my obligations to the Marchioness of Dufferin and Ava, C.I., for her wise advice before starting, and subsequent gracious approval.

M. F. B.

MILFORD HOUSE, STRAND,
November, 1894.

CONTENTS.

LIST OF ILLUSTRATIONS.

WOMAN IN INDIA.

CHAPTER I.

HER BIRTH AND INFANCY.

"May I, as I increase in this my house nourish a thousand. May fortune never fail in his race with offspring and cattle. Thou strong woman hast borne a strong boy. Be thou blessed with strong children, thou who hast blessed me with a strong child. And they say of such a boy, 'Ah, thou art better than thy father, ah, thou art better than thy grandfather.' Truly he has reached the highest point in happiness, praise, and Vedic glory who is born as the son of a brahmana that knows this."—*Brihadâsanyaka Upanishad.*

THE Indian child, whether boy or girl, may be said to come into the world amid a cloud of strange superstitions, and for the latter there will be no loving welcome from parents or grandparents. For weeks before the mother and mother-in-law have toilsomely observed every mystic ordinance which should propitiate the divine powers to bestow a little son; they have wreathed flowers at every auspicious shrine, they have lit lamps, they have burned spices, and when after all the tiny girl has come into the world, it seems in the gloom of the zenana, where the doors are jealously closed and the atmosphere is heavy with the stifling fire that must be incessantly burnt, in order to exclude the evil spirits which might exercise a baleful influence upon the child's future, that the gods are angry, and it is the poor young mother who has offended their majestic wrath.

Still, there is a little progress to be recorded in the

native mental attitude even on this point. Time was, and not so very far back either, when it was regarded as quite justifiable to end a baby girl's unwanted life by some such summary process as strangling. Upon that view advancement has assuredly been made, though still even, if the little one die, her little body is often thought not worth the expense of burning, and, with incantations and charms, it is carried out by some of the women folk to the jungle, where it is left to jackals and carrion birds with the words—

> **"Thus we drive you forth, O daughter!**
> **Come not back, but send a brother."**

That infant mortality is very high, is not on account of evil intent, but is due to the appalling ignorance of the *dhais*, the professional class of midwives or monthly nurses, whose methods of treatment are simply barbarous, and, indeed, viewed in the light of our western scientific knowledge, seem as if they would be enough to kill every unfortunate victim upon whom they were practised.

In an Indian house of any pretensions to being anything more than a mere hovel, the women's quarters, known to us as the zenana, and in colloquial Hindustani as the *bibi-ghar*, are always, architecturally and artistically, its meanest part. In one of its poorest and remotest apartments the poor woman will wait her hours of trial, while outside the door symbolic foliage and flowers will be twined. To these, the Hindus of the north-west add a swinging sickle, the sharp edge outwards, as a barrier against malignant demons, while as night comes down, and the feeble flicker of the rank-smelling cocoanut oil-lamps and the birth-fire kindled inside the close chamber penetrates the outer gloom, the other women move about with quick noiseless tread, and stand chattering to one another in eager curiosity.

"Only a girl, after all!" Prayers, offerings, pilgrimages, have been of no avail; but it seems like a sturdy little life, and there is much talk about the omens with which its birth was surrounded, for these are all-important. If the baby's ears first heard pleasant sounds, if its eyes rested upon white things, or such objects as rice, flowers, fruits or honey, or if crows or pigeons flew over the room from left to right, the signs were propitious, and some of the disappointment would be mitigated. If, on the other hand, a snake or monkey crossed the road, or a vehicle went by carrying a cot or stool with the legs upwards, or flowers associated with funeral observances were brought into the house, then life would seem to promise little worth having for the youthful arrival. An astrologer, too, must be consulted among many tribes and castes, who will foretell from the stars, and there is a fixed rate quite understood among all classes for his fee.

Not only the women of the household, but friends and relations from far and near come to visit the mother, crowding into the close little room which is often kept at such a degree of heat that existence must be well-nigh unendurable. This is not only due to the absence of ventilation, for which, as a rule, scarcely the slightest provision is made, but on account of a belief that whenever the child cries more fuel must be put upon the fire. Observances like this, however, are regarded not merely as sanitary, but as religious obligations, and accordingly many of the *dhais*, who may be classed as true Oriental prototypes of the late Mrs. Sarah Gamp, alike in ignorance, cruelty, and avarice, will often stop in the performance of necessary offices to haggle for higher payment than was bargained for, and will refuse to proceed with their duties until a guarantee has been given them that their exorbitant demands shall be satisfied. These and many more practices, which would be criminal were they not sanctioned by long custom, prevail throughout India, and are common to almost every creed and class. They are the broad outlines of the picture which touched the heart of the Marchioness of Dufferin and Ava, as they go straight to the sympathies and feelings of every other woman, and to recognize them at the outset of any effort to understand the conditions of woman's life in India, gives a degree at least of respect for the gentle fortitude that, in my opinion, is one of the most admirable traits in the native female character.

In minor details birth customs, however, are diverse as the tribes, sects, and septs of the dependency. In North Malabar, where a proportion of the population are Karavas, the woman is taken to a shed at some distance from the house, and is left absolutely unaided for twenty-eight days. Even her medicines are thrown to her, and beyond placing a jar of warm water near her about the expected hours of delivery nothing whatever is done for her. Ideas as to pollution from birth I found very strongly held all along the Western shores of India, and, in fact, worse uncleanness was supposed to be conveyed by it than from the touch of death itself. To trace the customs of isolation of the mother, and the still more curious one which also obtains of regarding the father as also impure for fourteen days, only to be freed at the end of that time from his defilement by holy water supplied by Brahmins from temples or consecrated tanks, would be a study well worth undertaking; but, for my own part, I think that some of the exceeding severity of convention in the matter here is clearly traceable to Jewish influence. At Cochin, long a great centre of industry, commerce, power, and fighting, are to be found two colonies, side by side, of black and white Jews. The origin of their respective settlements there is lost in dim antiquity, though it is the tradition of the latter that they are descended from those who came out with King Solomon's fleets, that "navy of Tharshish," which brought "gold, and silver, ivory, and apes, and peacocks." The Jew of to-day makes his personality felt in any community, and even though these Cochinese representatives of the Chosen People have a far more recent birthright in India than the one they claim, there is at least a sufficient community of practice to give one grounds for the belief that modern Malabar systems found their source in ancient Hebraic ordinances.

The participation of the father in the mother's uncleanness is not confined to the West Coast. It is found among the Kols of Eastern Bengal, though the paternal disability with them only lasts for a clear week, during which time the man has to cook for and wait upon his wife. With the Goalas, the great pastoral caste of the dependency, the father for three weeks is not regarded as eligible for his usual vocations. With these people, the expectant mother is put into a separate house, which is heated highly and kept closely shut, while certain symbolic plants and foliage are hung about the door, and the newly born infant is bathed in water in which other leaves and seeds have been boiled. Among the Rautias, whose legendary extraction is from Ceylon, but who are probably a degraded offshoot of the proud Rajput race, the richer a man is the longer is he unclean. While the middle classes can be purified about the twelfth day, a really wealthy man may have to wait for twenty-one days, or even longer, to be pronounced cleansed.

Among the Hindus the most important person in the birth ceremonials, after the *dhai* herself, is the barber. These form a caste to themselves, known in Bengal as the *Napit*, and standing socially in a good position. He is the first male, after her husband, to see a woman after her confinement, and he has to pare her nails on the day that this has taken place, repeating this operation on the ninth and thirtieth days after. Should the baby be troubled by fits or convulsions, he will be consulted, his method of cure being usually by spells and incantations. For the nail-paring, his poor neighbours know that he has a fixed charge of two or three pice, but from his richer patrons he looks for a larger fee, often receiving as much as a rupee and a piece of cloth, besides further doles of rice, salt, and spice.

The Muslims have a curious usage, which they call *thikra*, for which all the female relations of the prospective mother come to the house. Should the newly born baby prove to be a girl, it is optional for any one of these relatives, who may chance to have a son of her own, to slip a rupee or more into a small earthen pot called a *thikra*, where it becomes the perquisite of the *dhai*, and she who succeeds in doing this first has secured the first right in later life to the little girl as a wife for her own boy. The word itself, I should explain, is scarcely ever heard outside the zenana, and is one that men never employ. *Purdah nashin* ladies have, however, almost a language of their own in the *chota boli* that they talk to their children or to one another. One soon learns the long drawn out "*oui-i-i*" of assent or exclamation, but it is a little puzzling to the ordinary student of Hindustani, whether this has been studied under a tutor and with books and paper in London or picked up from the everyday talk to be heard around, to find that even the names of the months have synonyms peculiar to feminine phrase. In women's lips, the eleventh month of the Mahommedan year (*Zikād*) becomes *Thāli*, or "empty," it being the month that comes between the religious fast and feast of *Shawwal* and the rejoicings of *hijja*, and similarly the second month, *Safas*, is changed to *Terah tizi*, from a superstitious belief in the ill luck of its opening fortnight. A child born during those days is believed to be doomed to a life of misfortune, and save upon the direst emergency no wedding or family festivity is ever held upon them.

The first ceremony in the child's life is, so far as I could see and ascertain, common to both Hindus and Mahommedans, and is called *chatthi*, when the mother eats meat for the first time. The child, too, receives its name, though this is often changed or added to in later life. Most, if not all, of the names given have some special meaning, as "Khurshad Begum," "Queen of the Sun," or "Chandebi," "Daughter of the Moon," among the Mahommedans, unless they adopt such designations as Fatma Begum, Khudaeja Bee, or Aesha-Bee, to perpetuate the feminine names in the family of the prophet; Miriam Bee is another favourite name. Popular Hindu names are Motibai, Tanki, Munna, Kumari, and Ramabai, the suffix *bibi* being often added in colloquial use.

Among many Hindu castes the actual birth ceremonies terminate with *Ekaisi*, or the twenty-first day; but with the Mahommedans *Chila* is the fortieth day, when the mother washes and the child has its head shaved. Feasting and amusement often enters into this, but there are several curious rites common to certain castes and sects, such as *Kua Jhankna*, or peeping into the well of the Mussulman women, which, so far as I could gather, was a kind of consultation of the oracle, while the Hindus daub red lead upon the well itself. The whole house usually undergoes a thorough cleaning or purification, and life then resumes the even tenour of its way.

Thus, with so much of strange custom and profound superstition, it is not a matter for wonder that lying-in hospitals should have been somewhat slow in winning the support of the native women. Still they have made great progress within the last few years, and those of the presidency towns, supported by Government, are generally well filled by women of the working classes. Among the foremost of these the Eden at Calcutta claims a place, not alone for the admirable accommodation it gives to all women in their hours of greatest need, but for its work as a training school for *dhais* or native midwives. Free instruction is given here as well as pecuniary assistance towards maintenance while under tuition, and the work is taken up by Hindu as well as native Christian women. The services of these trained *dhais* are finding satisfactory appreciation by those for whose benefit they are intended, and probably through them the way will be paved for a fuller recognition of the value of qualified medical help. Sister Muriel, of Clewer, is chief hospital directress, and neither in the native nor Eurasian wards does one often find a bed vacant, while the health statistics concerning mothers and infants—always a crucial test of the management of a hospital of this class—are notably good. This point is of especial interest here on account of the high ratio of difficult cases that it receives.

Besides owning a fine State-supported hospital of this class, where Surgeon-Colonel Branfoot has rendered useful encouragement to Eurasians desiring to qualify as monthly nurses, Madras, through the generosity of Sir Savalay Ramasawmy, K.C.I.E., has been endowed with one of the best institutions of this class to be found in all India. It was opened by the Duke of Buckingham in 1880, and so well were caste scruples and customs respected that, although women of high caste would usually have died rather than enter a public institution, as many as a hundred and fifty resorted to it during its first year of existence. The Hindu women of Southern India, unlike the Mahommedans, do not regard it as a fatal sin to be seen or attended by a man, and the hospital was accordingly placed under the direction of Surgeon-Colonel Cook, whose kindliness and skill rapidly won for him the deepest gratitude of the native women, who, as the

A WARD OF SIR SAVALAY RAMASAWMY'S HOSPITAL.

repute of the institution spread, came from great distances to benefit by it. By 1887 another ward became necessary, and this Sir Savalay Ramasawmy added as his personal offering in commemoration of the Queen-Empress's Jubilee. Yet another ward was wanted, and this its generous founder gave in honour of the visit paid to, and satisfaction expressed at, the hospital by the late Duke of Clarence and Avondale.

Year by year the numbers who have benefited by its treatment have increased, and up to the day of my visit in November, 718 patients had passed through its wards—an increase of 120 upon the corresponding date of last year. Very homelike and orderly are the wards, which contain accommodation for thirty-two patients, with their comfortable spring beds, pretty chintz-printed coverlets, and distempered walls, while bouquets of beautiful tropical flowers show a greater attention to comfort than is usual in an Indian hospital. The staff of the hospital, under Surgeon-Colonel Cook, comprises his assistant, Mr. Wynn, the matron, Mrs. Kelly, who holds very high certificates of nursing skill, two Eurasian and one native nurses, and six Dufferin nursing scholars, who retain their native form of dress, but have made it smartly uniform by wearing little red jackets over their shoulders, and the white linen sari bordered with dark green. Ample space and perfect ventilation are secured to each patient, while a salutary rule, considering the malnutrition of many Indian working-class mothers, and the extreme youth of others (one or two girl-wives of only fourteen have been in its wards), enjoins that each woman shall spend a fortnight at the hospital before her confinement is expected. In numerous other small details the institution shows evidence of the most thoughtful care, while Lady Ramasawmy herself takes care that every little new arrival shall find a sufficient supply of suitable clothing ready for it, and does much of this work with her own hands.

At Bombay, again, there are those notably good institutions of this class, the Motabai, under charge of Sister Gertrude Anna, being the largest. This forms a section of the great aggregate of homes of healing known collectively as the Sir Jamsetjee Jeejeebhoy's Hospital. Then there is the Cama Hospital, to which is allied the Allbless Hospital for obstetrics, the two together providing accommodation for about a hundred patients.

The buildings of the two institutions form a handsome pile, and were both erected through Parsee munificence. Inside the wards are bright, lofty, and airy, with easily cleaned encaustic tile floors and distempered walls. To this Miss Annette Benson, who formerly held a public appointment under the London County Council, has lately been sent by the Secretary of State for India, as this is a Government recognized institution. She is assisted by Miss Cama, a young Parsee lady, who has lately returned from England after a course of study at home marked by much success. On account partly perhaps of its name and associations, it numbers a rather large percentage of Parsee women among its patients, but its advantages are sought much also by the Hindus, some even of high caste entering its wards, and in rather rarer instances still by Mahommedans.

In these hospitals the training of midwives holds a most important place, and it is very satisfactory to know, in connection with the Allbless department, that really progressive steps are being made. In its first year of work (1887) only two pupils, and those both Europeans, presented themselves for instruction, and at the present moment it has sixteen upon its rolls, of whom two are Brahmins, two Marathis, two of other good Hindu castes, and one of the Rajput race. In 1893 certificates of efficiency were granted to nine nurses, and further gratifying evidences of advance are shown in the facts that although the period of instruction has been recently extended from one year to eighteen months, and with it a higher level of merit in examination has been demanded, the change has not deterred pupils from entering;

while formerly the National Association of the Countess of Dufferin's Fund had to bear almost all the cost of feeding, and even clothing, the nurse pupils, the maintenance fees are now almost entirely met and defrayed by the nurses or their friends. These fees amount in the case of native nurses to twenty rupees a month—a high figure for an Indian woman's support—and examinations are held each six months to test the progress made. The three last months are devoted to instruction in midwifery, and it is with the help of a knowledge of this branch of medical science that the truest progress towards wiser methods of treatment in other directions will be made. That the women find good scope after training is shown by the fact that out of the eighty or so who have passed through its school, only some half a dozen have abandoned their career, while the rest who have persevered are to be found practising at distant stations and remote villages, or holding positions in civil or Dufferin hospitals. Among those who passed out certificated last year was a young African woman, one of two rescued from an Arab slave dhow, who is taking the knowledge she acquired to Mombasa. The other saved at the same time entered with her, but unfortunately never recovered fully from the misery and privations she had had to endure, and died ere her course of study was completed.

Besides these, there is a strictly Parsee lying-in hospital, which was founded to combat certain unnecessary superstitions and rites which had grown up concerning birth, and to bring about a more hygienic and common-sense course of treatment. In this it is proving successful, as, however, one would expect as one sees that within the past five and twenty years or so the ladies, as well as the humbler classes of this race, have made progress towards Western ways and customs that is little short of remarkable, especially in comparison with the intensely gradual advances of the people surrounding them.

So much, very briefly sketched, both for native theories and practices in ushering a child into the world, as well as for some of the more important efforts that British influence has provided to ameliorate these trying hours of a woman's life. To bear a son has been, of course, the girl-mother's highest hope, and great indeed is her joy if the new little arrival proves to be a boy. It enhances immeasurably the importance of her position in the eyes of the family, and though she may have been a poor little household drudge before, the Cinderella to her older sisters-in-law, she rises at a bound to a factor of consideration in her circle. If, however, the first-born is only a girl, there is far less satisfaction. Looking into the far future, the family see that she must be endowed with money and jewels, that a husband of her own caste and status will have to be found for her, and that at present the father is not assured of the son whom he regards as essential to the carrying on after him of religious obligations. But it is better to bring daughters into existence than to be childless. That to an Indian woman, whether Hindu or Mahommedan, is the cruelest of all curses, and I shall never forget the piteous look of agonized disappointment with which a young Santal woman of about twenty, who had been five years married, turned away to avoid telling me the, to her humiliating, truth, in answer to my inadvertent question, how many children she had.

Certain deities of the Hindu Pantheon are supposed to be susceptible to the prayers of barren women, who, to invoke the desired blessing of fruitfulness, will often make long and painful and costly pilgrimages to special shrines. The Seven Pagodas, between Madras and Masulipatam, are a particularly favoured place for this purpose, and I have heard Southern Indian women aver that auspicious results very frequently follow. But the rites and ceremonies that take place there are, according to all accounts, of a somewhat tantric or phallic character, and it is perhaps best not to inquire too closely into the details of the sacrifices that have to be offered. On the banks of the Ganges, too, at Benares, close to the Nepaul Temple and the Burning Ghat, there is a huge recumbent figure of the god Bhim, which is believed at particular seasons to possess peculiar virtues in this direction. At these times women, young and comparatively middle-aged, will come hundreds of miles to implore the earnestly desired boon, making offerings of oils, spices, and flowers. Very quaint and pretty are the baskets which the women use in all their ceremonials associated with Mother Ganga and her shores. They are of brass-work, made quite round, with the sides charmingly cut or fretted. On either side of the handle there is a tiny cup to contain the more precious gifts of spice and oils to be bestowed. There are many other resorts in different parts of the dependency which are believed to possess this same efficacy, and to them in all faith, and with much preliminary preparation of fasting and devotion, hundreds, even thousands, yearly make journey.

It is not difficult to understand the Hindu or Mahommedan woman's intense desire for motherhood. There is every possible influence directed to foster her innate sentiments, for one of the first of her life's lessons is that child-bearing is her chief purpose in the world. It has religious advantages to her, and removes, according to Brahmanical ideas, some of the disabilities attaching to her in the future state as a mere woman. Strongest, however, of all forces in quickening the passion for maternity is that should she, after a few years of wedded life, prove unfruitful, her husband is considered, even in the most civilized castes, fully justified in taking to himself another wife.

There are many tribes and sub-castes who prohibit polygamy under penalty of loss of caste or caste expulsion, as,

NATIVE WOMEN TAKING OFFERINGS TO MOTHER GANGA AT BENARES.

for instance, the Agarwals, the Baruis (the growers, by the way, of betel for chewing), the Binds (an agricultural and Hinduized non-Aryan tribe), the Kumhars (the potter caste of Bengal), and the Nagars of Bhagalpur, among many more. Others there are who nominally permit polygamy in theory, but never bring it into practice unless the first wife proves childless ; while with the whole Mussulman race, whose religious prohibitions allow to a man "not more" than four wives at once, it is quite the exception to find any zenanas where there is a plurality save for this reason. In fact, at Calcutta, where one branch of the Church of England Zenana Mission has devoted far more, and more personal, pains than usual to learning the conditions and winning the friendly confidence of the Mahommedan population, I only heard of one case where there were two wives, and these ladies I was taken to visit, under the impression that, like the majority of travellers out from England, I should not be satisfied that I had seen genuine native life unless it was shown me under a polygamous aspect!

The childless woman is, moreover, looked upon with feelings that are, if possible, more painfully humiliating to her than those of her Western prototype, who also, in the humbler orders, endures more than a little of stinging suffering through the not always nice or refined commentaries of her neighbours. In the East there is the added misery of the idea of directly divine wrath visiting itself in this calamity, which may extend itself further through her to the rest of the household. Then her cup of contumely and sorrow is full, if she finds herself not only dethroned from incontested wifely dignity, but her rival also bears the desired heir, and one hardly wonders if at the end she terminates a life which, according to all she has been taught, is a terrible failure, by charcoal fumes, or hanging, or drowning.

Happily for the individual, sterility in the native women is comparatively much rarer than it is in the more artificially living nations of Europe. To quote an official authority: "There is an abnormally high birth rate, not due to the youth of the married couples, or to their fertility, so much as to the great prevalence of marriage. . . . This rate amounts to between forty-four and fifty per mille, and may be attributed to the encouragement given to marriage first by the religious idea that a son is necessary to the spiritual welfare of the deceased after death, and still more by the fact that in a

THREE GENERATIONS.

society organized as is that of India, a wife so far from being an additional burden on the resources of the household, directly or indirectly adds to them." It may be remembered, too, that a very appreciable ratio of women of the child-bearing age, among the middle and upper classes, as widows, are not adding to the high birth-rate, and certainly, from all that I saw and heard, the numbers who have failed to increase the population by at least one or two is relatively a very small one. Ovarian disease and internal injuries, attributable to unduly early marriage, tend, however, to keep families smaller than might be imagined, when it is remembered that no time is lost, as with ourselves, in beginning the obligations of maternity. This last is an article of the *istri-a-char*, the unwritten but binding woman's code. The men know its existence, and the wiser among them recognize how futile it is to attempt to traverse it. In these traditions of the zenana, however, there is a distinct antipathy to immature union, and in the north-west, indeed, there is a special and an opprobrious term used to denote the weakly fibreless infants that are the results of too youthful a marriage.

Against the large and steadily maintained rate of fruitfulness there is also to be considered a very heavy scale of infant mortality. With parents immature in one, if not on both sides, a high average standard of vitality is not to be expected. The revolting and ignorant practices of the *dhais* may be held responsible for a large number more of deaths that could be avoided, and the mothers who have learnt the comfort to themselves and the greater safety to their offspring of the more scientific Western methods, are certainly showing a willingness to accept them, which they do not accord to other innovations of education or freedom. The multiplication of trained midwives to go out into the villages and districts will certainly mitigate the waste of baby life that goes on, and may in time, and so gradually as to be almost unperceived, effect other salutary changes in the women's condition.

Once out of the *chatthi ghar*, the child of course takes its chance of infantile ailments, as well as of the greater scourges of cholera or small-pox, which at intervals or in unfavourably wet seasons stalk like destroying spectres through the land. But medical skill and amended sanitation, better water supplies, and the daily improving means of food distribution, which every year is making the gaunt image of famine a less terrible vision, are giving yearly a cleaner bill of public health, which is not only reflected in a slowly declining death-rate, but gives promise of sounder stamina and physique for the generations to come. The infant is of course invariably nursed at the breast by the mother when she can possibly fulfil the function, and so soon as it can walk, it enters upon a joyous and untrammelled childhood.

Throughout Western, Southern, and Eastern India the children, boys and girls, disport themselves literally naked until five years of age. In Bengal it is not unusual at about two or three to put upon the boys a piece of cord, sometimes with a key or a small metal charm; and round Madras and in Eastern Ceylon the little girls are generally to be seen with a little zone or circlet of silver or bell metal round their podgy little middles. The girls begin to wear clothing sooner than the boys, and their earliest raiment is usually a comically shapeless sacque of coloured print. Innocent in the sense understood of European children they never are, for reticence or mystery towards them are quite unknown, and one might almost say that they babble artlessly over subjects that elderly matrons at home would discuss under all reservation. The knowledge of, and admission of this fact, is absolutely necessary for the comprehension of much that seems puzzling and suggestive of moral degradation in the Indian character. A knowledge of what one may euphemistically write of as "the facts of life" gives the women a habit of thought which makes them seem perfectly natural and everyday things, and as such they discuss them, but not merely from a morbid love of nauseous detail, as those who do not understand at once define it to be.

I do not know whether those noisy and assertive persons who have lately started the theory that the Western woman's disabilities arise largely from the "ignorance" in which well-brought-up girls are kept, are aware of this. If not, it may give them some difficulty to reconcile their demonstrative sympathy with the Indian woman's "down-trodden" condition, with the knowledge that she sooner and more fully learns the mysteries of existence than any others of her sex in the world. Yet, from their point of view, she is the "awful example" of humiliation! I give them the information, and leave them to argue over it.

The Hindu mother is generally affectionate to weakness, but she possesses very little control over, or direction of, the child after infancy. This is vested in the grandmother—the father's mother—and she has generally become a stern disciplinarian who must be obeyed unquestioningly. Respect to the father and love to the mother—though the prejudiced outsider would discredit this—with of course the elements of religion are the child's first home lessons. The girls are put very young to simple household duties, and the merest children may be seen cleaning the rice and pounding the corn with a dexterity and confidence curiously at variance with their youthful years. In better-class households there is often one at least among the women of the zenana who can read, and should this be the case, she may impart her knowledge to some of the little girls. If it is intended to send a girl to school, she generally begins to go at about six or seven years of age, but it is still far more exceptional for her to do this than to remain at home.

CHAPTER II.

HER EDUCATION.

> **"Drops of water falling, falling, falling brim the chattie o'er,**
> **Wisdom comes in little lessons—little gains make largest store."**
> **(*The Shlokas of the Hitopadesa.*)**

INDIAN social reformers are wont to express the view that when education is generally accepted by parents for their daughters, the complete emancipation of the sex will have come into measurable range. One is reminded a little of a trite old saying as to what pigs would do if they had wings, but those who most glibly speak of the widespread advantages that are to accrue from knowledge fail to see that the women have to be convinced in the first place of the desirability of it at all. And how deeply seated is actual prejudice against it in many quarters still, is one of the last facts that the well-meaning apostle of progress will admit. There are plenty of Mahommedans yet to be found whose educational views are expressed in the idea that women may be taught to read with benefit, since they can improve their minds by the study of the Koran, but it is not wise to allow them to learn to write, lest they should communicate with unadvisable acquaintances, and even be able to make assignations of deceitful purpose. Over the latter disability, the wit of the zenana has triumphed by attaching meanings that are unmistakable to the initiated to the most innocent of everyday things. It was discussing Rudyard Kipling with an educated Ranee, that I learnt first that the "object letter" described in his story "Beyond the Pale," in which a broken glass bangle, a red dhak flower, a pinch of cattle food, and a number of cardamons was intended to be construed into a widow's request for a visit at eleven o'clock, was a perfectly probable missive.

To such and many other objections to female learning *per se*, there is yet to be added a still stronger element of difficulty to be overcome before learning is generally sought for girls. This lies in the fact that Indian woman possesses no practical incentive yet to pursue book learning. She is taught that her calling in life is marriage, and learns to look on that as the end and aim of her existence. Unlike ourselves at home, she is not for ever crying out in newspapers and on platforms for new openings of occupation, nor is she influenced by American examples to endeavour to enter upon vocations vastly better filled by men. In fact, in all my wanderings, I only saw one woman filling a clerk's position, and she was a bright young Tamil who assisted Mrs. Brander, the Chief Inspectress of Female Education to the Government of Madras, in her secretarial department. Even domestic service, save for the inappreciable per centage of ayahs employed, is not fulfilled by women. The woman who fails to marry, and in consequence must earn her daily bread, is far from being regarded as a commendable example to her sex. Rather, she is a social failure, who must explain herself and behave with humility beside mothers who have realized the true mission of womanhood. It is not characteristic of the true Hindu or Mahommedan woman to desire to be independent of man, and education therefore falls to the level of a mere prop, useful only where a better hope has failed.

Moreover, the native temperament measures everything by its utilitarian value. Learning, therefore, for learning's sake, is a merely academic luxury, and one into which elements of danger to accepted traditions may lurk with insidious possibilities.

Still, in spite of the weighty obstacles against which it has had to contend, the educational movement is undoubtedly making way among the sex. Chief among the factors which have tended to break down the barriers of mistrust and objection I should unhesitatingly place the much higher standard of education, which has been gradually raised among the men during the past quarter of a century or so. With the students who have come to England for university or bar studies there has been undoubtedly a regrettable tendency to choose English wives, with results it is to be feared generally very far from satisfactory. For the white girls who go out find themselves in the very awkward position of being better educated and more advanced in thought and freedom than the female part of the family to which they have allied themselves, while, unless they are of singularly adaptable nature, or their husbands have abandoned their own national habits and customs far more than usual, the system of domestic life and the household ways must of necessity present features unpleasant as well as unexpected. European society in India is exceedingly severe upon these mixed marriages, and save in one or two notable instances that might be mentioned, where the lady has had singular force of character and the entire courage of her opinions, it declines to receive either the man or the woman under any circumstances. With the young men who have profited by the splendid schools and colleges open to them now in all parts of India, there has not been the same temptation to which their more travelled and enterprising brothers and cousins have been exposed in this direction; though, in defence of those who have succumbed to it, be it said that English women at home have been very ready to flatter and accept these Oriental suitors. But the home-taught young man, for all the domestic conservatism, which even civil service appointments and national congresses scarcely seem to shake, must gradually come to desire a more even level of companionship on the part of his wife. It is one of the Western misconceptions to regard the wife as of no importance in the family circle. On the contrary, *purdah* though she may be, she is a factor of consideration alike as a dowried girl-bride and later on as sons' mother, as mother-in-law, and grandmother. While her husband's learning did not carry him into wider interests than the immediate market prices current, or the last bit of litigation upon which his neighbours had embarked, he found in his wife all the sympathy he desired. But now that he is himself a judge it may be, or a deputy-collector on special duty, involving perhaps a really high degree of specialized scientific attainment, he begins to think he would like his wife to know a little more also of the world's broader affairs. I saw several instances in which the ladies of the Church of England or other Zenana Missions had been asked to instruct in English and other branches of knowledge the girl-wives of young men at the universities.

The present position of female education in India may be summed up by saying that it has long left the stage of being actively opposed, and has passed through its phase of passively indifferent neglect to one of toleration. There is no enthusiasm, general or even widespread, for it as yet, and the women who pursue it to its higher walks may be said to bear the same position to the masses of their sex, as those do here, who preach in chapels or wear uncompromising trousers to ride bicycles astride through the city, who are looked upon as unfortunate aberrations by their less go-ahead sisters.

To understand and grasp properly the present aspect of the question a few figures will be useful, and in quoting them I would like to thank the India Office for the ready and ungrudging help it gives to any one in search of information regarding the dependency. Going back to reports of 1877–78, I find that the number of girls at school throughout British India was set down at 66,615. In 1882–83 the numbers had advanced to more than double, and some 3487 schools had then an attendance roll of 162,317. In the mean time an important commission on public instruction, under the presidency of Sir W. W. Hunter, had been appointed, and several valuable recommendations on the subject of female education were made in the report, with the result of very marked increase both in the numbers of girls' schools and the pupils attending them.

From the latest statistics available, namely those of the years 1891–92, one learns that the total number of girls attending public and recognized private educational institutions was 339,043. Resolved into its factors, this mass gives some interesting details. For instance, only 76 of the sex are yet to be found in the collegiate establishments of first grade, and of these 29 are medical students. Entered, however, in the technical and other schools, are 461 young women, of whom 51 are set down as studying art, a branch of knowledge to which Indian girls are at present curiously indifferent. In fact, except in the high school at Bombay, where one or two Parsee girls had taken it up and showed me a few examples of still life and drawing from the antique, I saw no evidences whatever of a native aptitude or inclination in this direction. Certainly no native woman has so far distinguished herself in it, but an Indian creative female artist, should such ever arise, would be an extremely interesting phenomenon.

In the normal schools for the training of school teachers, 819 are put down as under instruction; and then, coming to the section devoted to private instruction, are two particularly striking entries. The one is that 355 girls are pursuing advanced studies in Arabic, Sanscrit, Persian, and the other Oriental classics which, as these attainments are of no special utilitarian value in the modern system of Anglicized education, shows that even among the women are to be found a few who love learning and literature for its own sake. The other bears silent but eloquent testimony to the Mussulman indifference to female knowledge. Only 8117 girls are to be found attending the private Koran schools, a small proportion indeed to the millions of Mahommedan women.

Put in form perhaps more easily to be comprehended, 99·44 per cent. of the entire female population of India—enumerated at 113,406,669—is illiterate. Under instruction at the present time is 0·22 of the whole, while of those beyond the school-going age, only 0·34 are able to read and write. Stated thus, it is a startling record enough, even beside the male average of 11 per cent. who are not illiterate.

It is in the Madras and Bombay Presidencies that female education has made its best advances, and in both these the percentage of females over five years of age and not illiterate stands at 1·2. This, however, really gives a better ratio of strictly native educated women to the southernmost tract, as in Bombay, it must be borne in mind, are included the Parsees, who in the past quarter of a century or so have completely emancipated their women from *purdah* traditions, and have accepted for them the advantages of learning quite as unreservedly as for the boys. Madras has, however, been the centre of Indian mission efforts far longer than any other part of the dependency, and indeed we may go back for its commencement to 1542, when St. Francis Xavier's name was first associated with Madura and the Páravás tribes of the Tinnevelly district. The earliest two of the Protestant mis-

MISSION TEACHERS AND SCHOLARS AT CALCUTTA.

sionaries, who by the way were Lutherans, began their efforts at Tranquebar, and to two of them, Ziegenbalg and Schutze by name, is due the credit of having translated the Bible into Tamil and Hindustani.

Even the sternest critics of modern missionary methods are compelled to admit how much the evangelizing agencies have done in the direction of female education. Going back to the year 1850, I find that the Protestant societies then possessed only 285 educational establishments. In 1880, the numbers had risen to 1120, and ten years later to 1507, while the numbers of pupils in the corresponding years were 11,193, 57,893, and 104,159. In the last-issued report of the Department of Public Instruction in Bengal, official recognition of the value of these mission efforts is ungrudgingly given, but whether the British subscriber, who, often self-denyingly, supports these undertakings, grasps how much larger is the work of teaching than that of preaching is another matter. Personally, my own bias was to have admired and defended all missionary labours. Brought up and still an attached member of the Church of England, I would far rather have set it down that the various societies are realizing all that they undertake upon the platform of Exeter Hall. But they are not. Their individual zeal and earnestness is not, as a rule, to be discredited, though I have met instances in which social prestige was ranked as of more moment than the slow winning of native confidence, and servants and horses as things to be appraised rather than a bazaar congregation. It is according to the point of view from which the question is regarded, whether it is advisable to keep Christian dogma discreetly veiled and in the shadowy background or not. There are insidious possibilities in the precept that the reading of a chapter in the Bible and the "force of silent influence" is enough when coupled with prayer, and it is certain that the religious influence exerted in the schools has but the scantiest results.

I was talking one day to a very intelligent Parsee machinist in Delhi, and he mentioned to me that his children attended a certain missionary school there. This somewhat surprised me; and I said, "But you are not Christian converts, surely?"

"No," he replied, "I hope we are all as good Zoroastrians as any; but, you see, it is a great advantage to the boys to know English, and *they get no harm if they have to hear a little of your religion.* It is very little expected of them in return for what they are taught, and they will forget it all in a couple of months."

One point, however, was forcibly borne in upon me, that the insistance upon religious instruction is invariably slacker where missionary schools are rivalled in the field by Government ones. In Madras, for example, the Education Department is exceedingly active, and here there is a decided tendency to keep the elements of proselytizing in a subordinate position. In Bengal, on the other hand, where the Administration does next to nothing for the advancement of female education, a far bigger pill of Biblical and ecclesiastical learning can be and is given with the jam of general teaching.

As mere teaching agencies, the mission schools that I saw from Negapatam to Delhi, from Calcutta to Calicut, are deserving of the highest commendation. Modern European methods have been skilfully brought into harmony with native needs, and ideas even of punctuality and truthfulness—virtues in which the average native character is not strong—have been imparted. Yet, ungracious and paradoxical as it seems to allude to the fact, in face of all that has been done for female education, there is an existent drawback to wide development of the movement in its association with evangelization. For there is no denying that even if Hinduism is being imperceptibly weakened, Christianity is not being accepted in its place. On the other hand, the native Christian is viewed with undisguised contempt by his former co-religionists, and we are brought face to face with the undoubted truth that the large proportion of native Christian women who are in the position of school-teachers is the very reverse of a tower of strength in the situation. Till one has moved and lived among the people, it is almost impossible to realize the deep-rooted prejudices against a woman's doing any work outside her own home sphere. All down the centuries, since the Rig Veda taught that woman had won her right to rise to the world of life when she had fulfilled her duties as a wife to her husband, the traditions have strengthened, till it has come to be regarded as an unnatural and a sinful thing for her to look for other interests. She who has accepted Christianity has in the first place to cut herself away from her own people by her change of faith. Far from being honoured for this, she has become to them as out-caste, and teaching by her, instead of being the commendable work that it is with us, is rather degraded to the aspect of being the one calling into which she could enter.

On the other hand, there is of course to be considered that if converts are made, they must not be placed at any unfair disadvantage to the rest of the community in the struggle for a livelihood. It is not a matter for wonder on any grounds that the missionary agencies have fostered schoolmistress-ship as a female profession, as they have done by means of normal schools and university scholarships. Not only does the adoption of the calling relieve the converting pastorate of the immediately serious questions of maintenance, but it is promising of a possibility of further evangelizing. Moreover, one is asked whether it is not better to have native Christian teachers than none at all.

To my mind only one answer presents itself. So long as the vitality of the female education movement is preserved from outside, and European money and energy are forthcoming to fan the precarious little flame, the present system will last, and a certain amount of progress will be recorded. But before we can view the subject with any genuine satisfaction, and feel that from being an artificially fostered production it has become a living reality, we must have created both a genuine desire for learning for its own sake and further provided the means by which it can be naturally and on the spot supplied, according to the inherent prejudices and beliefs of the people.

It is therefore that an experiment, initiated by Ramabai in the Sharada Sadan, at Poona, was of particular interest. Of course Ramabai herself, with her knowledge, her independent views on marriage, and her contentions for women's rights, stands somewhat in the same position towards the ruck of her countrywomen as the extremely advanced of the progressive sisterhood bear towards everyday womankind with ourselves, and it may be taken for certain that it will be very long before her pronounced emancipation finds favour with those of whom it has been well said, "Her sway in her own immediate circle is complete, her social aspirations are restricted within immutable limits, while those of her inferiors are similarly kept from encroaching, and she has no conception of any social grievance with which the elders of her caste are not competent to deal." For Ramabai's idea was no less than the training as teachers of children-widows and childless—therefore often unvalued, cruelly treated, and even deserted—wives. Of the caste Hindu widows' lot enough has been written. It is the one point in the domestic system that the sensation-monger feels himself or herself to be upon quite safe ground, since it can always be said it was bad enough to require amended legislation. No doubt, too, with a race which places the sexual pleasures in such paramount estimation, a girl would feel that to live life as thousands of European "old maids" do, her fate was specially hard; while, moreover, in either her own or her dead husband's house she might be viewed as a useless encumbrance, the drudge, the slave, and the despised.

Now for Ramabai to bring such to her home was to do a double good. In the first place, it took the unfortunate girl away from where she was probably not wanted, and placed a useful vocation in her hands; in the second, by only receiving those of caste, she had commenced a band of teachers who can go into the zenanas of their co-religionists on equal social terms. Most unfortunately, I was unable to go to Poona, but my knowledge on the subject is derived from a reliable official source, and it was less value after all, in such an inquiry as I had been commissioned to make, to see the small home details of such an institution than to know in broad outline what were its intentions and purpose. There were some forty inmates till quite recently, ranging in age from twelve to twenty. English was added to the general education given to them in their own vernaculars, and Ramabai herself instructed them in Sanscrit, the language of their own sacred books; but since I left India I have learned that the "Home of Learning" is in a state of collapse. Forgetting, evidently, that there were plenty of evangelizing seminaries in the field, Ramabai was induced to abandon her original plan, which guaranteed that Hindu religious and caste observances should not be interfered with, and to introduce Christian prayer and instruction. The work by this means has been shaken to its foundations, her pupils have left, and what might have been the seed of a valuable indigenous influence has withered away.

There are considerable differences in the general system

pursued by the three presidencies, the lieutenant-governorships, and the native states, and it is perhaps not necessary to institute any lengthened comparisons as to their divergencies. It will suffice to say that there are two views from which elementary instruction through the vernaculars is regarded. One is whether it is to be a merely useful scheme of teaching that should assist the masses in their humble and everyday vocations; and the other is, whether it shall be treated as a possible basis leading to higher stages, possibly even the university degree itself.

Under present conditions, I am of opinion that, so far as the girls are concerned, the former is the better fundamental idea. There are few women at this time better competent to speak on such a subject than Mrs. Wheeler, the native lady who fills the post of Inspectress of Schools to the Government of Bengal. In her own words, she is "but one generation removed from all the narrowness of orthodox Hinduism," but she enjoyed the benefit of a father who felt that his daughters were worthy of being taught. He was an exceptional linguist, holding an important post in connection with the Civil Service examinations, and became a convert to Christianity. Mrs. Wheeler was married to one of the chaplains of the Society for the Propagation of the Gospel. During her brief wedded life she did much in connection with his school-work, and on his death, leaving her with two little children to provide for, she was anxious

MRS. WHEELER, INSPECTRESS OF SCHOOLS IN BENGAL.

to find occupation which should give her enough to educate them fittingly. Almost by chance she heard Sir Richard Temple express the wish that some suitable lady could be found to fill the post of inspectress of girls' schools, and she offered herself for it, being immediately accepted. When she took up her work she found there were no standards of instruction, no uniformity of books in use, and everything slipshod and haphazard. She had a hard battle to fight in introducing systematic courses, and had to live through much calumny and acrimony; but she triumphed over all, and to-day has the pleasure of seeing all that she has proposed in the code. She has visited England and the Continent twice to see all that she could of European methods, and her inherited knowledge of native character and ways of thought have given her especial advantages for her work.

Under Mrs. Wheeler are the strictly zenana and purdah schools, but for the ordinary day-schools, to which these conventions are not rigidly applied, she has the assistance of the male inspecting staff. As the outcome both of her racial knowledge and her actual experience, she deprecates strongly the tendency to push the girls on to university distinctions. The results are showy, no doubt, and look well in school reports; but in practice the young women become arrogant, are seldom successful as teachers, and very frequently develop hysteria and nervous complaints. It is too great a brain effort without any hereditary preparation, and to exhibit these girls as triumphs of the system is far from advantageous as an object-lesson to thoughtful eyes. Exceptions there are of course, a very notable one being another remarkable native lady, Miss Chandramukhi Bose, M.A., the first of her sex to win this coveted degree, which she did in 1884, before it was even officially opened to women. She is now directress of the Bethune Collegiate School at Calcutta, a well-attended and prosperous establishment, departmentally supported, which may be said to touch the high-water mark of women's education as it exists in India. Its primary school is conducted upon the most approved of modern ideas; but of more general interest is its collegiate aspect, and the work it does in preparing girls for the First in Arts and B.A. degrees of the Calcutta University. Since

A BENGALI GIRL STUDENT.

these examinations were thrown open to women a steadily increasing number of girls, from eight in 1889 to twenty in 1893, have entered the college, paying only three rupees a month for their tuition. It can claim the credit of having turned out twelve young lady B.A.'s, three of whom passed during 1893. There is a percentage of Christian girls among its collegiate students, but the majority are Brahmos, the most emancipated and advanced of the Hindu community.

In consultation with Mrs. Wheeler, Sir Alfred Croft and

the Bengal Education Department recently revised the vernacular standards for girls' schools and zenanas, and as a comparison with our English corresponding grades, it will be of interest if I give it in full (see Table opposite). That comparatively few go beyond the fifth standard is due to the prevailing custom of child-marriage, which seldom leaves a girl at school after her thirteenth year, though she will probably not be a wife till after she is fourteen.

Mrs Brander Senior Inspectress of Schools. Madras Presidency.

Madras has always prided itself upon keeping well in the van of educational progress, and it is therefore not surprising to find that both for its central and northern circles it has appointed a lady as inspectress of its schools. This post is held by Mrs. Brander, who came into prominent notice both as an advanced exponent of sound knowledge and a sympathetic and accomplished English gentlewoman when she took the control of the Madras Normal Training College for Teachers. Immediately under her supervision are some 590 schools, with an attendance roll of about 28,000 pupils. As showing, however, the occasional energy and ability shown by native-women, it is worth mentioning that during Mrs. Brander's last furlough an acting appointment was given to Miss Govindurajula, a Tamil lady of high qualifications, and she fulfilled the very exacting and responsible duties of the position with full credit.

HIGH CASTE HINDU GIRLS, MADRAS.

The higher caste Hindu girls are among the brightest and most satisfactory of native pupils, and they possess certain hereditary advantages in the respect that learning has always maintained among their race. From recently compiled figures, furnished to me by Mrs. Brander, I find that out of the total number of 8458 girls receiving public instruction in Madras city, 168 are classified as coming from the "richer" and 2975 from the "middle" classes, and of these by far the larger proportion are Hindus; but perhaps even more interesting is the movement on behalf of the Mahommedan girls.

To reach even the lowest of this race was very hard; to gain the *Gosha* girls seemed well nigh impossible. The first effort made, certainly in this Presidency, and so far as I am able to learn, in any other, dates from about eighteen years ago, when a little band of ladies, at the head of whom was Lady Hobart, conceived the idea of a school where the strictest Mussulman could be as sure of seclusion from male intrusion as behind the purdah itself. Not only should it be a school, but a training college for mistresses also; and under the name of the Hobart Training School it has been one of the most entirely satisfactory features in the educational scheme of Southern India. Such was the fear on the part of Mussulman parents of their daughters being seen in the streets that the school had to provide covered conveyances to fetch and take home the pupils, and even to-day, when there are nine such homes of instruction in Madras city alone, with 498 pupils, this has still to be done. The Church of England Zenana Mission is well to the fore also in this work, and in the schools under Miss Oxley's care the drill and singing are notably good. It must be admitted, however, that Mahommedan girls' education in the northern and central circles of the Presidency showed in 1893 a falling off to the extent of six schools and 179 scholars upon the figures of the previous year.

The code of Madras differs very little from that of Bengal,

and it is not necessary for me to repeat it, but over and beyond this I found in the southernmost Presidency three

Mohamedan Pupils at the Hobart Training School.

interesting and recent innovations in kindergarten, drill, and needlework. The first has been warmly adopted in the schools, and an admirable little manual on the subject has been written by Mrs. Brander, who, it may be mentioned, has also written a capital little work upon domestic economy for native households, published by order of the Indian Director of Public Instruction, a subject which is also beginning to receive attention in the schools. Miss Rajagopaul has also compiled a collection of kindergarten and action songs, which have been popular, and form a decidedly original line for a native lady teacher to have taken up. As to drill, I cannot do better than quote from the inspectress's last official report, in which she says "a decided change for the better has taken place in girls' schools in the matter of physical exercises. They are practised now in almost every girls' school in the central circle, and in secondary and upper primary schools they are generally well organized and suitable. . . . Many managers are now introducing light dumb-bells, rings, and poles into native girls' schools, thereby improving the exercises and rendering them more popular. Grants amounting to Rs. 128 have been distributed among four schools during the year for the purchase of calisthenic apparatus."

I think, however, that the most noticeable point in the claims of Madras to be considered a pioneer in matters educational lies in the movement that has been made towards continuing education after school. So long as girls go to live with their husbands at the age of fourteen, no matter how sound a foundation of learning may have been laid, the ultimate result can never be more than superficial. It is a matter therefore of importance as well as interest to record that a really earnest effort in the direction of home education classes has been made, and four different sets of teachers are at work in this direction. At the present time about a hundred and twenty women are studying thus, carrying their reading on to English, arithmetic, history, and geography, being visited at home weekly by the native governesses and occasionally attending lectures. I was present at one of these of a series organized by the Hindu Reform Association, given in Tamil, upon the world and its movement, and a fashionable as well as much interested audience of about fifty higher caste Hindu and Brahmin ladies it was. They came in handsome carriages, wore splendid jewels, took copious notes, and showed really intelligent interest in it by frequently asking questions on points they wanted to understand more fully, till one little event proved too much for their and my own gravity. One of the ladies had come attended by an aged widow, who was doubtless an old nurse and attendant, and whose shaven head, flowing white garments, and total absence of jewellery in any form showed that she belonged to the Brahmins, and was respecting all their rigid traditions as to how a woman who has lost her husband ought to appear. An austere and unhumorous person indeed she seemed, but she listened intently to the lecture, while she furtively watched her young mistress, until, in an interval when there was no astronomical diagram upon the screen and it was filled by a round bright circle of light, she made with her thin bony hands, in its exact centre, the shadow of a goose's head! It was one of the best I ever saw done under any circumstances, and she allowed it to rest open-beaked for a few seconds as if amazed at what it was hearing, and then set it wagging as though it were fully endorsing all that the lecturer was saying. Even the quiet Hindu ladies broke into a soft low laugh, and the lecturer, who was a clever young Tamil woman, who had taken a good certificate at one of the Scotch training-colleges, could only pause and smile, till with swift tact she called upon her colleague at the lantern for the next slide of the series. But the old lady was not at all abashed, and at the conclusion of the demonstration, came up to ask of the assistant if she would kindly show her once more "how the moon and the earth ran round the sky!"

Another useful insight into home education was afforded me by being present at the annual inspection by Mrs. Brander of a set arranged under the auspices of the Free Church Mission. Papers were in English, with dictation in Tamil and Telegu, including a certain amount of literature, composition, and poetry, and arithmetic up to fractions, and the *vivâ voce* work was certainly highly creditable, while the papers were handed in looking remarkably neat. Government assists this work, which costs about six thousand rupees a year, by a grant of over two thousand rupees, and the pupils show great interest in their studies, especially in English, which the greater number of them take up. In this connection may be mentioned the foundation of a women's magazine in Tamil called the *Maharani*, which has been started to meet the difficulty of finding bright and useful reading for girls. It is effectively illustrated, and contains articles on history, natural science, and social topics, as well as a serial story, though the dress, which fills so large a space in English girls' papers, does not form one of its departments. That may come in time!

Bombay treads closely upon the heels of Madras in the encouragement it bestows upon female education, and stands well in advance of Bengal. Curiously enough, Bombay city gives the lowest percentage of girls attending school to the population of girls of the school-going age of all the headquarters of the five educational divisions of the Presidency, with only 8·2 per cent. set down as scholars.

Poona stood highest, with 24 per cent., but there are various reasons for the extremely good proportion of students to girls here. Not only is the place an especially active centre of much and various mission work, but its branch of the National Indian Association is a very vigorous one, and its municipal administration, unlike that of many boards, is thoroughly in earnest in encouraging the movement. It also possesses a very large Parsee community as well as several notably good schools for girls of this race, to which they are sent from all parts of the Presidency. Moreover, when Mr. R. G. Oxenham, Acting Director of Public Instruction, gave me the statistics from which these figures were compiled, Ramabai's school was crowded and thriving.

At the present time, those of administrative influence in Bombay lean rather to the encouragement of primary education. The Government is strongly supported, so far as Bombay city is concerned, in its movements on behalf of education in general by the Joint Schools Committee—a body on which are four members (three of whom are native gentlemen) appointed by the municipal corporation of the town, and four nominated by Government. Twelve schools are devoted exclusively to girls by this committee, and though chiefly attended by Hindus, they include among their pupils Mussulmans, Jews, and aboriginals.

All possible assistance and information concerning these municipal schools was placed at my disposal by the Hon. N. B. Masani, the secretary to the committee, whose views that education among the native women will not be "rushed," agreed with the opinion I had myself formed early, and which was confirmed as I went along. The schools as I saw them are modest in extent and scope, and I was glad to find in most of them that there were either head mistresses or qualified female assistants. I paid a long visit to one of the largest, where the discipline and tone seemed in all respects commendable, and where the informal little examination I was asked to make brought me intelligent and correct answers. That the teaching given in these schools is satisfactory is, however, shown by the fact that one of the valuable Mary Carpenter Scholarships, and another bestowed by the National Indian Association, were won by girls taught in them. Bombay, however, stands behind the other two Presidencies and the North-West Provinces, in not including in its official *personnel* a lady to act as inspectress to girls' schools. To a certain extent this deficiency is met by some of the ladies belonging to the National Indian Association, who have kindly undertaken to visit the schools occasionally; but I found the need of more feminine direction, especially where needlework was concerned. Nothing creditable in this direction was put before me, but some very commonplace embroidery and some absolute horrors of Berlin wool cross-stitch were brought out as the best they could show. The two vernaculars in most general use in Bombay are Marathi and Gujerati, and five of the municipal schools are for pupils of the former and seven of the latter.

As a glimpse of what the people are doing for themselves in the direction of education, I was much interested in a visit that I paid to the Goculdas Tejpal Free School, an institution maintained by the trustees (every one of whom is a Hindu gentleman, not only of high caste, but of considerable official and social status) of the enormous fortune left by the late Mr. Goculdas Tejpal for educational, benevolent, and religious purposes. The school itself occupies a flat in one of the huge many-storied houses one finds in the native quarters of Bombay, and the light and well-ventilated rooms had many pictures, European as well as native, illustrative of scenes from Hindu religious books. It has upon its register 125 girls, most of whom are under twelve years of age, though there are two or three young married women who have reached the sixth standard and who are pursuing their studies at their husbands' desires. The head mistress is a Hindu, and a qualified teacher, as, indeed, the results of the last Government examination, when 78·9 per cent. of the candidates presented passed, are enough to show. Besides the knowledge prescribed for the girls by the Education Department, kindergarten teaching is given to the infants, and greatly enjoyed by them, while needlework of a practical and useful character has a prominent place among the day's lessons. The girls were taught to cut out and make their own *cholis* (little jackets), to darn rents in their saris, and do simple embroideries. I asked what the school was doing in the way of physical education, a point on which one generally finds the most marked backwardness, and found that, so far, very little had been attempted. Still, to prove to me that an effort had been inaugurated, they went through the *gurba,* a curious performance that is more than an action song and less than a drill, a religious exercise and yet a game. In this the girls place a large brazen vessel, with a fire alight, in the centre of their class-room or playground. They join hands and circle round it, stepping sometimes forward, sometimes back, and changing places in an intricate system of movement.

In Bombay, as in all other parts of India, one finds that the Mahommedan girls are the most backward to avail themselves of educational advantages, despite missionary and all other effort. Still, a little progress even here may be recorded, and I learn that a really satisfactory advance has been made in the Presidency in the number attending secondary schools. In the Surat district there are two Hindustani schools for girls, one of which is in charge of a Mahommedan lady teacher, while there is another under similarly qualified management at Karachi. Scattered, however, through the Presidency are a number of small establishments of teaching, under native management, and known as Koran schools. Of these, whose average attendance varies from twelve to fourteen scholars, twenty are for girls, and though the instruction they give may not be of the highest order, still it is an encouraging sign to note any unaided effort on behalf of female learning.

Nothing strikes one more in Bombay than the simply marvellous strides which the Parsees have made towards the complete equality and emancipation of their women. But a quarter of a century ago Parsee ladies were to all intents and purposes *purdah nashin*—not perhaps as rigidly and narrowly as the Mohammedans, but in spirit debarred from any place in social life. To-day one meets them everywhere, from a Government House ball or dinner to a seat on the tramways as they start out, with all the frankness and independence of English women, to do their daily work of teaching, nursing, or study, and I have even heard of one or two who fill book-keeping or secretarial posts. I have met several of them who drive and even ride fearlessly and well, and as hostesses in their pretty and well-ordered drawing-rooms I have found many who are charming and cultivated to the highest degree. Only in 1893 a young Parsee lady, Miss Cama by name, went over to England to pursue her medical education, and has returned to Bombay with the distinction of a high British diploma, and instances, from Miss Sorabji (though she came of a Christianized family) onwards, of girls who carried off the highest honours in the native universities could be given.

For the most part, the schools are managed without aid or grant from Government, and consequently are exempt from official inspection, but the quality of instruction is maintained by the examinations of the science and art classes and colleges for which the pupils are encouraged to enter. I visited the largest of the three vernacular schools, which have together an attendance roll of something over a thousand scholars. At this particular one there were over four hundred upon the register, and the building, which had been erected by private Parsee munificence in 1885, had cost over a lac of rupees. The class-rooms were excellent, their light and ventilation leaving nothing to be desired. I listened to the lesson in geography which was being given to the fourth standard scholars, and it struck me as being taught with remarkable clearness and ease. . The subject was the island and harbour of Bombay, but instead of making her lesson a dry statement of areas and population, the teacher had provided an enormous shallow pan of water, and with modelling clay, tiny houses, trees, and ships, was making one and another of her little charges construct quite an admirable representation of the island. The kindergarten formed a large department, and in no London school or institution have I ever seen one better equipped and supplied than this is. Its completeness is largely due to Mr. Darasha Chichgur, a Parsee gentleman who has visited both England and Germany in order to study Western developments most likely to be of use for his own people. Here the needlework was useful as well as artistic, and I saw several charming examples of gold and silver embroideries upon ribbon-velvet as used by the ladies of this faith for the borders of their saris. Another very good institution is the High School, at which the majority of the students are Parsee girls, some of whom are learning drawing and painting.

It would not be fair to conclude this brief summary of educational work in Bombay without passing reference to the useful labours of the various missionary bodies who are in the field, but I have, both in Madras and Calcutta, indicated the scope and character of the efforts usually made by them, and which in broad outlines do not greatly vary. In Bombay the Society for the Propagation of the Gospel, the Free General Assembly, and the American Mission, among others, are doing notably valuable work. If, however, I have not spoken specifically of their schools, it is not from any intention of under-estimating their usefulness, but simply because I have thought it more significant to speak of movements official or indigenous. In the work of training native women as teachers, philanthropic bodies stand conspicuously well to the fore. At Ahmedabad is an excellent training college, and from another in Rajkot some notable examinational successes were obtained. The Karachi municipal female normal class had on its rolls at the close of last year no fewer than eighteen Mohammedans and fourteen Hindus, under supervision of Roman Catholic sisters, and the official comment upon it is that it is "doing admirable work in the way of disseminating knowledge among native women." Commendable institutions exist also in Kolhapur and Hyderabad. So far, indeed, as the supplies of future teachers are concerned, the Bombay Presidency stands very well, as it does also in point of the quality of education and its good intent of encouragement. Where it lags behind is in its ratio of girls attending school to those of the school-going age.

Then, lastly, is to be considered what the native States are doing in the matter of education. Hyderabad, with its preponderant Mussulman population, lags behind; and in Baroda no very striking progress is as yet recorded. Mysore and Bhaunagar lead the way, and though, unfortunately, I had no opportunity of visiting the former vast territory, I enjoyed the pleasure of a chat with its clever and far-seeing Maharajah, and learnt from him that all possible encouragement by means of grants in aid and scholarships are devoted by his assembly to the fostering of female education. The result in practice of this wise policy is, that while Hyderabad can only return three per mille and Baroda five per mille of their female population who can read and write, Mysore stands comparatively high with seven per mille. Mysore, moreover, led the way in another direction, which was the official discouragement of early marriage of both sexes, and while I was staying in Madras, the question how far legislative intervention was to be regarded as justifiable was engaging considerable attention. The example in this direction, or in that of education of the native States, has a more weighty influence than is often admitted, and innovations launched from them are likely to be accepted far more readily and with better grace than anything directly initiated under British prestige.

In Bhaunagar, which is very rarely visited by English tourists, I spent some days, which I rank among the most interesting of my experiences, for the vast Katthiawar district, which is bounded on the south by the Gulf of Cambay, and on the north by the Gulf of Cutch, has played no small part in the making of India, and its rulers earned no small fame in that memorable conflict of 1303, which has given to a good Rajput in the oath "by the sin of the sack of Chitor" the most binding tie he can lay upon his conscience. It was in later days than this that we first hear of Bhaunagar, its premier state, coming forward to help the British. Its ruler, Akherajii, in 1771, lent valuable assistance to our forces in subduing the pirate stronghold of Talaji, as well as in other ways. His son, who died in 1810, also cultivated the friendship of the English, then holding Surat as a chief trading centre, so that hereditary influences and associations have helped, doubtless, the enlightened gentleman upon whom in 1886 the Queen-Empress conferred the honour of Grand Commandership of the Star of India, subsequently bestowing upon him the formal title of Maharajah, while the State itself was advanced in official recognition to first-class degree. Compared with such kingdoms as those of Baroda or Hyderabad, Bhaunagar may seem but small, with its population of about half a million, and area a little under three thousand square miles; but it is fairer to estimate by prosperity than by mere size, and a revenue of forty-five lacs of rupees is by no means to be despised. It may be safely said that in no State of India are the funds more generously managed or with a more public-spirited consideration for the welfare of the people than in Bhaunagar, and one's first impression on arrival is the extraordinary appearance of well-to-do comfort on all hands. There is one proverbial standard in India for judging of a place's affluence or the reverse, and that is the proportion of earthenware to brass or copper *lotahs*—the water-vessels carried by the women to the wells—metal ones indicating comfortable circumstances. In all my drives and walks during nearly a week's stay in the capital I did not see one made of clay! The attraction, however, to me to visit the State was the excellent accounts I had heard of the advance that women's education was making there, and these I found had not been in any sense over-coloured. The system pursued showed the best features of progress allied with wise discretion as to the dangers to be feared from undue pressure.

In the State I find that there are sixteen schools for girls, having a total number of 1468 pupils. According to statistics which I have at hand, the proportion of girls attending school throughout India is one to every 343 of the population, so that this number, compared with the 224,803 women of the State, gives the more satisfactory ratio of one girl in each 153. The Maharajah, together with his council, have, however, placed their system, so far as girls are concerned, upon a footing which is, I believe, unique in India, and that is by the appointment of a lady superintendent of female education. This office, which is a State one, is filled by Miss Brooke, who, before its institution, had occupied an important post at the Female Training College at Ahmedabad. The nomination, now of some five years' standing, has proved most fortunate, as Miss Brooke is not only a lady of wide culture, but she has a pleasant sympathy with the ways and workings of native character, while she grasps, as many well-intentioned English ladies fail to do, that the teaching suited to girls at home is not of necessity the best for their sisters out here. Her aim has been to make learning a practical reality. Rather than strive for striking examination effects, she has tried to render knowledge pleasant, and to induce bright, intelligent native girls to come forward as teachers. In this she has succeeded already in a manner which justifies her in hoping for yet better results in the future, and she looks forward to a time when female teachers or assistants will be available for all the schools in the State.

One of the most admirably ordered schools that I saw

throughout India was the Mahjiraj School in Bhaunagar city, which has upon its rolls no less a number than 283 scholars, of whom almost all are drawn from the leading and wealthy families of the place. A most public-spirited example has been set by the Maharajah in sending his own daughter, the Kumari Shri (Princess) Kasaba, a pretty and intelligent

SCHOOL GIRLS IN BHAUNAGAR.

young lady of about fifteen, to study here, in addition to receiving private tuition from Miss Brooke. The princess takes her place in class with the other girls, earning or losing her marks with complete impartiality, and is a good English scholar already. She showed me some of her exercise books, and her handwriting is extremely good, while she recited some difficult lines of Mrs. Sigourney's in the sweetest of voices and with excellent expression. This school, I learnt from Miss Brooke, was the oldest in the Gujerat province, and had been established as far back as 1857, and in its earlier days had had a hard battle to fight against prejudice and indifference. When she took up her appointment she found about 170 scholars attending, but every year has seen a notable increase up to the present figures. In the last Government examination held, 83 per cent. of the candidates passed. An interesting feature in a recent prize distribution was that ladies only were invited, and the awards were presented by Princess Ramba, an older daughter of the Maharajah's, who was educated in the school, and is now married to the heir-apparent of the Rajah of Brebunder. It is very rarely that such ladies can be induced to take part in anything approaching a public ceremony, and the event therefore is one of sufficient importance to note in any record of woman's progress in India. The singing is made a great feature of this school, and besides an English lady teacher, from whom two or three of the Parsee scholars are taking private lessons upon the piano, two native musicians from the State band attend to give instruction. A song in Gujerati and a simple two-part ditty in English were pleasingly rendered by the girls, who did sums, read English, and altogether went through an informal examination for me. Still I think nothing gave me greater satisfaction after the hideosities I had seen in Madras and Calcutta as specimens of needlework than the altogether delightful embroideries and stitchery laid before me. But I am old-fashioned enough to believe in such teaching as worthy of a place in any code, and its prominence is undoubtedly appreciated by those for whom the school exists, as upon its attendance registers are to be found Brahmins, Rajputs, Jains, Levanas (the wealthy trading caste), Parsees, and Mahommedans, the growing readiness of these to accept education being a source of great gratification to all. Several girls in the school had reached the sixth standard—practically equivalent to our own—and thirty-one were learning English.

The Wadwha school, on the outskirts of the town, which I visited, is more exclusively a working-class school, and numbers about 150. Unlike the experience of many other parts of India, it is less easy in Bhaunagar to secure the attendance of the lower castes than the upper, for, with its docks, public works, and other sources of labour, the people are so prosperous and well-employed that they want their daughters at home. Still, this school, which was opened in 1868, shows a

STREET SCENE, BHAUNAGAR.

steady increase since its foundation, and is giving a sound and useful education to its scholars, though it does not profess to teach beyond the fifth standard. Among its pupils are

STREET SCENE, BHAUNAGAR.

children drawn from the gardener and fruit-seller, the artisan, the basket-weaver, and other humble castes, though only two are set down as the children of agricultural labourers. A merry lot of little people were they, to whom a request to show me some of their games was more welcome than questions about the geography of the Bombay Presidency or the history of the Rajputs, and books were adjourned very readily for this purpose.

Bhaunagar, probably, will one day be in the field as a mart of worked silver, an art-industry which is developing there in a satisfactory manner. In conception and execution it is somewhat allied to that associated with Cutch in its palmier days, before European demands lowered its standards of design and craftsmanship. Vigorous and pleasing work is turned out by the Bhaunagar silversmiths in the form of cups, plates, and such accessories for the table as pepper-pots and finger-bowls; but when I was there its best workers were engaged upon the separate pieces to be used for a set of gates for a new temple then in the course of erection. These gates are extremely beautiful and are made of sandal-wood entirely overlaid with silver *repoussée*, chiefly representing scenes from the Hindu mythology.

Thus the movement has been initiated. Patience and tact are wanted for its development; and one little difficulty in the high education of working-class girls, especially when these are Mahommedans, ought not to be overlooked—that is, the danger of teaching them up to a more advanced standard than will probably be their husband's attainment. For again I can only repeat that the *istri-a-char*, the women's code, is opposed to innovation. Let me conclude this chapter with some remarks made before the National Indian Association by Mrs. Flora Annie Steel, who speaks with the knowledge of a quarter of a century of official connection with the Education Department of the North-West, and says—

"Your village matron is conservative to the backbone, and I doubt if even a revolting daughter would have a chance against a really stalwart Punjabi mother-in-law. I remember an example of this in Muzuffarghar, a district noted for its dislike to education. A boys' school was started in a certain village by the usual bribes to the head men of illuminated certificates, or possibly the still more coveted honour of a cane-bottomed chair to sit in at the district durbar, and a remarkably nice young man in a black alpaca coat went out to take charge of it, full of zeal and high imaginings. He returned to head-quarters next day full of bruises. The old women of the village had solemnly beaten him to the boundaries with their slippers. So far as they were concerned the schoolmaster was welcome to be abroad; he certainly should not be at home amongst them.

"Perhaps a beginning might be made by offering prizes at the village fair-time for proficiency in spinning, dairy work, cooking, and the preparation of simples. It is rather an opening of the siege by distant parallels; still I know of several cases in the West Highlands and Islands where the introduction of a churn thermometer has done more to shake the belief in witchcraft than the board school. For the A B C is not an Abracadabra; especially when the pupils leave the school long ere they reach words of five syllables."

CHAPTER III.

HER MARRIAGE.

"Enter, thrice happy! Enter, thrice desired!
And let the gates of Hari shut thee in
With the soul destined to thee from of old.

"Tremble not! lay thy lovely shame aside—
Lay it aside with thine unfastened zone,
And love him with the love that knows not fear.

"Because it fears not change; enter thou in,
Flower of all sweet and stainless womanhood,
For ever to grow bright, for ever new;

"Enter beneath the flowers, O flower fair!
Beneath these tendrils, Loveliest, that entwine
And clasp and wreathe and cling, with kissing stems;

"Enter with tender blowing airs of heaven,
Soft as love's breath, and gentle as the tones
Of lover's whispers when the lips come close;

"Enter the house of Love, O loveliest!
Enter the marriage bower, most beautiful!
And take and give the joy that Hari grants."

The Indian Song of Songs.

INACCURATE sensationalism reaches its climax over the system of child-marriage. The assiduously circulated idea of missionary reports and social grievance seekers is that the wretched girl-infant is married at about five or six years of age, generally to some one vastly older than herself, who takes her away whenever he pleases, and exercises whatever violence of brutal lust he cares for. We are bidden to imagine barbarous results of force too revolting to be set down on paper, too impossibly hideous in suggestion, one would have thought, for any human being to have believed of another. But that the ceremony of infancy is a mere form of betrothal, and that the second series of rites (the *rukhsati*, or bride's home-taking), immediately preceding the consummation of the marriage, is rarely proceeded with until the girl has given unmistakable physical evidence of having reached womanhood, is not explained, and in this fact lies the defence of the whole theory on which Indian matrimonial views are based.

Oriental sex-philosophy goes to primitive and elementary nature, and teaches woman that life without marriage is incomplete. Maternity, it proceeds to impart, is the object for which she was sent into the world, and this obligation, which she has no right to shirk or modify, if fulfilled, brings with it the best of happiness in this life and the best of rewards in the next. Indeed, it is only by the bearing of children that she can rise above her curse of disabilities as a mere woman, bearing in herself the taint of original sin, that demands for its expiation the gift of a son to carry the domestic worship of her husband's family. Mr. H. H. Risley, whose essay on "Caste in Relation to Marriage" is one of the most frank and common-sense contributions that have been made to this subject, scarcely regards the standard Brahmanical explanation that marriage is a sort of sacrament, and the earlier her mystical functions are accomplished in life the better, as a fully adequate one, and thinks rather that enforced competition for husbands—"hypergamy, or the law of superior marriage"—has tended to bring about the present deeply rooted system. His remarks merit quotation, as the opinion of one who has had opportunities altogether exceptional for arriving at sound conclusions.

"Enforced competition for husbands on the part of the higher groups, and the desire to imitate their superiors which animates the lower groups, combine to run up the prices of husbands in the upper classes, while the demand for wives by the men of the lower class, which ought by rights to produce equilibrium, is artificially restricted in its operation by the rule that they can, under no circumstances, marry a woman of the classes above their own. These men, therefore, are left very much out in the cold, and often do not get wives until late in life. An unmarried son does not disgrace the family, but there is no greater reproach than to have a daughter unmarried at the age of puberty. Husbands are bought for the girls, and the family gets its money's worth in social estimation. Bargains, however, must be taken when they are to be had; and no father dares run the risk of waiting till his daughter is physically mature. He is bound to be on the safe side, and therefore he marries her, child as she may be, whenever a good match offers.

"Many hard things have been said of infant marriage, and the modern tendency is to assume that a population which countenances such a practice must be in a fair way towards great moral degradation, if not to ultimate extinction. Much of this criticism seems to me to be greatly exaggerated, and to be founded on considerable ignorance of the present conditions and future possibilities of Oriental life. In truth, excluding the poetical view that marriages are made in heaven, two working theories of the institution are at present in existence—one which leaves marriages to make themselves by the process of unrestricted courtship, and another which requires them to be made by the parents or guardians of the people who are to be married. The first, which we may perhaps call the system of selection, is accepted, and more or less acted up to, by all Western nations except those who follow the French custom of *mariages de convenance.* The second, a system of avowedly artificial selection, is in force, with few exceptions, throughout the East. For all Hindus, except the handful of *declassées* who have adopted more or less completely European ideas on the subject of marriage, and seem now to be on the high-road to form a new caste, the bare idea that a girl can have any voice in the selection of her husband is excluded by the operation of three inexorable sanctions—by the ordinances of the Hindu religion; by the general structure of the caste system; and by the general tone and condition of social life in India. Religion prescribes that, like the Roman bride of early days, a Hindu girl shall be given (*tradita in manum*) by her father into the power of her husband; caste complications demand that the ceremonial portion of the transfer shall be effected while she is still a child; while the character of society, the moral tone of the men, the seclusion of the women, the immemorial taboos and conventions of family etiquette render it impossible that she should be wooed and won like her European sister. To persons of a romantic turn of mind, the admission that infant marriage in some shape must be accepted as an ultimate fact of the Hindu social system will sound like a final abandonment of all hope of reform. But there is more to be said for the custom than appears at first sight. A moment's dispassionate consideration will show that if any sort of controlling authority is to make people's marriages for them, the earlier it commences and completes its operations the better. Where the choice of a husband must in any case be undertaken by the parents, it is clearly tempting Providence for them to defer it until their daughter has grown up, and may have formed an embarrassing attachment on her own account. As for love, that may come—and, from all one hears of Hindu unions, usually does come—as readily after marriage as before, provided that opportunities for falling in love with the wrong man are judiciously withheld. This may seem a cynical way of handling the matter, but it is the only way that accords with the lines of Oriental life as at present ordered, and it were folly to dream of making all things new."

Certainly, so far as my own experience went in my travels, the Indian women are not dissatisfied with the present system; but the common reply, when one ventures that statement to superior persons who have not been in India, is, "Yes; but if they get a little education they at once want to alter it." On that point, however, I received some enlightenment at Bombay. I was invited, in a very prettily worded and nicely written note, to come with my hostess for the time being to tea with two young Mussulman women. We were received by them and the other women of their family in a beautifully furnished room, with a handsome Axminster carpet on the floors, and well-chosen English engravings on the walls, as well as pretty trifles of china and needlework decoratively employed. The two young ladies were exquisitely dressed in native costume, one being in white satin with a quantity of silver-embroidered gauze over her hair and shoulders, and the other in a cunning blending of pale pink and green. Both spoke English faultlessly, and I learnt that they had only recently been married, one being nearly twenty and the other over twenty-one; while I knew further that they were strictly *purdah* girls. It was too good a chance to lose, and I asked them if, as their husbands were both highly educated men, one holding a position under Government, and the other a barrister of rising practice, whether they would not now "break their *purdah*."

"Not at all," they replied together, and the older one continued, "Why should we? You English ladies don't understand how very little we really lose by it. We see the men of our own families as freely as you can see yours. Even our cousins of our own age we may meet; but where we differ is that you allow them to take what we should consider liberties, and, I believe, even kiss them. Now, a high-class girl is taught not to touch so much as the hand of a man, and that becomes simply a matter of habit as easy to preserve as any other good manners. European women don't think it hard that they may not sit on a man's knee, do they? Well, we don't think it hard to keep at a little distance, and that is only a question, I think, of degree. Our husbands would willingly let us go out, but we have been taught all our lives that men other than they are as nothing to us; and you see we have not any inclination or desire to ride or drive or walk in the streets. We go to our family parties, and can see and receive all our women friends. I don't see what there is to be dissatisfied about. And so far," she continued, "I don't think you can call the working results of our system a failure. Take our own family, and we can carry our pedigree back for twenty generations—that means a great many daughters—but never has one of them discredited or dishonoured our women's fair name. Are there many European families who could say as much?"

Of course, with the aristocracy of the Muslim race, marriages seldom take place outside their own circle, and I fancy it would upset some pet theories as to the results of continued intermarriage to trace the complications of blood-relationship in some of the high-class families of the north-west. If I speak here first of the Mahommedan marriage customs, it is because they vary much less than do those of the Hindus, and can therefore be more quickly dismissed. Where there are more sons than daughters in a family community it becomes necessary to seek an eligible *parti* from outside; but the utmost care is always exercised in this, and the closest scrutiny invariably made concerning the relative social status of both sides. I have already described the advantage that the thikra ceremony gives, and supposing that the child duly lives, it is generally about the age of ten that the mother of the prospective bridegroom makes formal proposal on his behalf. On this point, I may correct an erroneous impression concerning the usual age of the bridegroom. He is generally from five to eight years older than the bride in the ranks of all above the very poorest, so that when she can be taken to his own house he is generally from nineteen to twenty-two, against her thirteen to sixteen. In the case of ruling princes, one often finds them fully married as young as fifteen to seventeen; but the general tendency—doubtless largely influenced by the longer time required for a modern professional education—is, as with us, to raise considerably the average of the male marrying age. As a consequence perhaps of this fact, the young man's consent to his parents pursuing the customary preliminaries is now almost invariably asked by them directly or indirectly.

While she is alive, it is always the mother of the bridegroom who opens the negotiations, and she takes with her as many of her nearest relations as she can. It is seldom that she is not so sufficiently sure of her reception by the bride's family as to render this a merely formal step, but instances arise at times when a pushing or intriguing woman has secured the privileges of the thikra, and the girl's parents had other views as to her disposal. In such case there is often bitter feud, as the prejudices in favour of the old custom are very strong, and at the same time parents may have good reason for not desiring the offered suitor.

Supposing, however, that no opposition has been raised, the mother comes home triumphantly, and the preparations for *mangni*, or actual engagement, are at once begun. An auspicious day is carefully chosen, and one that is equally convenient to both families. It is incumbent on the bridegroom's parents to contribute largely to the feast that will be held at the house of the bride, as their own particular

A BIT OF A WEDDING PROCESSION.

friends, as well as the relatives of their side, will participate in it, and their offerings, which consist generally of the choicest fruits in season and procurable, both fresh and dried, as dates, raisins, almonds, and nuts, are sent in large *bhwans* (trays, with closely fitting covers). The mere public announcement that such a marriage has been arranged suffices to constitute the betrothal, and between the young people themselves no formal ceremony takes place. When this, however, has been made, it is imperative etiquette that the bride and bridegroom shall not see one another. So intensely strong is this curious convention, that the young man's family can insist upon the match being broken off if he has caught a glimpse of his wife that is to be, and as it would be greatly to the disrepute of the contracting family for such a thing to occur, the utmost care is exercised as to the girl's seclusion in the zenana.

There her young mind is fed with ample details of what married life has in store for her. She, and all the older women of the household, watch eagerly for signs of physical development, and hail her attainment of womanhood as an event of great joy, which may be discussed without the slightest reticence. With the Hindus the chief difference of preliminary detail is only that betrothal has probably taken place at an earlier age. Meantime both prepare their *trousseaux*, to be in readiness immediately that it may be required. Very beautiful indeed are some of the draperies that are put into these bridal outfits; and I recall a *sari* that I saw at Calcutta of *malmal*, the soft silk muslin of the Punjab, in a full rich shade of myrtle, only to be produced with indigo, and the native yellow dyes of *asbarg*, the flower of the Cabul larkspur, and *narsingar*, the sweet-scented blossom of one of the *nyctanthes*. The bordering was a subtle blending of orange and yellow, and the more misty hues of vermilion, into which each of the same dyes entered, and was a harmonious result that could never have been obtained with any mixtures of unallied anilines and chemicals.

During the years that elapse between *mangni* and *shadi*, as the Mahommedans term the second part of the ceremony, presents of fruit and other things are continually passing between the contracting parties. On festival days the young man is always expected to visit his future parents-in-law, and it is regarded as good manners on his part to do so on frequent other occasions.

When the bride's family are satisfied that the time has come that the marriage rites can be completed, there is much talk and discussion as to the details, and the first consideration is that of a day and date. The *nek saat*, or good omens, in each family have to be brought into accord, and mutual convenience must not be overlooked. The wedding-day is generally fixed some weeks or even months before, to allow of ample preparation; but meantime an entertainment is usually given to the chief relations and friends on both sides, when it is decided who else outside the immediately contracting families are to be asked, and invitations issued. Among wealthy families, too, it is not unusual to commence *naubat*, or the wedding music at the gates, quite a fortnight before *barat*—a word used as the generic term to cover both the feasting and processions of the actual ceremony.

Shadi itself embraces several minor observances, of which the *sachakh* is the first. People hired for the purpose assemble at the bridegroom's house, and are then deputed to carry to the residence of the bride sweetmeats, dried fruits, and sugar-candy, and jars, in which are henna leaves, with which native women are wont to stain their hands and feet. A complete outfit, of all the richest and costliest materials available, is also sent for the bride, and in return her family send back an equally beautiful dress for the young husband-elect to wear. This procession, which is generally joined by several members of his family, is always accompanied by music, and the offerings are received formally and taken into the zenana, where the ladies examine them with keenly critical eyes and much interest.

Barat is the next stage, and unless the distance between the two houses is very great, it is a point of etiquette that all the men attending should walk, the bridegroom alone riding on horseback. The women follow either in closed carriages, or *palkis*, richly decorated and closely curtained, and music by professional performers constitutes an important feature of the display. Elephants, camels, floral trophies, and banners are requisitioned wherever possible to add to its pomp and circumstance, and if the procession has

GIRLS GOING TO A WEDDING IN PALKIS.

to pass through a town, it perambulates all its streets rather than taking a direct course. At the house of the bride a hearty welcome is accorded to all; the guests are ushered inside, and food is available for all the servants and retainers, as well as in many cases for the attendant rabble who follow to see what they can. Indoors an entertainment of music and singing, with very often a dance, is arranged; but I must admit that Eastern dancing is as a rule woefully disappointing to European eyes. When one has seen the splendid classical grace of movement among the women as they carry their water-pots upon their heads, or marked the easy swing of well-developed limbs, it is difficult to think that they could ever be wanting in charm of movement. And yet when they come to pose and posture as "dancing," all this seems subordinated to mere wrigglings and contortions, supposed, I believe, to be voluptuously suggestive to the Oriental male mind, but rather resulting in monotonous muscular spasms.

A BIT OF A WEDDING PROCESSION.

This enjoyment generally begins in the late afternoon or early evening, and its delights are long drawn out into the night; so far, indeed, that there is often but very brief interval before *nikah*, or *ajd*—the wedding-service—takes place, early next morning. The kazi, whose position in the internal regulation of Mussulman affairs is a little difficult to define, since he is priest, arbitrator, and judge, arrives and seats himself before the bridegroom, and the question of *mahar*, or the marriage settlements, are brought forward.

The demands of the bride's family are generally exorbitant, and out of all proportion to the bridegroom's paying possibilities; and as a consequence these unreasonable sums, such as half a million rupees, are seldom even in part set aside at all. It is supposed, however, to be more in accordance with the bride's dignity to ask a very high figure for her portion. Both bride and bridegroom are separately and formally asked if they consent to be united, and on an affirmative reply from each, there is a short office of prayers and excerpts from the Koran. Songs appropriate to the occasion are also sung by the professional musicians engaged, and a quantity of *hatashi*—a peculiar form of sweetmeat—and dates are thrown over the head of the bridegroom and picked up by the guests. He is then congratulated by all assembled, and is expected to shake hands with the kazi and embrace all his nearest relatives.

Meantime, however, the bride has remained in the zenana, and for a shy youth the worst part of the ceremony has now to be faced. For he must enter it alone, and here the women make it a point of honour to accord him a "warm reception." It is usual for several of the girls to stand behind the door and to meet him with a shower of stripes from little switches, to which long silken tassels have been tied, while others throw shoes at him, and inflict all the small torments possible upon him. However annoying these may be, he must accept them good-naturedly, though he is allowed the consolation of encouragement from one or two of the older women, who whisper to him of the loveliness of the bride and of the delights that are in store for him when he may behold her. This detail of the ceremony may be undertaken by any of the elderly relatives; but in the towns of the north-west it is more usually performed by ladies professionally engaged for the purpose. Both bride and bridegroom wear the *sikra*—a floral garland from which a veil falls over the face—and with this on they are seated opposite to each other.

Thus seated, the *Kutam Majid*, or holy book, is brought before them with respectful reverence, and both their veils are raised. Then it is that the husband beholds his wife for the first time; but it is considered very bold and indecorous for the girl to lift her modestly bent head or to open her closed eyes at this time, and she thus remains, even when he, in survival of old ideas of marriage by capture, lifts her to carry her to the carriage, or *palki*, in which she is to be taken to his house. However slight he may be, or whatever are her proportions, he is allowed no assistance of any kind in this. The returning procession is made yet more imposing by the addition to it of all the bride's presents, which are usually very numerous. The day after the marriage the bride is brought home to her parents' house for a short time, and the significant rejoicings and games of *chanthi* are held. She goes back, however, with her husband, and enters the zenana of his father's house, where for the first year or so of her married life she has many hard lessons of discipline and forbearance to learn.

The Hindu marriage customs differ in many essential points from those of the Mahommedan race, and great divergencies exist again between those of the various castes. Further variations there are still between the pure Aryans and the aboriginal tribes, even though, as in Orissa or on the Malabar coast, these may have accepted Hinduism either fully or with modifications. It would not be difficult to fill a whole book with these diverse ordinances, or to find reasons and explanations concerning most of them. It will, however, suffice if I describe a few of the most characteristic that came under my personal observation, and particularly interesting are those of the Brahmins, whether in well-known Eastern Bengal or upon the seldom-visited slopes of the Western Ghats.

Among the nine qualities which the Brahmanical statutes ordain as essentials of right conduct, *avritti*, or the observance of legal marriage, is one. The ceremony has in consequence been hedged round with a vast amount of ritual, but, provided that a girl is wedded before she attains to womanhood, it does not much matter at what age her marriage takes place. After the preliminaries and mutual agreement between the contracting parties have been settled, the first step to be taken is the anointing of both the bride and bridegroom with turmeric. I believe that according to strict custom this should be done to the boy or young man first, and that some of the same preparation as he has used should be sent to the girl, unless he lives at too great a distance for this to reach her the same day. This has always been selected for astrological reasons, and it is essential that both be anointed upon it. Then begins a sequence of entertainments that last, according to the circumstances of the two families and their friends, from three days to a month, the rule being that a great dinner should be given, first by the parents of the young couple, and after that, that kinsfolk and acquaintance should arrange such a series that neither eats again in their own house till the wedding takes place. The night previous to the wedding as many of the married women friends of both families as possible meet and eat together, and are given betel-leaves and areca-nut, in return for which hospitality they are expected to invoke prosperity and happiness for the pair to be wedded. A *sraddh*, or service of offering, is performed on the morning of the day on which the bridegroom

A CALCUTTA ZENANA.

will go in procession to the bride's house, and the favour of the household gods and the departed ancestors for three or four generations back is besought.

The *bar jutri*, or bridegroom's procession, sets out usually in the evening, and he takes with him a "best man," who, as a rule, is his younger brother and a mere boy. The women of the bride's family receive him with noisy shouts of "*Ulu, ulu!*" (Joy, joy!), but he takes a place upon a raised dais called in Bengal a *masnad*, and waits until the moment arrives at which the ceremony can be proceeded with auspiciously. The first step in this is for the girl's father to take him into one of the inner rooms of the house, where he stands upon a board that has been smeared with rice-flour, symbolic of the plenty that may surround his steps; and water for washing his feet, and a syrup, into the composition of which honey enters largely, are offered to him, both of which he touches as sign of their acceptance.

Meantime, however, the women have their special usages, and the mother of the bride welcomes her future son-in-law by pouring some curds at his feet. The full ritual then gone through is called *satusi*, or, as we might render it, the seven lights of Hymen, and is extremely curious. Seven married women, all in festal attire, one of whom must be the bride's mother, unless she is a widow and so debarred from fulfilling any public function, in which case her place is taken by an aunt, each hold a torch of small twigs and cotton waste. The mother or the aunt leads the way, and bears upon her head a flat basket, round which are twenty-one small lights. Seven times round the bridegroom they walk, all of them assisting to cast the lights in the basket over his head, while water is sprinkled, and one of the number blows a conch-shell, the rest vociferating, "*Ulu, ulu!*" This cry is continued by all of them, while the bride's mother (or aunt) touches the bride-groom's brow with an oddly heterogeneous collection of things, which include betel and areca nut, curds, sandal-wood, oil, a bit of clay from the Ganges, a looking-glass, and a cluster of plaintains. This ceremony, I am bound to say, I have not

A FLORAL TROPHY IN A WEDDING PROCESSION.

seen, and knowing the Brahmanical caste hatred for Europeans, I imagine that very few not of their own *jat* have done so. My information on this point has been derived from separate and reliable sources, however, and I give it without hesitation. The next step I believe is that the mother places a weaver's shuttle between the young man's hands, and binds him hand and foot to symbolize the fetters he has imposed upon himself, and he then indicates his humility in the situation by bleating like a sheep. There is another and perhaps prettier form, in which future happiness is indicated when she lays upon his lips a padlock and turns the key, so showing that the door of unkind speech has been closed.

A Brahmin bride wears red silk upon her wedding-day, and after these observances concerning the bridegroom have been carried out she is brought in seated upon a board by attendants, who circle seven times round the bridegroom. When she is set down before him, a large cloth is quickly spread over both for a few seconds, and in that moment is supposed to come to them the love that will last them for life. They then exchange garlands, and come out into more public gaze, after which there is little secrecy or mystery even in the highest caste rites.

The next stage is the *sampradan,* or the gift and its acceptance, in which the father of the girl, following the words recited by the priest present, offers her to the bridegroom, and his formula of reception runs, "Who gave her? Love gave her. To whom did he give her? To Love he gave her. Love is the giver: Love is the taker. Love pervades the ocean. With love I accept her. Love—may this also be thine." Presents are then exchanged, and the couple are escorted to the bridal chamber, a corner of her *sari* being knotted to his cloth, but it is a part of this item of the ceremony that a number of young women are already in the room, and it is their business to keep the wearied lad from obtaining any sleep for the rest of the night. Lastly comes the *kusandika,* observed among all the higher castes as the final and most binding portion of the whole ceremony. Fire, under priestly manipulation, is kindled from a sacred source, and *ghi* (clarified butter) poured upon it in offering. From it seven points are marked off, upon which the bride must tread, and, treading upon her heel in token of her whole subjection to him, follows the bridegroom reciting certain prescribed forms. Then the newly made wife changes her *gotra*, or family sign, for that of her husband, and the lad with his own hand makes a mark in vermilion upon the parting of her hair. Three days after marriage the young people are laid upon a bed surrounded with flowers, and afterwards a final feast is given, for which the rice must have been prepared by the girl-bride. If the bridegroom's family eat this, it is a sign that they are satisfied that all ceremonial and caste observance had been properly regarded.

Among the Nambutiris, as the Brahmins of the Malabar coast are called, the early details involve a handsome dowry honestly paid in full by the girl's father. The bridegroom's procession and the feasting and first ceremonies are much the same as in Eastern India, but he carries also a bamboo staff in his right hand and has a thread tied round his right arm, while the bride holds a mirror and an arrow, and wears the sacred *tali*, or string, round her throat. This, with the Brahmins and higher-caste Hindus, and an iron bangle among the lower ones, is the usual equivalent of our wedding-ring, though the right to draw a line of vermilion down the parting of the hair is another outward and visible sign throughout India of marriage.

To proceed, however, with the Nambutiri rites, the father of the bride hands her with her dowry to her husband, the two take seven steps forward together, an offering is made, and as the procession leaves the house for that of the bridegroom he is bidden in set phrase to show her all kindness and consideration. Arrived here, there is further eating and drinking, and the pair are led by a priest to their own room, where a rug is laid on the floor with quantities of rice and paddy round it. The pair seat themselves on this, the priest goes out and locks the door, and then chants in a loud voice passages from the sacred books, which the bridegroom audibly follows. Then the wife has to serve her husband with his first meal, and the union is a completely valid one.

With the Hindus, however, whether of high or low caste, it is only in rare instances that the girl-bride goes to her husband's house until she has attained to full womanhood. Certain sub-sects and particularly devout families perform at this period of her life an office of purification known as *garbhadhan* or *punarbihaha*, or a kind of penance, varying in severity, but, so far as I can learn, usually consisting of seclusion from the rest of the family and a fasting diet of rice and *ghi*, all sweets being forbidden. Even the enlightened Parsees of Bombay have not overcome their racial prejudices as to a woman's occasional pollution and uncleanness, and isolate their girls at certain periods.

So much for high caste ceremonial, and a few words may now be spared for that of the lower orders and working folks, among whom *purdah* is not observed. The first and most important functionary in village or bazaar life is the *hajjam*, or barber, who knows to a nicety the circumstances of all his neighbours. The parents of the girl tell him they are looking for an eligible *parti* for her, and he, in the pride of his knowledge, names to them the two or three he has good reason to think would not be unfavourably inclined. He receives his instructions to negotiate in the matter, and goes to the parents of the bridegrooms in prospective to discuss it, and eventually decides which he considers in every way the most desirable alliance for both sides. Then the question of *tilak*, or bride's dowry, comes into consideration, though so various are the practices sanctioned by custom upon this point that it is almost impossible to lay down any hard and fast rules concerning them. With many of the non-Aryan but Hinduized tribes, for instance, the system of the bridegroom's paying a bride-price—a survival clearly of marriage by purchase—obtains; notably among these I may mention the Doms, a large Dravidian caste; the Kols, a hard-working and industrious people, much employed in mining; and the Santals, a really interesting and very large jungle race; and in each of these the bridegroom pays to the girl's parents from three to ten rupees. With the last-named he has in addition to present to her mother and both her grandmothers, if alive, a new *sari*.

By all, save the very lowest Hindus, it is deemed essential to the validity of the marriage that a Brahmin priest should be present. When the marriage has been brought about through the agency of the *hajjam*, he assists the priest in counting the bride's dowry, and this constitutes a part of the ceremonial. On the west coast, however, with the Kadupattars, who are a humble school-teaching caste, the barber is himself allowed to perform certain of the rites, though the *tali*, the symbol of marriage, is always with them tied by a near female relative of the bridegroom's.

On this Malabar coast the Nayars form one of the most interesting studies in racial characteristics to be found in British India, as they, almost alone, preserve in their present day customs evidences of the polyandry they formerly practised. Early history has something to say of them, since the Sheikh Zin-ud-din, somewhere after the middle of the sixteenth century, stated that it was customary for each woman to have from two to four men as husbands, and that these seldom quarrelled, while later, Hamilton, writing in 1727 his "New Account of the East Indies," observed that the husbands, who might not exceed twelve in number at once, "do agree very well, for they cohabit with her in their turns according to their priority of marriage, ten days more or less, according as they fix a term among themselves, and he that cohabits with her maintains her in all things necessary for his time, so that she is plentifully provided for by a constant circulation."

Now, as I saw these Nayars on the coast between Tellichery and on to somewhere beyond Cochin, they are a shy race, the women noticeable for their scanty clothing, and remarkable because even to this day the husband has no legal rights and responsibilities according to the tribal understanding of the law, which is merely undoubted custom, towards his wife or his children. In the early stages of the marriage rites there is little difference to be noted in those that one has seen in other parts of the dependency, neither does there, unless one has been warned of it, seem anything unusual in the tying of the tali round her neck. Yet she is not married to the man who has done this, and the mere fact that he has done it constitutes an insurmountable barrier to his becoming her husband in later life. He is merely an east-coast Brahmin, whose profession in life is to act a part in this pseudo-ceremony, and in return to take a fee for his services.

Still, by the strict technicalities of other castes, the girl is the wife of a plurality of husbands, for later on, and when she is of an age to decide for herself, she chooses a man whom she will wed. In the phrase employed to denote the short office of this comparatively civilized system of marriage she passes the door of good and of bad, and the contract is made by the mutual exchange of two pieces of cloth in the presence of kinsfolk and friends.

It is so common to think of Indian women as deprived of all voice in the choice of their husbands that I may go back again to Central Bengal to mention both the rites and the rights of the Santali and Kol women, whom I saw in the coal-mining district of Girideh.

The former tribe is divided into twelve septs, nearly all of which have passwords of their own, and marriage may not take place between two members of the same sept. The girls, who do not wed at a very early age, are allowed a certain choice of their own in the selection of their husbands. Two whom I saw, who were shortly to be married, were approaching sixteen years of age, and were fine, well-grown girls, who had no shyness in standing for the photograph I wished to make of them. Some of their marriage customs are curiously primitive survivals, and one of these is that while a price, as I have already stated—usually three rupees, with a new sari each to her mother and grandmothers—is paid for the bride, in the case of a widow who is permitted to re-marry only half that sum is asked. The argument on which this is based is that such ladies can only be regarded as borrowed, and each will have to be returned to her first husband in the next world, so that as the second one only enjoys her companionship temporarily, he is only to be expected to pay a reduced price for her. In what is known as a "bazaar marriage," which, though quite binding, is only resorted to when the girl seems shy and "holding off," the young man dips his fingers into red paint or earth, and watches his opportunity when the young lady is out walking or shopping to make a mark upon her brow. He has, however, to run away at full speed to escape the thrashing that her male relations would administer to him for his audacity. If the girl declines to live with him she has to go through a ceremony of divorce, and I heard of one or two cases in which girls had been thus wedded out of spite in order to compel them to subject themselves to this indignity.

It should never be forgotten that the law nominally protects a girl until she has passed the age of twelve. In the absence, however, of a thorough system of birth registration, and in very many instances the existence of a superstitious unwillingness to state age correctly, it is always exceedingly difficult to ascertain what the true years of any native may be. Nor must the fact be overlooked that, with poor parents especially, it is advantageous to them to hand over their daughters to the custody of their husbands, and thus obtain relief from the cost, small even as it may be, of their maintenance. The Indian girl develops and ages very rapidly, and it is very rare to see a woman over thirty who is not wrinkled, wizened, and unlovely, either in exceeding skinniness or excessive *embonpoint.* The youngest instance of motherhood that I saw was a girl who had just passed her thirteenth birthday, when it happened to be one of the rare cases in which an age could be definitely fixed, and in her arms was a lusty five-months'-old infant. So far, however, from this being an "awful example" of the evils of the system, it was very much the reverse, for the girl-mother was tall, strong, and vigorous, nursing her child adequately, and looking in every sense the picture of robust animal health.

Sentimentality, and that insular habit of thought which decides that what is right in England is of necessity the only right course anywhere else in the world, has launched a big weight of prejudice against the system, which is not at all borne out, viewed in the dispassionate light of working results. If one half of the evils set down as associated with it were true, the Indian race must have been effete, if not extinct, generations ago. He would be regarded, however, as a rash man who ventured any doubts to-day as to the virility, fighting qualities, and capacities for enduring hard strain, of Ghurka or Sikh, Pathan or Rajput, even beside those "raw bhoys that don't know fwhat a bullut manes, and wudn't care av they did," as no less an authority than Private Mulvaney says. In fact, with these fighting races marriage takes place very young, and the tradition concerning the last named is that even, if not now, at least until very recently, premature consummation was the rule and not the exception. Yet to see the stately carriage of the men, and the fine figures and swinging walk of the women, as one traverses Rajputana, as I did, from Jeypore to Ahmedabad and Bombay, gives one no inclination to support the approved paper theories. I hold no brief for child-marriage, and think it would undoubtedly be to the greater happiness of the girl in the long run to let her enjoy two or three years of light-hearted absence from care before she assumed the responsibilities of motherhood. Such, however, is not the view taken of it by Hindu or Muslim religion or custom, and I have tried to view the question as they do, and see the advantages they find in it—for it is idle to suppose that they would have maintained a system down so many of the centuries if it had not possessed certain recommendations in their eyes—rather than to look at it from the strictly European standpoint, and as a peg for all the critical fault-finding to be hung on.

Meantime the advocates of Western "reforms" may take

note of a tendency to raise the age of marriage among the thoughtful and educated of the two races. It is as it should be that the movement has started in two of the native States, namely, Mysore and Hyderabad. Not only will this have a swifter and deeper influence, coming from such quarters, but with the smouldering ashes of hatred buried darkly, and seldom perceived, as they are against the British rule, any effort in this direction, initiated from our side, would have been undoubtedly met by more than covert hostility. In both these States the age of marriage has been placed at fourteen. In Hyderabad it is true that, by safe-guarding clauses which nullify one another, the act virtually reads: "You shall not marry your girls younger than fourteen, unless your family wants to do so, and then you may." But the point to be noted with satisfaction is that the germ of an idea is there, that excessively early marriage may not be an unmixed good, and that it should be discouraged rather than fostered.

Of the Parsees and their marriage customs there is not much to be written. Zoroastrian ethics recommends marriage on the ground that wedded life is more likely to be happy than unwedded, and the encouragement of matrimony is a meritorious act. Consequently several rich Parsees have founded endowment funds for the purpose of providing poor but deserving girls with *dots,* and it is unusual to find unmarried women in this community. Fifteen is the lowest age at which a girl may marry; but to find one actually wedded at this period is exceedingly rare, and twenty to twenty-five is the general age. As a result the Parsee women retain their good looks and graceful carriage far longer than those by whom they are surrounded.

The Parsee marriage ceremonial is in itself simple and

impressive, though it is usually, even among the humblest, made the occasion of much pretty pageantry. The bridegroom is escorted by a bevy of the bride's girl friends, who wear their most charming saris, and carry flowers from his house to that of the bride, or wherever the rite is to be performed. From him they receive gifts, which also they present, and make certain offerings of rice, rose-water, and other symbolic things, while his own gifts to the bride, of a new sari and articles of household use, are brought in on flower-decked trays and laid down in all due formality before the assembled company. Both bride and bridegroom receive the benedictions and good wishes of their parents, and are then taken to a raised dais, which has been decorated with all the resources of flowers, gold paper, and coloured drapings at command. The service is conducted by two priests, who recite from memory several long chapters and prayers, based upon a verse in the *Gatha*, which runs: "I say these words to you marrying brides and to you bridegrooms. Impress them in your minds. May you twain enjoy the life of good mind by following the laws of religion. Let each of you clothe the other with righteousness, because then assuredly there will be a happy life for you." Between each section of the service rice is cast towards the young couple, to signify plenty and prosperity; but, with the adoption of European ideas, the fashionable tendency of the Parsees is to abbreviate and simplify the service as far as possible. It is followed by a dinner, at which the newly-married couple are present; and they are generally accompanied to their future home by a number of their friends, who continue their merry-making far into the night.

CHAPTER IV.

MEDICAL AID AND ASSISTANCE FOR THE SICK.

"And those things which have long gone together are, as it were, confederate within themselves, whereas new things piece not so well; but, though they help by their utility, yet they trouble by their inconformity. . . . It were good therefore that men in their innovations would follow the example of time itself, which indeed innovateth greatly but quietly, and by degrees scarce to be perceived."—BACON.

WHENEVER the history of the social life of India comes to be written, the influences and developments of the movement for supplying medical aid to the women will constitute a factor of weighty consideration. I am not prepared to say that even yet are the problems of the situation all solved, nor that enlightened and scientific methods are everywhere superseding the superstitious and harmful practices of ignorance. Still, an appreciable beginning in the right direction has been made; the Dufferin Fund has laboured long enough to allow of a fair estimate being formed of the results in actual working of its noble intentions. Zenana medical missions have long realized that the healing of the body seems more apparently, to the native mind, making for righteousness than the healing of the soul; and to-day there exists a sufficiently large body of native female practitioners to demand attention in any discussion of present conditions and future outlook.

Of the inception of the Dufferin Fund it is unnecessary to write much. The scheme, so broad in its scope, so profound in its sympathies, and so high in its ideals, was surely one of the finest ever evolved from woman's brain and heart, and

THE MARCHIONESS OF DUFFERIN AND AVA, C.I.

because it has not hurried on to its complete realization with the speed that its generous foundress, in her deep womanly pity for the suffering she had seen around her, would have wished, rather let it not be written of in the bald terms that relate to negative success, but spoken of as only another confirmatory evidence in the long list of experiences that in India, as elsewhere, the best progress is made by gentle steps.

The fund was first started in 1885, under the direct patronage of the Queen-Empress, and a well-considered list of high British officials and native rulers and gentlemen as vice-patrons and central committee was drawn up. No less a sum than two lakhs (200,000) of rupees were given very readily by the Nizam of Hyderabad, the Maharajah of Jeypore, and the Maharajah of Ulwar, and their good example—quite as much, be it fairly stated, from a genuine admiration of the disinterested kindness of their popular vicereine, as from the native characteristic of emulation, which leads the ruler of one petty state to try and outdo his neighbour of another—was promptly and generously followed. Ere long, the committee found itself able to invest five and a half lakhs of rupees, and, thanks to further liberal gifts, its capital now stands at 11,96,300 rupees.

At the risk of criticism to the effect that I am here only stating what is accessible in yearly reports, I think it advisable to dwell a little on the working plan of the fund. Misconception is so pitifully rife as to its purpose and system, and while people are to be found who ask whether it does not train missionaries or provide hospital nurses for the British troops in the East, or send soldiers' wives to homes on the hills, there is at least some occasion to say plainly at the outset both what it does and does not do, to render further remarks properly intelligible. As stated in its own articles of association, the three primary objects of the fund are as follows:—

1. *Medical tuition*, including the teaching and training in India of women as doctors, hospital assistants, nurses, and midwives.
2. *Medical relief*, including—
   (*a*) the establishment under female superintendence of dispensaries and cottage hospitals for the treatment of women and children;
   (*b*) the opening of female wards under female superintendence in existing hospitals and dispensaries;
   (*c*) the provision of female medical officers and attendants for existing female wards;
   (*d*) the founding of hospitals for women where special funds or endowments are forthcoming.
3. The supply of trained female nurses and midwives for women and children in hospitals and private houses.

It does not pretend to be evangelizing or sectarian, and it frankly faces but does not attempt to crush the grave difficulties with which it is confronted by *purdah* conventions and caste prejudices.

Next, it must be understood that the Indian Government maintains a very efficient state-supported service of medical aid. By this, over eighteen hundred institutions are kept up, in the larger towns in the form of civil hospitals, under the chief medical authority of the district when it is "up country," and under the professors, physicians, and surgeons of the medical colleges of the Presidency towns. During the last few years small dispensaries, generally affording accommodation for a few in-patients and under the control of an assistant-surgeon or a hospital assistant, have multiplied exceedingly. Now, to such institutions as these the poorer and working class women could go, and in the case of the hospitals they could feel assured of special female wards. But—and that "but" covers very much—the doctor would inevitably be a man. To the secluded and low caste women of the community this did not greatly matter, though even such have certain inherited dislikes and what I may call the *purdah* spirit upon the subject. These, therefore, already in a measure provided for, Lady Dufferin could regard as presenting less immediately pressing claims, and the great vital principle underlying her whole splendid effort was to carry help and alleviation into the remote chambers of zenanas and *bibi-ghars*, behind whose jealously closed doors no men, save those of the family, might pass, and to which, if such assistance were to be taken, it must be at the hands of trained women.

It would serve no purpose to trace the growth of the idea along its various stages, for under Lady Dufferin's energetic guidance it took firm root, and spread out branches from Madras to Quetta, from Karachi to Calcutta. Lady Lansdowne took over the work with loving zeal, and though her name may not have come so prominently into English notice in connection with the fund as it deserved, I think none who had seen even a tenth part of what I did of its administration and general working, could fail to be impressed by her whole-souled interest in and wise fostering of the growth of the movement. In fact, in certain ways the task, as Lady Lansdowne undertook it, required quite as much anxious thought as did its initiation and launching, since upon her shoulders fell the details of modification, enlarging, curtailing, or revising according to the knowledge gained by actual experience.

In dealing with the three aspects of the fund, I would take the second one before the first, as it is in that direction that the most tangible results are to be noticed. It is not my purpose, nor would it be specially interesting, to embark upon statistics, inevitable as they are to render the educational position of the dependency clear; but the time has now come when the best friends of the fund are asking whether the building, the equipment, the endowment of the magnificent hospitals of the greater towns has wrought all the benefit that was expected of them. The best answer to the question lies, I think, in a remark made to me by one of the highest medical officials under Government, who said that the Dufferin Fund, alike in scope and practice, was fifty years in advance of its time. So far as patronage of the hospitals goes, it is admitted with all regret that the higher caste and zenana ladies of the East have not availed themselves as freely of the advantages that they offered as Lady Dufferin and her more hopeful advisers expected they would do.

It is not that anything is wanting in the hospitals; for native architects and advisers have directed the building of the *purdah* rooms, and caste traditions are scrupulously regarded in the nursing and cooking arrangements. Stringent regulations have been framed to exclude those not of position or undoubted respectability; while the most jealous husband, father, or brother knows that the patients are absolutely secured against intrusive male eyes. The comparative want of success is due, not to any failure on the part of the promoters to secure it, but to innate ideas and customs which prevent those for whom these benefits were intended from profiting as fully as they might by what is available for them.

Nor, I think, is this surprising, if we look at home. Even with ourselves, and the knowledge that we have of the skill and the kindness and the attention of our hospitals, there are still very few of the middle or upper classes who will voluntarily enter one, even with the privacy of the paying ward. With the native and *purdah* women there is also an intense shyness of strangers even of their own sex and their own race, as well as the sense of home sickness in its most exaggerated form when away from their usual surroundings. Indeed women doctors throughout India told me that it was one of their greatest difficulties to keep their patients after they had been in hospital a few days, on account of the almost irresistible longings of intense nostalgia that came over them. Moreover, the idea is still a new one. The customs and traditions to be overcome are those that have hardened and crystallized through the centuries, and against those the innovations of a decade are still scarcely realized as existent.

Meantime, while the undiscerning reader in England is looking at the scrappy paragraph which the average reporter culls in a quarter of an hour from the annual Report, and thinking, if the beds are filled all the year, if the numbers in the out-patients' department show an increase, and if there is no specific fault or grievance laid down, there can be no cause for anxiety as to the movement, others there are who are asking, Why is the Dufferin Fund "wasting" money on building hospitals that are not doing what it was reckoned they would accomplish? For no one doubted for a moment that hospitals could be filled; but those who knew the characteristics of native women feared well lest they should be occupied by the special classes that Lady Dufferin so earnestly desired to benefit. The critics who deprecate the outlay on bricks and mortar do not grasp how very frequently the fund has had large donations from wealthy natives conditionally upon the whole or the greater part being devoted to the erection of an hospital or a dispensary. Only to mention a few specific instances in which this has lately occurred, let me name the gift of the Babu Durga Prosad, who gave ten thousand rupees to the Gaya branch of the fund in order that an hospital should be erected in that town, to be called the "Pavitra," after his mother; while at Baranagore the Babu Benode Lal Ghose, vice-chairman of the municipality, laid down a similar sum, as well as all that was needed to purchase a site, the whole there also to be the memorial to his mother. At Comilla the Nawab Faizunnissa Saheba and three other ladies jointly offered the whole amount required for the building of an hospital. Four thousand rupees were presented to the already existing hospital at Naiserabad by the Srimali Biddaza Chandhrani, that a new ward should be added to it, to be called the Biddaza Morgee Ward; and at Cawnpore, Pershotam Rao Fantia Sahib, Subadah of Bithoor, has given five thousand rupees towards the building of a better hospital for that place of bitter memories.

The fact is that the erection of fine buildings, with their invariable memorial stones and flourishing inscriptions, is the favourite form for Indian native charity to take. With the Parsees on the Bombay side some few have founded scholarships, and some few have bestowed handsome and even anonymous gifts in other useful directions. But to rear an hospital, to put up a fine hall, to present an institute to a town, are all tangible hereafter as monuments, and thus commend themselves vastly to the Oriental mind. The best answer, however, to any strictures on this point is furnished to me by Lady Dufferin herself, who says that in no instance has the fund put up an hospital that was not urgently needed, nor has it ever sanctioned outlay in this direction disproportionate to its developments on other sides, while it has not encouraged even native gifts of buildings unless there was due prospect of their means of maintenance. Hospitals must necessarily be the schools for the teaching of the future practitioners, and therefore they constitute an integral part of the Dufferin scheme, for, to come back now to the first clause of its intentions, it will be found that women are to be taught and trained *in India.* Lady Dufferin grasped what few Indian social reformers do, in that, if the stream of medical aid was to be an abundant one, spreading its benefits far and wide, the source must be from within, and not one dependent upon the precarious supplies from home charity or Englishwomen's enterprise. One of the most interesting aspects therefore of the whole situation is how far the more emancipated of the educated native women have been worthy of the confidence that Lady Dufferin thus showed in their ability, and have responded to the calls of their suffering sisters.

There are five Indian universities, namely, those of Calcutta, Bombay, Madras, Agra, and Lahore, which give medical degrees to women. At the present time there are close upon three hundred young women under instruction for these degrees, and if it must be admitted that of them a rather large proportion belong to the mixed Eurasian race, I think that that must be accepted as a necessary halfway step. There is a rather unkind legend current in India of a typical street urchin transported to Calcutta who said, "God made white men, and God made coloured men, but English Tommy, he made d—d half-castes," and as a race they seem to possess the faculty of uniting the worse qualities of both sides. Here and there may be found one superior to the usual attributes, and in the case of the women, those who overcome their tendencies to a backboneless, flabby inertia generally have energy and perseverance enough to carry them through the course of study. Provided that they possess these recommendations, there are several distinct advantages in their entering upon the profession. In the first place, it affords them an honourable and useful vocation—a matter of considerable importance when the problem of "what shall we do with our Eurasians?" is vexing many official minds. In the second, their knowledge of the vernacular most spoken around them, and their innate acquaintance with the habits and prejudices common to half or possibly three-quarters of their ancestry is directly in their favour, even against the more highly skilled woman doctor coming to the East for the first time, and with no more knowledge of Hindustani or Bengali, Tamil or Gujerati than she has picked up from books.

So far as the experiment of training native girls as doctors, assistant-surgeons, and hospital assistants has gone, it is satisfactory. As with school teachers, however, I cannot regard it as an unmixed advantage to the ultimate status and foundation of the movement to allow it to become identified with any propagandist movement, but the same difficulty is encountered as with the other calling. A livelihood must be found for convert girls; must we not at present accept whoever comes forward? Altogether it is a puzzling problem, but I am inclined to think it will be the Parsees who will do the most towards its solution, provided only that they are wise. Of course Hindus and Mahommedans are united in antagonism to this shrewd and far-seeing race, who are amassing money and making themselves almost the rulers of trade, but for all that they are received in every day dealings with an amount of fraternity that is never shown towards the Western race. The Parsees have adhered consistently to their religious principles, which are less hateful in Hindu eyes than Christianity, but they have ceased to keep their women *purdah*, and have extended to the sex the same educational privileges as their men enjoy. Meantime, the women have not succumbed to the temptation to travesty

European dress, but they have freed themselves from many of the conventional fetters, and several of them have succeeded notably well in the direction of medicine. On the Bombay side at least, therefore, the Parsee girls have it very much in their power not only to mitigate present suffering, but to show the possibilities to other women of a remunerative and honourable career.

There are many who maintain that it would be better to try to make nurses first than hospital assistants, the grade that is at present passed by very few of the native women students. In this I cannot wholly concur. We must face the situation as it is; and so far the idea of trained nursing assistance is not yet borne in upon the native mind, which regards that as one of the intuitive accomplishments of a wife or mother, and would be very much averse to seeking skilled help from outside. No less important as an item to be taken into account are caste prejudices; and even if a woman had overcome her inherent dislike to giving water or performing certain offices for patients of lower caste than her own, it must be remembered that patients of higher religious grade than her own might be unable to accept her ministrations. So rigid are these rules, that in the *purdah* wards of the Victoria Hospital of Calcutta each one has been provided with its own kitchen, in order that no outrage shall be done to these ideas. The hospitals naturally require nursing staffs; but as long as these customs survive as matters of vital consequence, there are grave difficulties in the way of extending the profession.

My own conclusions in the matter are that the fund has done well in establishing so many fine hospitals, even though these may not have always attracted patients of the ranks it was desired to reach, in that they constitute a magnificent foundation-ground for the training of the women doctors of the future; and that the time has now come when encouragement may be specially and well directed towards inducing more girls to qualify as practitioners. At present I would not demand a very high degree of knowledge; but whatever is taught should be simple and commonsense, and equal to the everyday ailments of women who are not overwrought with "nerves," nor have ruined their constitutions by unnatural habits. Women of the hospital-assistant class should go out now far and wide. They do not despise fees of two or three pence a visit; their wants are modest, and they can sustain existence on resources that would be starvation to the English lady doctor. And if their skill is but small, be it remembered that what little knowledge they do possess is at least free from superstition and positive danger to life. They will create a demand for something better, and in due time that will be met.

How great this mass of superstition to be combated is perhaps only to be realized after one has seen something of native midwifery. This as a science is supposed to belong to the Chamains, the women of the Chamars, the tanner and leather-working caste of Bengal, Behar, and Upper and Central India. In the North-West Provinces there is a rhymed couplet proverb which says it is unadvisable to cross a river in the same boat with a black Brahmin or a fair Chamar, and by their higher-caste neighbours they are regarded as very lowly folk, who are only fit for the most menial and degrading occupations. There are certain necessary offices connected with childbirth which caste Hindu women are prohibited from performing, but the Chamains have no scruples of this description, or indeed from rendering any "assistance" required. In the absence of a Chamain, a woman of the Chandal or Sudra castes—both servile orders—will be called in; though these latter seldom make a regular profession of the calling, but the orthodox Hindus have a saying to the effect that the household becomes unclean unless a Chamain has been present at one birth at least in its circle.

The Hindu or lower class and Mahommedan non-purdah woman is not affected by any feelings of reserve as to her condition. She pursues her daily and domestic avocations up to the last, so late indeed that all the lying-in hospitals can record instances in which the child was born before the mother arrived at the doors. It is generally stated that Indian women suffer very little in comparison with Europeans, and possibly, in a perfectly natural and healthy mother, this is the case. In the hospitals, however, the proportion of difficult cases involving the use of instruments is unduly large, and malformations and internal injuries are appallingly frequent. These are often the result of the barbarous treatment resorted to by the ignorant *dhais* or midwives, who, on the first indications of approaching labour, take the poor woman to the *asancha ghar* or *chatthi ghar*, the house or room of confinement, and as a kind of preliminary assistance, roll and rub her regardless of the additional torture inflicted. When the Marchioness of Dufferin and Ava stated, as one of the reasons of her appeal for medical help, that among other atrocities perpetrated by these women was that of placing a heavy beam upon the poor creature, an attendant sitting upon either end, the fact was questioned from the exceeding horror of the idea, but the practice is far from infrequent when parturition is delayed. To stop hæmorrhage after birth, there is a dangerous system among them of applying great pressure.

The newly-confined woman is made to stand against the wall, while the *dhai* with her head or bent knees exerts her whole force against the lower part of the stomach. Among their other details of treatment, they employ, to bring about the contraction of the uterus, an embrocation made from the leaves of *Artemisia vulgaris,* and to lessen superabundant flow of milk, a plaster made of pea-flour and the dried bark of *Cucurbita* is employed.

Altogether opposed to our ideas of sanitation is the birth-fire kindled with charcoal, which east and south, west and north, with Tamil and Punjabi, with Brahmin and Mussulman women alike, smoulders beneath the *charpai,* or bed, on which the mother lies. In Bengal it is placed at the door of the *chatthi ghar*, while within an oil-lamp is kept brightly burning night and day, as darkness is supposed to favour the entrance of evil spirits. Among many castes nothing whatever may be removed from the room, and no washing is permitted unless it be that of some of the infant's clothing, and that even must be dried within the stifling chamber. A Mahommedan woman must endure this purgatory for ten days, her more fortunate Hindu neighbour escaping with six. Not until after the third day since confinement may the mother eat her ordinary pulse and rice, for up to that time turmeric, molasses, spices, and various highly stimulating condiments are given. That fever is not far more frequent than it is, is one of the medical problems of India, as puzzling as the reason of the immunity from typhoid enjoyed by the pilgrims at Benares.

After a premature or still birth, it is a very usual practice on the part of the *dhais* to administer a decoction of bamboo leaves, in which a copper coin has been soaked, the underlying idea of this seemingly risky practice being to correct the internal poison which caused the mischief. Death in childbed is regarded as a curse of wider effect than merely to the woman's own circle, and among the Santals and Kols, it is believed that the spirits of such women, as *kitchni,* are capable of the most diabolic mischief in a district. Among the Oraons any woman dying within a fortnight after a birth becomes a *chorail,* and such are reputed always to walk upon inverted feet, that is to say, with the toes behind. Hardly any tribe or caste, however, could not be named that did not view such a death as a peculiar misfortune.

At present, too, it must be borne in mind that the native girls who come forward to qualify in medicine seldom possess a good preliminary general education. There is no medical school in the world that can make satisfactory doctors out of persons who are ignorant of simple arithmetical calculations or elementary science, and many of the pupils who present themselves are really as untaught as this. The result is that valuable time, which ought to be spent in medical studies, has to be given up to the acquirement of knowledge that should have been attained in the schoolroom.

The requirements of the Indian universities which grant medical degrees to women are high, and as a fair sample of what is demanded by all, I will give the outline course that is followed at Calcutta for the female certificate class.

FIRST YEAR.

Anatomy.
Materia Medica.
Dissections.
Chemistry (thirty elementary lectures).
Compounding (six months).
Test examinations in Anatomy, Materia Medica, and Chemistry.

SECOND YEAR.

Anatomy.
Physiology (elementary).

Materia Medica.
Chemistry (full course).
Dissections.
Attendance at six *Post mortem* examinations.
Hospital attendance (including out-door departments) twelve months.
Pass examinations in Anatomy, Materia Medica, and Chemistry.

THIRD YEAR.

Medicine and Clinical Medicine.
Surgery and Clinical Surgery.
Medical Jurisprudence (demonstrations).
Midwifery (with attendance at three labour cases).
Hospital attendance (of which three months in the Ophthalmic Wards).
Pass examinations in Pathology, Physiology, and Medical Jurisprudence.
Pathology (with attendance at six *Post mortems*).
Physiology.

FOURTH YEAR.

Medicine and Clinical Medicine.
Surgery and Clinical Surgery.
Midwifery (including six labour cases).
Hospital practice (of which six months in the Medical and Surgical Wards *minus* fifteen attendances at the Dental Dispensary; and six months exclusively in the Midwifery Wards, when the students are to take regular turns of duty, night and day, assisting the regular work of the hospital).
Dentistry (optional).
Pass examinations in Medicine, Surgery, and Midwifery.

Thirty-three per cent. of marks must be obtained to pass, and there are somewhat stringent rules as to failures. For a lower grade of practitioners, who would be unequal to passing the Entrance Examination of the Calcutta University, or an equivalent test, admission to the Eden Hospital is allowed. Here they receive a year's course of midwifery instruction, and, if found proficient, are entitled to a certificate as fully qualified *dhais* or midwives.

The matriculated female students of the university follow precisely the same course for the final M.B. or L.M.S. examinations as the men, and in this one or two Bengali girls have distinguished themselves. This occupies five years, which are thus filled :—

FIRST YEAR.

Descriptive and Surgical Anatomy.
Chemistry.
Botany.
Dissections.

SECOND YEAR.

Comparative Anatomy, Comparative Physiology, and Zoology.
Descriptive and Surgical Anatomy.
General Anatomy and Physiology.
Chemistry.
Practical Chemistry.
Materia Medica.
Botany.
Dissections.
Pharmacy, three months.
Preliminary Scientific L.M.S. and M.B. examination.

THIRD YEAR.

Materia Medica.
Dissections.
Physiology.
Hospital practice, one year.
First M.B. and L.M.S. examination.

FOURTH YEAR.

Medicine.
Surgery.
Midwifery.
Medical Jurisprudence with demonstrations.
Hospital practice, twelve months.
Final M.B. or L.M.S. examination.

FIFTH YEAR.

Medicine and Clinical Medicine.
Surgery and Clinical Surgery.
Midwifery and six labour cases.
Medical Jurisprudence with demonstrations.
Pathology with demonstrations.
Ophthalmic Medicine and Surgery.
Hygiene.
Dentistry.
Post mortem records.
Hospital practice, six months.
Out-door and Eye Infirmary practice, three months each.
Final M.B. or L.M.S. examination.

At this juncture, however, I am met by the necessity to allude to the greatest of all India's wants for girl students, and that is an institution upon the lines of our own London School of Medicine for women. The point was first borne in upon me in Madras, where, after some pressure from outside, the university opened its medical classes to women, but—contrary to the strongly expressed opinion of Lady Dufferin and other ladies competent to speak—compelled the male and female students to study together. There are numerous scholarships available for women students; the curriculum is a well-devised one, and the knowledge derived from its training leaves nothing to be desired. Some forty young women, chiefly Eurasians and Hindus, are entered there as students, and some show decided promise. But the point felt by all who have the best interests of the movement at heart is, that until the sexes are permitted to pursue their studies apart, the class of native girl who will take up medicine will not be that most likely to inspire the highest confidence of her co-religionist sisters. They regard it as an extremely "emancipated" thing for her to take up such a calling at all; but when they find that she has prepared herself for it by study side by side with a number of men, they view her conduct as reprehensible; and, rather than advancing the cause of female doctors in India, this course of action (in which, however, Madras stands no worse than the various other universities of the dependency) is decidedly retarding it.

The same I found at Calcutta, where the European and Eurasian far outnumber the native ladies, and I am inclined to think that the better class of these who might be willing to enter upon the medical profession are much deterred from doing so by the knowledge that their studies would have

THE EDEN HOSPITAL.

to be pursued side by side with the male students. Certain it is that the district board of Pabna for some months was offering a scholarship of ten rupees a month to any native girl to assist in the medical course, and no one suitable had offered herself for it, while I believe that similar help from the boards of Puri and Mymensingh went a-begging. In the report of the Director of Public Instruction, I observe too that the Superintendent of the Campbell Medical School states with regret that so far it has not been found practicable to raise the standard of female entrance. On the other hand, he is able to mention with satisfaction that in the final Licence Examination only eighteen out of fifty-four male students were successful, while five out of the seven girls who came up were passed with credit. A great and desirable addition to the comfort and well-being of the Calcutta lady students is the Surmo-moyee Hostel or boarding-house for their accommodation, the generous gift of the Maharanee of Cossimbazar, C.I., to advance medical education among the sex. It is situated close to the Eden Hospital, in which, of course, the students have to see much of their practice, and its well-ordered arrangements under Miss Taylor have been keenly valued by its inmates of such varied races and creeds.

I might say the same of the Grant Medical College at Bombay, where, to quote from a *précis* statement, with which I was furnished by official favour, I find that "at the date of the last report the number of female students in attend-ance was twenty-nine, which was increased to thirty-five by the admission of six new students. Of these thirty-five, six left, one obtained the degree of L.M.S. of the Bombay University, and two have qualified as 'certificated practitioners,' thus leaving twenty-six on the college roll—

twenty-two matriculated and four non-matriculated." It is, however, only fair to say that the greater number of these young ladies, whose diligence and conduct are pronounced in every way satisfactory, are Europeans and Eurasians. A few are Parsees, and only one or two are Hindus.

Scattered through the dependency one finds many of the zenana missions maintaining lady doctors, but these are almost invariably Englishwomen who have had their training at home. Here and there, as at Benares or Lucknow, they also support hospitals; and although at one time certain of the evangelizing bodies were rather blamed for their practice of sending out women who did not possess full medical degrees, that objection seems now to have ceased. It may sound inconsistent to advocate the sending out by the Dufferin Fund of women of the hospital assistant class and not commend the missionary societies for acting upon the principle of half a loaf better than no bread, but the cases are hardly analogous. The native practitioners know well that they are responsible to the Civil Surgeon of their district, and that they only treat their female patients under his advice and control. On the other hand, English missionary doctors have been known to attempt cases and even operations of the highest complexity merely upon their own slender knowledge, and the results have not always been wholly satisfactory. However, I visited various zenana hospitals, and generally without any warning of my call, and I certainly saw and heard nothing open to any adverse criticism upon them. Convert women patronize them much, and in this connection may be mentioned a curious little difficulty that the Dufferin Fund had to face, and whose solution excited a certain amount of unfavourable comment.

Knowing equally that numerous hospitals supported by

mission agencies are available for native Christian women, that the civil hospitals present no obstacles to such that *purdah* or *gosha* women would experience, and that caste Hindu and high-class Mahommedan women regard as something like pariahs those who have accepted Christianity, the Dufferin Fund decided to check the admission to its wards of those who were converts. This of course gave rise to much bitterness in certain circles, but there was no other course open in the matter. The fund had been established to benefit the majority, who would still less have participated in its advantages had they found the hated minority sharing them also. There was consequently no alternative, and it seems unreasonable that there should ever have been any difference of feeling in the matter.

To describe in detail all, or even only the principal hospitals that I inspected while in India would be tedious, and so I will take those only of two of the Presidency towns as representing all that is best and most advanced. I take these in the order that I saw them, and in Madras a place of honour belongs to the Victoria Hospital, which was started in 1885.

Encouragement was given to the movement by the ready and public-spirited action of some of the native princes, including the Prince of Arcot, the Maharajahs of Vizianagram and Travancore, and the Rajah of Pudakòta. Very fine buildings were erected, providing all accommodation for general diseases as well as for lying-in, and the medical superintendence was placed in the hands of a staff of highly qualified lady doctors. Gradually the *gosha* women began to appreciate the benefits offered them, and the number of cases treated annually has shown a satisfactory increase.

Intensely and tragically interesting too is the Leper Hospital maintained here, and which by the courtesy of Surgeon-Colonel Cook I was permitted to visit, under his own escort. This magnificently planned group of buildings is controlled by Surgeon-Colonel Cook, and is, I believe, the only hospital of its class officially kept up in British India. Its inmates, several of whom he would not allow me to see on account of the hideous repulsiveness of their appearance, are divided as follows: 22 East Indian (or Eurasian) men, 8 East Indian women, 134 native men, 50 native women, 6 children—doomed, alas! probably to a long life of loathsome disease—and 9 prisoners; the entire number of leper criminals throughout British India. My chiefest interest lay, of course, among the wretched women sufferers, and there was a touch of affectionate pathos in the answer of one soft-voiced Eurasian woman, who had been an inmate of its wards for over twenty-two years, when Surgeon-Colonel Cook asked her if she had "any complaints." She said, "I don't think, sir, we could have a thing more done for us in the world than we get here." All were wonderfully cheerful, and evidently valued the excellent and abundant food and the many comforts provided for them. The men have laid out a pretty garden, and the Eurasian patients occasionally get up little concerts and dramatic entertainments, while kindly hands from outside have helped to fit up modest chapels for the members of every creed within its walls. It is, perhaps, not the least of the testimonies to the breadth and toleration of our Indian Government that in one of the wards a little enclosure should have contained a sanctuary of the Church of England; that another should have had a high altar of the Church of Rome, with jewelled cross and fragrant flowers, while the heavy perfume of the incense just used was still lingering in the air; and a third had concealed behind artfully disposed hangings the signs and symbols of Sivaism; while in yet another were emblems common to all Mohammedan mosques.

At Calcutta the chief female hospital is the Dufferin Victoria, where a great feature is made of its out-patients' department. Here the attendance numbers over twenty thousand yearly. Miss Hamilton, M.D., who was its chief medical officer until she accepted a post as resident physician to the zenana of the Ameer, had a large native private practice, and her great skill and gentleness in dealing with the diseases peculiar to women won widespread confidence in her knowledge. Here, again, arises a difficulty, for though in the wealthier classes large fees are willingly paid for relief from pain or a successful operation, those of middle or humble order seem to imagine that advice should all be gratis.

It is impossible yet to get away from the fact that female life has no very great value in the East, and there are plenty of men still to be found who argue, why should they pay heavy doctors' bills for their wives when, if they die, they can so easily replace them? It is on this ground that I do not think India offers an unlimited field of work for English lady doctors. So long as these are attached to missions, associations, or hospitals, and are doing philanthropic work, all is well; but it is a matter of greater difficulty than is generally realized for them to build up private practices among the better-class women in their homes. Some few ladies there are who have done it, and whose gentleness at the sick-bed and skill in surgery have earned for them a far-reaching reputation, but these chiefly have settled and worked in the bigger cities of the dependency, and far more depends upon the individual tact of the lady than many would admit. The movement has passed experiment into permanence, and if it be not going forward as rapidly as we in the vigour of our Western energies think it ought to be, I can only say again, it is only adding one more experience to that long list of trials of patience which tell us that progress in India is only to be made very slowly indeed. By slow steps, however, the women will learn to seek medical help when they want it.

There is only one other aspect of this work upon which I need touch, and that is its indirect educational purpose. On this I will not use my own words, but rather quote a private letter written to me by the editor of one of the leading newspapers of India, in which he says, "The chief value in my eyes of the movement has always lain in the promise and hope it afforded of at last invading the seclusion of the zenana, and thus gradually lifting its inmates out of the appalling depths of ignorance and superstition in which they have for centuries been steeped. For what is it at present that hinders all real progress in the country but the overpowering influence of the zenana. Once break down *that*, or rather shed light into it, and give it a healthy and upward direction, and I believe that progress and enlightenment will make such bounds in this country that the regeneration of India will be a living reality. It is the *educational* influence of the Lady Dufferin movement that I have ever regarded as its chief value (though, curiously enough, I have never seen this idea put forward by any of the professed supporters of the fund, either on the platform or in the press), and I believe that that influence will yet prove to be, when the dark recesses of the zenanā shall have been penetrated by reason and light, the most powerful lever to progress, and the greatest stimulus to the spread of

Christianity throughout the land that it would be possible to discover. What is it but this influence of the women, moulded in the ignorance and superstition of the women's quarter, that is at present, and will continue to be until it is given a right direction, the great hindrance and drawback that is fatal to all real progress? Get at the women then; educate them, bring them to a more enlightened frame of mind. Show them the *beauties* of Christianity, appeal to their hearts by wisdom and the personal example of beautiful lives, and you will see such an era of progress set in that the regeneration of India will be a reality, and the conversion of its people an accomplished fact. When *that* is done, England's great mission in India will have been accomplished, and it will be the proudest achievement that was ever entrusted to a great nation to perform in the history of the world."

CHAPTER V.

WIDOW-REMARRIAGE AND DIVORCE.

"Alone upon the housetops to the north
I turn and watch the lightning in the sky;
The glamour of thy footsteps in the north;
Come back to me, beloved, or I die.

"Below my feet, the still bazaar is laid,
Far, far below, the weary camels lie;
The camels and the captives of thy raid;
Come back to me, beloved, or I die.

"My father's wife is old and harsh with years,
And drudge of all my father's house am I;
My bread is sorrow and my drink is tears;
Come back to me, beloved, or I die."

The Love Song of Har Dyal (Rudyard Kipling's Version).

THERE is nothing perhaps that gives a thoughtful observer in India a more convincing sign of the utter superficiality of what European influences have effected in regard to native Hindu social customs and habits, than the attitude that they maintain towards the remarriage of widows. Their helpless, hopeless lot has been the theme of more eloquence at Exeter Hall, and upon missionary platforms, than perhaps any other single aspect of the whole evangelizing field. The strong arm of legislation has been evoked upon their behalf, and widow-marriage has been legalized. Schools and educational establishments have been founded for them upon the theory that if they were competent to earn a living, the hardness of their fate would be mitigated, and perhaps as independent and self-respecting members of society they might even be sought in marriage after all. A pen so weighty and unsentimental as that of Professor Max Müller has been enlisted upon behalf of "that strange product of India, and of India only, the child-widows, children who are formally married to elderly men belonging to good families, who often never see their husbands, but who, when their husbands die, are doomed for life to an existence which in the best cases is one of joyless drudgery, excluding all hope of renewed happiness, and fully accounting for the eagerness of Indian widows in former times to die on the same pile with their husbands, or, as the law does no longer allow this, to end their life by slow starvation, or by jumping into a well."

Nothing that public opinion at home or in high official circles in India could do towards modifying the deep-rooted rigours of the system was left unattempted, yet what are the facts to-day? Simply this, that not only have we failed to amend matters in the slightest degree, but there is to be noted an even growing prejudice against widow-remarriage.

To understand this fact, for fact it is, and borne out by statistics as well as observation, one must know that the prohibition of widow-marriage is a sign of social position and good caste. Among the Brahmins it is completely interdicted, and the Rajputs, with their exceeding jealousy of their women, do not allow it under any circumstances. But under the greater prosperity and the more affluent conditions which settled rule has given to the humbler working orders, these latter can now indulge in the luxury of imitating those above them, instead of as of yore, regarding their examples as impossible of realization. It is this prohibition that evidently appealed to them as a supremely desirable virtue; for it is almost, if not the very first of the aristocratic customs that they adopt, just as I believe they would go back to the practice of suti were they left to themselves. The heartiest burst of approval that I heard in a theatre in India, was when a young woman on the stage, believing her husband to be dead, said, in a fine burst of well-acted grief, that she would follow him through the funeral pyre, a sentiment which her audience evidently thought the most praiseworthy she could have uttered.

As showing, however, how essentially the antipathy to remarriage exists in Hinduism, it is remarkable that it is not only the poor of the orthodox creed who take advantage of bettered circumstances to enforce it, but the aboriginal and semi-aboriginal tribes, as they rise in social status, make it a matter of principle. My inquiries in Bengal brought me a good deal of curious information upon this point. Professor Max Müller has succinctly laid down the theory of the subject, as laid down in the Mahabharata, by saying that "a woman in India always belongs to somebody. She cannot exist by herself. In her youth, it is said, she belongs to her father; if her father dies, to her brother; if she is married, to her husband; if her husband dies, to his family." *

Mr. Risley, whom I have already cited as the most outspoken and unconventional authority upon the "true inwardness" of native opinion and custom, points out that the doctrine of spiritual benefit requires her to devote her life

* "There is not a single woman in the three worlds that deserves to be regarded as the mistress of her own self. The father protects her while she is a maiden. The husband protects her while she is in youth. Sons protect her when she is aged. Women can never be independent as long as they live."—*Mahabharata—Anucasana Parva* (prose rendering by Pretāpa Chandra Ray, C.I.E.).

to the performance of his sráddh, while the very character of the Brahmanical marriage-rites in themselves constitute a technical barrier. "That ceremony being regarded as a sacrament ordained for the purification of women, and its essential portion being the gift of the woman by her father to her husband, the effect of the gift is to transfer her from her own *gotra*, or exogamous group, into that of her husband's."

Further evidence on this point by an orthodox Hindu gentleman, in the inquiries set on foot by Government as to infant marriage and enforced widowhood, is contained in this argument. "But if her father is out of the question, it may surely be said that she may give herself in marriage. This, though, she cannot do, because she never had anything like disposal of herself. When young she was given away, so the ownership over her, vested then in the father, was transferred by a solemn religious act to the husband, and he being no more, there is no one to give her; and since Hindu marriage must take the form of a religious gift, her marriage becomes impossible."

It becomes, therefore, quite clear by what process of reasoning a tribe, as it emerges from servility and degradation into full-blown Hinduism, raises the importance of this doctrine, even as the Church itself gave to marriage a mystical symbolism to lift it from a mere union of the flesh for the gratification of the passions. Only to mention a few of the instances of sub-castes or tribes who within recent years have assumed this badge of respectability, may be named the Kapalis, who are cultivators of jute and weavers of canvas and matting; the Chandals, of whom one sees much on the cruise along the turbid waters of the Hughli, where they own boats of the strangest variations upon the strict lines of naval architecture that it seems possible to construct.

The name of Chandal has always been associated since the days of Manu with "the vilest of mankind," and it is not surprising, therefore, that they endeavour to ignore their low origin and, when they migrate into new districts, to find fresh titles and callings. They may be found as grass-cutters, potters, carpenters, and pedlars, and as they drift into these vocations, they endeavour to assimilate its more exclusive observances. With them, the prohibition of re-marriage has come into practice within the last generation,

A CHANDAL VILLAGE ON THE HUGHLI.

as it is also doing with the Rajwars who are scattered throughout Chota Nagpur, Western Bengal, and the tributary states, even as far as Darjeeling and Chittagong. These, however, are innovating gently, and began by the interdiction of the marriage of widows with children. The *dhobis*, or washermen, socially almost the lowest of all castes throughout the dependency, in that, as Mr. Lesfield says, "no Hindu, even of the lowest caste, will wash his own clothes, and so the *dhobi* has been formed into a caste which shall bear the impurities of all," are also now forbidding remarriage, and among the Kurmis of Upper India, the custom is gradually coming into effect.

Other tribes also, without placing a stringent veto upon it, are bending to the principle involved by laying down who a widow may marry. This is almost invariably a younger brother of the late husband, wherever it is sanctioned, and it is at least a little curious to find so marked an agreement on the part of the aboriginal and Dravidian peoples, who alone permit it, with ancient Jewish ordinances. With the Santals, Kols, and Oraons, though theoretically perfect freedom of remarriage exists, it is "good form" to make choice of this kinsman, but the first named are among the few tribes of India, like the Nayars of the Malabar coast, whose customs retain any evidences of former polyandric practices. Whether a younger brother of the late husband has already a wife or not, he can, by mutual agreement, wed the widow.

But among the castes which do not absolutely forbid widow-remarriage there exists a form, legal and valid in all respects, known in Bengal as the *Sanga*, and in other parts as the *Sagai* rites. Much of the ceremonial of a girl's wedding is dispensed with, the pacing round the sacred fire being invariably omitted, and the whole observance often resolving itself into no more than the husband's marking the bride's brow with red lead. Even, however, where a greater amount than this enters into the proceedings, it is all on the bridegroom's side, and though he may give feasts and entertain his friends, the bride herself has no part in them, nor does she even appear at the one on the eve of her marriage in her own relations' house. She is sought at dead of night by him in her own room, and before two or three of her closest female relatives he puts the vermilion or some similarly sticky red substance upon the parting of her hair. Among the Santals this is varied by marking a flower and placing that in her hair.

In one very strange form of marriage practised by this non-Aryan people it is the woman who takes the initiative, and if she finds her affections unrequited, she takes a vessel containing rice-beer, enters the man's house, and sits down. The beer shows the object of her visit, and if the women of the house do not favour her intention they may resort to any means short of physical force or personal violence, which are forbidden by custom, to eject her. They may burn red pepper on the fire, drench her with cold water, or apply the most odious names to her; but if she remains passive for two or three hours she has accomplished her purpose—the marriage cannot be set aside. Only a few weeks before my visit to the coal-mining district, the village communities of Girideh were much perturbed over a case in which a widow had thus secured a husband who was very far from reciprocating her attachment. Councils were called, and innumerable palavers held; but no precedent for ignoring such a wedding could be found, till at last an astute young Christian Santal, of rather better education than some, suggested that this form of marriage could only be gone through by a girl, and there was no other known instance of a widow practising it. The loophole of excuse was thankfully accepted, and the designing widow endured her discomfort for nothing.

In the case of a child-bride there is always a certain amount of ceremony connected with the *rukhsati*, or home-taking of the bride, but this, in the case of a widow, is not performed.

There is one respect, and perhaps one only, in which the Hindu widow stands at an advantage to her prototype in

Europe, and that is, that if she has had children, the burden of their support falls upon their father's family. It is only in rare instances that any attempt is made to evade this responsibility, even where the widow marries again, but should they accompany her to her new home, they are debarred from participation as members of the family in the acts of domestic worship.

Lastly, in this connection, is to be considered the attitude taken up by the Hindu community in general upon the question, apart from the technically religious difficulty to which I have before referred. It is due I think chiefly to the intense competition which exists in the highest castes for eligible husbands, and a fear of increasing that by rendering another and somewhat large class available for marriage. In India, as almost everywhere else, women are numerically preponderant. There are no vocations for them sufficient to make any appreciable difference in the situation, nor are they, like their sisters of the West, able to give their energies to, and find even full happiness in the unmarried state. The education of the men must in due course affect their views upon the subject, but it will be a very gradual work to effect any change in marriage habits, for the superficial reformer, who introduces bills to raise the age of marriage or to legalize widow-remarriage, does not see that these are more than merely social customs to be dealt with by legislation. They are vital elements of religion itself, and to attempt to tamper with them is to lay rough hands upon the heritage of the centuries, and principles that are bound up with all that is most sacred in a Hindu's faith. If ever there was a system over which the plea that patience might have her perfect work was specially to be urged, it is the social order of India.

Meantime, here and there, a little step forward in improving the status of the widows is made. At present I fear that the training of them to be school-teachers is too closely identified with the missionary movement for it to be regarded as standing upon a satisfactory basis, from the point of view of future native development. One would rather see the humblest indigenous effort of this kind made than the most magnificent of buildings reared by the subscriptions of the generously disposed in England, since the one would indicate a genuine desire, while the other, however nobly intentioned, has all the time an artificial position in the general economy. Some few widows are taking up the work of nursing, though this involves an independence of caste prejudices that at present is very far from general. It is possible, however, that in less wealthy caste families the recommendations of an independent and remunerative livelihood may outweigh these inherent objections, and so far as an effort has been made in this direction, I should be inclined to regard the outlook as certainly promising. A few also, possessing means of their own, have taken up medical studies, and though it may be but a day of small things, such beginnings are not to be despised.

With the Mahommedans there is not the slightest objection to the remarriage of widows, as indeed one would expect, when one remembers that the favourite wife of the prophet himself had been previously wedded. In the case of a young widow, all reasonable effort is made by her family to find her another husband, and this fact should not be forgotten in any attempt to appreciate the degree in which the prohibition of widow-remarriage presses upon the population. Again, with the Parsees, there is a like independence, and in this charitable community there are many institutions and funds for the help of those left without a bread-winner. It is argued, without I believe any reliable statistical information, that an unduly large proportion of Hindu widows are driven to prostitution. This is a statement that in the absence of really convincing inquiries should only, I think, be taken with extreme reservation, for two reasons. The first is the tendency of caste—in some respects quite as much the safeguard as the curse of India. Now, with the long-cultivated habits of thought among the people that a potter's son shall be a potter, and that it would be highly unbecoming for a potter to turn his attention to basket-making, this calling is itself a caste which is greatly against those not of it joining themselves to it. The second is family pride, which would prevent it; and even in the instances where the girl-widow would get more kicks than halfpence as her share, there would be, for the credit of the name, care exercised to prevent her thus dishonouring the reputation of her late husband's kith and kin. To quote Professor Max Müller once more, "Who would deny that there are thousands of well-conducted families in India in which the young widow of any member of the family is treated with respect and kindness—nay, with a mixture of pity and reverence? No doubt they are made to work, and in many cases the work, which was formerly done by them without demur, appears now, particularly if they have received a better education, irksome and degrading to many of them. To say that all widows, and more particularly all child-widows, are ill-treated by relatives, or encouraged to lead a disreputable life, is certainly a falsehood, and a falsehood that could find no credence amongst people acquainted with the true Indian character, and with the very strong family feeling that prevails among the better classes."

Speaking broadly upon the subject of divorce, it may be said only to be allowed by those who permit the re-marriage of widows. The view commonly obtains that a vast amount of immorality and intrigue is fostered by the zenana system, but I am not at all prepared myself to endorse this hastily-passed verdict as a fair one towards the average standard of native female rectitude. The zenana system *per se* is, I take it, rather a survival in idea of the protection that men gave to their women-folk in days when every man's hand was against his neighbour's, and a woman was quite lawful prey to her captors. Men have inherited a tendency of mind which leads them to mistrust one another's honour and good faith where women are concerned, and this I think is more the basis of the theory of rigorous *purdah nashin* than a fear of infidelity on the part of the women themselves. It is at least a fact, that while a native gentleman will talk freely about the women of his family to English ladies, and admit them gladly enough to the zenana, he would regard it as a personal insult for even an English gentleman to make the slightest inquiry upon the subject. No man, according to strict native idea, has any legitimate right to desire information concerning another man's wife, daughter, or sister, and if he seeks it the inference is that he has unlawful reasons for doing so.

Several causes contribute towards maintaining in practice a very fair level of feminine morality. To say that the lack of opportunity is a factor of leading importance in the result may be taken to imply that, were the conventions of seclusion relaxed, there would be a revolt against chastity; but this is, I think, a very unfounded and unworthy conclusion to draw. I am quite certain that if all present zenana restrictions were withdrawn, the Indian female population would stand woman for woman upon quite as high a platform as ourselves in this direction. What I mean to convey is that women live their lives so closely under one another's ken, that there is not the possibility for anything like a widespread laxity to exist. Where women of varying ages, tempers, and ambitions are living together, whatever they may do in annoying one another over petty spites and jealousies, it becomes a certainty that neither will venture on a course that would give all by whom she was surrounded the most powerful handle of all against her. No punishment is thought too brutal for unfaithfulness, and of this fact the women are well aware. I have myself seen instances, especially in the North-west Provinces, where a husband has cut off the nose of his wife, not even upon actual proof, but upon mere suspicion. Hands are sometimes cut off, and other horrible forms of mutilation are resorted to, while every judge or chief magistrate can tell of cases in which actual torture, ending even in death, has been practised. The woman, robbed of her fair looks, is ruthlessly cast out. A living she may find if she can, for she is branded with a mark more indelible than the Scarlet Letter itself, and alms that would not be withheld from the most impudent of self-asserting "holy men" are denied her.

It follows, therefore, that in the higher castes divorce by law is not much sought. The Rajputs summarily dismiss a woman guilty of adultery from being even a member of the caste, though in cases of incompatibility of temper they allow a couple to separate, each professing to regard the other as a parent. The wife then goes back to her parents, and the husband takes to himself another spouse. A somewhat similar custom exists among the Santals, where the pair, who for any reason of misbehaviour or personal interests desire to separate, upset a jar of water and tear in half three leaves of the Sa'l tree in the presence of their neighbours, saying as they do so, "Now become we to one another even as brother and sister."

Another notable variation is to be noted among the Tharus, a Himalayan hill tribe, who, like almost all the Nepaulese folk, view marriage with extreme laxity, and permit divorce upon almost any pretext. Mr. Nesfield, who has pursued a close investigation into the manners and habits of Upper India, has shown at length that such women with them may marry again by the same rites as widows, and the designation of *urari*, or "selected," is applied to such unions, to distinguish them from the *byalir*, or originally made matches with girls. There is, however, a precedence of respectability about the latter in their favour. A *urari* wife is not accepted in a family unless the chief relations have accorded their consent to the marriage, which they signify by holding a special ceremony called *bhatana;* but if this is withheld, she is simply regarded as the man's mistress, and he cannot take cooked food or water from her hands without lowering himself in social standing.

Most curious of all, however, are the divorce proceedings of the *Nambutiris* or Vedic Brahmins of the Malabar coast. Western India is now the least-visited part of the great dependency, and of the characteristics of its people perhaps less is known than of any others of the population. But they possess in Mr. W. Logan one of the most sympathetic and erudite historiographers of all India. His account of the whole conduct of a matrimonial cause is so full of detail, and the official report in which it appeared is so inaccessible to the vast majority of English readers that I make no apology for quoting it in full, long as it is.

"When a woman is suspected by her own kinsmen or by neighbouring Brahmans of having been guilty of light conduct, she is, under pain of excommunication of all her kinsmen, placed under restraint. The maidservant (*dasi*, or *veshali*), who is indispensable to every Nāmbutiri family, if not to every individual female thereof, is then interrogated, and if she should criminate her mistress, the latter is forthwith separated, and a watch set upon her. When the family can find a suitable house for the purpose, the *sadhanam* (the thing, or article, or subject, as the suspected person is called) is. removed to it; otherwise she is kept in the family house, the other members finding temporary accommodation elsewhere. After further examination of the maidservant, authority is granted in writing to the local *smārthā* (*e.g.* president of the assembly at which caste offences are tried), who in turn calls together the usual number of *mimamsakas* (persons skilled in the law).

"They assemble at some convenient spot, generally in a temple not far from the spot where the accused may be. All who are interested in the proceedings are permitted to be present. Order is preserved by an officer deputed by the chief for the purpose, and he stands near the smārthā and members of the tribunal. The only other member is a Nambutiri, called the agakkoyma, whose duties will be described presently.

"When all is ready, the chief's warrant is first read out, and the accused's whereabouts ascertained.

"The smārthā, accompanied by the officer on guard and the agakkoyma, next proceeds to the accused's house; the officer on guard remains outside, while the others enter. At the entrance, however, they are met by the maidservant, who up to this time has never lost sight of the accused, and who prevents the men from entering. In feigned ignorance of the cause of being thus stopped, the smārthā demands an explanation, and is told that a certain person is in the room. The smārthā demands more information, and is told that the person is no other than such and such a lady, the daughter or sister or mother (as the case may be) of such and such a Nambutiri, of such and such an illam. The smārthā expresses profound surprise at the idea of the lady being where she is, and again demands an explanation.

"Here begins the trial proper. The accused, who is still strictly *gosha*, is questioned through the medium of the maid, and she is made to admit that there is a charge against her. This is the first point to be gained, for nothing further can be done in the matter until the accused herself has made the admission.

"This point, however, is not very easily gained at times, and the smārthā has often to appeal to her own feelings and knowledge of the world, and asks her to recollect how unlikely it would be that a Nambutiri female of her position should be turned out of her parents' house and placed where she then was unless there was some cause for it.

"In the majority of cases, this preliminary stage is got over with little trouble, and is considered a fair day's work for the first day.

"The smārthā and his colleagues then return to the assembly, and the former relates in minute detail all that has happened since he left the conclave. The agakkoyma's task is to see that the version is faithful. He is not at liberty to speak; but whenever he thinks the smārthā has made a mistake as to what happened, he removes from his shoulders and lays on the ground a piece of cloth as a sign for the smārthā to brush up his memory. The latter takes the hint, and tries to correct himself. If he succeeds, the agakkoyma's cloth is replaced upon his shoulders; but if not, the smārthā is obliged to go back to the accused, and obtain what information is required.

"When the day's proceedings are finished, the members of the tribunal are sumptuously entertained by the accused's kinsmen, and this continues to be done as long as the inquiry lasts. A trial sometimes lasts several years, the tribunal meeting occasionally, and the accused's kinsmen being obliged to entertain the members and any other Nambutiris present on each occasion, while the kinsmen themselves are temporarily cut off from intercourse with other Brahmans pending the result of the trial, and all *sraddhas* (sacrifices to benefit the souls of deceased ancestors) are stopped. The reason for this is that until the woman is found guilty or not, and until it is ascertained when the sin was committed, they cannot, owing to the probability that they have unwittingly associated with her after her disgrace, be admitted into society until they have performed the expiatory ceremony.

"The tribunal continues its sittings as long as may be necessary; that is, until either the accused confesses and is convicted or her innocence is established. No verdict of guilty can be given against her except on her own confession. No amount of evidence is sufficient.

"In former days, when the servant accused her mistress, and there was other evidence forthcoming, but the accused did not confess, various modes of torture were had recourse to to extort a confession, such as rolling her up in a piece of matting and letting the bundle fall from the roof to the courtyard below. This was done by women. At other times live rat-snakes and other vermin were turned into the room beside her, and even, in certain cases, cobras, and it is said that if, after having been with the cobra a certain length of time, and unhurt, the fact was accepted as conclusive evidence of innocence.

"In cases where the accused offers to confess, she is cross-examined and re-examined very minutely as to time, place, person, circumstances, etc., but the name of the adulterer is withheld (though it may be known to all) to the very last. Sometimes a long list of persons is given, and similarly treated.

"Innocent persons are sometimes named, and have to purchase impunity at great expense. In one case a woman, who had indicated several persons, was so annoyed by the continual 'Who else? Who else?' of the zealous scribe who was taking down the details, that she at last, to his intense astonishment, pointed to himself as one of them, and backed it up by sundry alleged facts.

"The persons accused by the woman are never permitted to disprove the charges against them, but the woman herself is closely cross-examined, and the probabilities are carefully weighed. And every co-defendant, except the one who, according to the woman's own statement, was the first to lead her astray, has a right to be admitted to the boiling oil, as administered in the temple of Sāchindram in Travancore. If his hand is burnt, he is guilty; if it comes out clean, he is innocent. Money goes a long way towards a favourable issue in these ordeals.

"The tribunal meets at the accused's temporary house, after she has admitted that she is where she is because there is a charge against her. She remains in a room or behind a big umbrella, unseen by the members of the tribunal, and the examination is conducted by the smārthā. A profound silence is observed by all present except the smārthā, and he alone puts such questions as have been arranged beforehand by the members of the tribunal.

"Sometimes the greatest difficulty is experienced in getting her to confess; but this is usually brought about by the novelty of the situation, the scanty food, the protracted and fatiguing examination, and the entreaties of her relatives, who are being ruined, and by the expostulations and promises of the smārthā, who tells her it is best to confess and repent, and promises to get the chief to take care of her, and comfortably house her on the bank of some sacred stream, where she may end her days in prayer and repentance. The solemnity of the proceedings, too, has its effect. And the family often come forward, offering her a large share of the family property if she will only confess and allow the trial to end.

"When by these means the woman has once been induced to make a confession of her weakness, everything becomes easy. Hitherto strictly *gosha,* she is now asked to come out of the room, or lay aside her umbrella, and to be seated before the smārthā and the tribunal. She sometimes even takes betel-nut in their presence.

"When the trial is finished, a night (night-time seems to be essential for this part of the trial) is set apart for pronouncing sentence, or, as it is called, 'for declaring the true frame, figure, or aspect of the matter.' It takes place in the presence of the local chieftain who ordered the trial. A faithful and most minutely detailed account of all the circumstances is given by the smārthā, who winds up with the statement that his servant will name the adulterer or adulteress. Thereupon the man comes forward, steps on to a low stool, and proclaims the name or names.

"This duty is invariably performed by a man of the

Pattar caste, as it is essential that he should be a Brahman, and as no Canarese Brahman would do it for love or money, a needy Pattar is found, and paid handsomely for doing it. Directly he has performed the duty, he proceeds to the nearest tank to immerse his whole body, and so wash away the sin he has contracted.

"The next proceeding, which formally deprives the accused woman of all her caste privileges, is called the *keik-kottal*, or hand-clapping ceremony. The large Palmyra palm-leaf umbrella, with which all Nambutiri females conceal themselves in their walks abroad, is with them the outward sign of chastity. The sentence of excommunication is passed by the smārthā in the woman's presence, and thereupon her umbrella is formally taken from her by a Nayar of a certain pollution-removing caste. With much clapping of hands from the assembly, she is then instantly driven forth from her temporary quarters, and all her family ties are broken. Her kinsmen perform certain rites, and cut her off from relationship. She becomes to them in future even less than if she had died. Indeed, if she happens to die in the course of the inquiry, the proceedings go on as if she were still alive, and they are formally brought to a conclusion in the usual manner, by a verdict of guilty or of acquittal against the men implicated.

"The woman thus driven out goes where she likes. Some are recognized by their seducers; some become prostitutes; not a few are taken as wives by the chettis of Calicut. A few find homes in institutions specially endowed to receive them.

"These last-named institutions are of a peculiar character. In one of the best-known of them, the members have baronial powers, and keep up a sort of baronial state, with two hundred Nayar followers. The members of this are recognized as of the Tiyan, or toddy-drawer caste; and the sons of the *machchiyars* (female inmates) become in turn *mannanars* (or barons). The women take husbands from among the Tiyan community. The women who are sent to this one are those convicted of illicit intercourse with men of the Tiyan or of superior castes. If the connection has been with men of lower caste than the Tiyan, the women are sent to another institution called Kutira Mala, deep in the jungles of the western ghats.

"Following on the hand-clapping ceremony comes the feast of purification given by the accused's people, at which, for the first time since the trial commenced, the relatives of the accused woman are permitted to eat in company with their caste fellows, and with this feast, which is partaken of by every Nambutiri who cares to attend, the troubles of the family come to an end.

"Apart altogether from the scandals which are thus dragged into the light, it is a very serious matter for a family to have to incur the expenses of such an inquiry, for the cost rarely comes to less than one thousand rupees, and has been known to amount to as much as twelve thousand rupees. Nothing but the dread of being deprived of their caste privileges by the general body of their community would induce a family to incur the odium and expense of such a trial, and this feeling prompts them unhesitatingly to cast out their erring members."

The side lights upon the inner prejudices and rigours of caste conventions thus revealed are instructive, and the severity of punishment meted out to an erring woman is distinctly against the unfair theory that lapses of morality are generally condoned. The procedure of supposing the woman to be guilty until she can prove her innocence, is the reverse of our own basic ideas of justice, but she is at least given opportunities, and is certainly not condemned unheard.

Concerning the Mahommedan practices and customs of divorce, popular knowledge is, I find, singularly scanty, and I have been at some pains to ascertain what these are. I am indebted to Mr. Syed Abdul Majjid Shah, of an old and honourable Mussulman family of Hyderabad, and himself a barrister, for the most reliable information on the subject, which I give as I received it from him.

"Divorce is allowed in the religion of Islam, but only under stringent conditions.

"All recorded sayings of the prophet show that he looked upon any system of divorce with extreme disapproval, and considered that any laxity in the binding nature of the marriage oath was calculated to undermine the foundations of society. He has repeatedly declared that nothing could be more displeasing in the sight of God than divorce. He laid down for aggrieved persons the distinct and separate periods at which they ought to make special efforts to become reconciled, and renew their conjugal intercourse; but should all endeavours in this direction prove unsuccessful, after a third and final attempt, a decree of separation could be pronounced. In cases of conjugal disputes he recommended that arbiters should be chosen on both sides, to endeavour to effect a reconciliation.

"According to the Muslim legists, the wife also is entitled to demand a separation on the grounds of ill-usage, the withholding of due and proper means of maintenance, and certain other causes. The kazi (the Mahommedan judge) is empowered to decree separation if the facts are established. In every case in which the proceedings for divorce are instituted by the husband, he has to give up to the wife everything he settled upon her at her marriage. This deterring influence against mere caprice, the frequency of the admonitions in the Koran against separation, and the reiterated recommendations to heal quarrels by private reconciliation, show how sacred was the marriage tie in the eyes of the Arab legislator, as extracts such as this prove: 'And if ye fear even a breach between them (man and wife), then send ye a judge chosen from his family, and a judge chosen from her family, that peace be maintained,' etc.

"As far as I am aware of divorce in practice, it is exceedingly rare; and the only case indeed that I can remember was one of a Mahommedan servant to a missionary, who, although he was married already, fell in love with a beautiful but low-caste Hindu widow, whom he induced to become a member of his own faith and then married. Some time elapsed before the missionary discovered the affair, and the sahib then told his servant that if he did not separate from the woman, he would at once dismiss him, and this, under pressure of his master, he consented to do.

"This, as my own experience alone, might perhaps be of little worth, but to support my statement I will quote what Mr. Justice Ameer Ali says: 'As regards divorce, speaking from a somewhat extensive experience of this province (Bengal), which alone contains nearly twenty-two millions of Mussulmans, I know of only half a dozen cases occurring within the space of twenty-five years among the respectable classes, one of which, however, emanated from the wife. In all these cases there were faults on both sides.'

"The language on the subject that I have heard often upon missionary platforms is not even decent enough to refer to. It is sufficient, though, for me to say that there is not the slightest foundation for the slander that I have more than once heard from missionary lips, that a Muslim can divorce his wife by repeating the word 'talag' three times!"

CHAPTER VI.

FEMALE LIFE IN FIELD AND FACTORY.

"Sing, Gunga! to the millstone
It helps the wheel hum,
Blithesome heart and willing elbows
Make the fine meal come.
Handfuls three
For you and for me,
Now it falls white,
Good stones bite!
Drive it round and round, my Gunga,
Sing soft to the stone
Better corn and churrak-working
Than idleness and none."

From the Sanscrit.

THE true economic position of woman in India has generally been judged under the dazzling glamour of a cloud of sentiment. The bare suggestion of working for three half-pence or twopence a day has sent well-meaning enthusiasts into frenzies, they have drawn imaginary pictures of ryots' grievances, they have bidden us think of all capitalists, whether British or native, as so many grinding slave-drivers, against whom no legislation could be too severely aimed, and in short the general idea that has been fostered has been that life among the Indian working classes, and to their women in particular, is simply the hardest work and semi-starvation. All qualifications as to differing standards of comfort and domestic surroundings are ignored, but when these are taken into consideration, and the situation of labour studied dispassionately, I am very far from being prepared to admit that the average Indian woman has any cause to envy her European sister.

Let me take two extreme cases. The Englishwoman in my mind, whom I have actually seen, is a woman aged before her time (for, relatively, child-marriage exists in our own country) and burdened with two or three young children to support. She lived in the East End of London, occupying one small room up a steep and rickety flight of stairs, for which she paid two shillings a week, and considered herself fortunate in being able to earn regularly five shillings and sixpence a week in a cardboard-box factory. And there are thousands of women in London whose weekly wage is not only no more, but often considerably less, as must be the case when matchbox-making is paid at the rate of twopence-halfpenny a gross, the workers finding their own paste, or mantles with elaborate trimming at sixpence each. Out of wages as scanty as these, the Englishwoman in winter must find fuel enough to keep something of the cruelly penetrating fog and frost out of her poor apartment; her food, even in its elementary simplicity of tea and bread, is to be bought; her own and her children's clothes and boots have to be provided, some furniture and bedding are a necessity—yet the slender pittance must suffice to purchase all. Then turn we to the other instance—a poor widow whom I saw at Berhampore. With industrious labour she could earn at reeling the pierced cocoons of silk from half to three quarters of an anna a day, which far more than sufficed for the simple diet of rice, grain, and vegetables which satisfied her. There was a corner for her to sleep in the family hut; she had nothing to provide towards the feeding and clothing of the children; the cost of firing was infinitesimal; except her simple vessels for cooking and eating, her furniture was a negligeable quantity, for among the points in which the balance of advantage distinctly lies on the side of the Indian woman is that of climate. It saves her in house-rent, fuel, and clothes. If she lives outside a town her palm-leaf hut costs her nothing save the labour of her men-folk in building it and keeping it in repair;

FOR THREE FARTHINGS A DAY.

if she be within the city walls, the mud walls and thatched roofs of the native quarter are far less costly than "two-pair backs" or even garrets or cellars at home. A few sticks or the slowly smouldering cake of dried cow-dung—the preparation of which is among the minor industries of the community—suffices for the cooking of the simple meal, and a pie or two buys a week's supply of this. Thin wheaten cakes in the North-west Provinces, or rice generally elsewhere, form the staple of the food, which becomes an almost luxurious meal if some curry, or a chili, an onion, or a little *ghi* (clarified butter) can be added. The desire for meat, which makes it almost a necessity in our own working people's existence, she knows not, and, indeed, many castes may not touch it at all. Even tea she does not want, while any form of intoxicating drink she never dreams of taking. If her cloth and sari were coarse they were clean, and she could dispose them with folds as graceful as the wealthiest ranee or begum of the East; and while she draws them round her for her midday rest and ease, she realizes the indefinable pleasure of the *dolce far niente* that the more energetic races rarely attain unto. Yes, for all her three farthings a day, I think that poor old Hindoo woman might sometimes have been envied by her who nominally was making twelve times that sum.

To take agriculture first, the greatest of all the "great" industries of the dependency, and in which hundreds of thousands, even millions of the sex are employed, it would perhaps afford a more exact parallel to place the Indian working woman side by side with the women of France, where the system of peasant proprietorship obtains, rather than to institute any comparison with those who toil upon the soil in England, as though occasionally they lend their labour for wages to the wealthier zamindars of their district, they more often assist their fathers and husbands. The Hindu or Mahommedan woman labourer has at least the interest of the family in her work, and the harder she strives the greater the common advantage. Moreover, there is not the same reason in her case that she should not work in the fields that there is in England. It used to be an accepted article of faith with the Dorsetshire labourers, in whose midst I was brought up, that there was no real gain to the household when the mother went out to labour, since the extra expenditure in "shop bread," and the wear and tear of the children's clothes, which were perforce neglected during her absence, quite swallowed up the apparent gain of her earnings. These drawbacks do not exist in a land where all food is so simple, and where clothes are put on without the necessity for cut, or fit, or stitch, and where the requirements of everyday comfort are so quickly realized.

CHEAP FOOD—NATIVE DEALERS AT MADRAS.

As to what their simple home-life in the villages or townlets really is, I know no description more charming, and could give none more graphic than that by Sir George Birdwood in his fascinating monograph on the "Industrial Arts of India." "Outside the entrance, on an exposed rise of ground, the hereditary potter sits by his wheel moulding the swift-revolving clay by the natural curves of his hands. At the back of the houses which form the low, irregular street, there are two or three looms at work in blue and scarlet and gold, the frames hanging between the acacia trees, the yellow flowers of which drop fast on the webs as they are being woven. In the street the brass and copper smiths are hammering away at their pots and pans, and further down in the verandah of the rich man's house is the jeweller working rupees and gold mohrs into fair jewellery. . . . At half-past three or four in the afternoon the whole street is lighted up by the moving robes of the women going down to draw water from the tank, and so going and returning in single file, the scene glows like Titian's canvas and moves like the stately procession of the Panathenaic frieze. Later the men drive in the mild grey kine from the moaning jungle, the looms are folded up, the coppersmiths are silent, the elders gather in the gate, the lights begin to glimmer in the fast-falling darkness, the feasting and the music begin, and the songs are sung late into the night from the Rama-Yana or Mahabarata. The next morning with sunrise, after simple ablutions and adorations, performed in the open air before their houses, their same day begins again." A wedding or a death breaks the monotony of an existence which in truth has its interests and its pleasures, even as our own villagers can be happy throughout the recurring round of winter and summer, seed time and harvest. Only in the chill days of the rainy season are the mud huts uncomfortable and the thin cotton cloths insufficient, and then the dread spectres of dysentery and fever claim their own; but even for this, the wide distribution of hospitals and dispensaries into the remotest country districts is bringing much mitigation.

In preparing the ground for the wheat, rice, paddy, millet, pulse, cotton, and sugar, the women take their part, and very curious throughout Bengal is the leading share that is assigned to them in the labour connected with irrigation.

A sufficient water supply is of course highly essential for all these main crops, and for rice, which occupies nearly sixty per cent. of the cropped area of this province, it is all-important. Government provides the main water system, but the tenant often has to bring the supply on to his own land. The canal runs, perhaps, a few hundred yards below the cultivator's rice patch, and he therefore digs for himself a little channel between the two. He knows, however, that the water will never run uphill to him, and he therefore makes a tank or two at convenient stages. A couple of women then stand on either side of the channel on the edge of the canal, with a common palm-leaf basket attached to two stout ropes of twisted fibre. This they sink into the canal, and by a swift, dexterous movement of arm and wrist, throw the basketful of water, with almost inappreciable waste, into the tank of the stage above them, from whence a couple more will probably pass it on in a similar fashion. Tons of water are often thus raised in a day, and it is exceedingly interesting to watch the ease and rapidity which the women have acquired in this work.

The ingathering of the crops, and the subsequent winnowing and grinding, is also largely done by the women, and, with the primitive tools that they have at command, they perform their tasks with a speed and skill that individual practice could hardly have imparted without the help of hereditary instincts. With a palm-leaf tray, not unlike a housemaid's dustpan, and a few shakes to and fro, the chaff or husk is easily separated from the grain, and one may see quite tiny girls in all parts of the dependency thus at work with hardly less speed or neatness than their mothers and grandmothers. The process of grinding varies a little in the different provinces, though I never saw it more strikingly and gracefully done than by a group of Tamil women at Kinaya on the shores of eastern Ceylon, up one of the back-waters of Trincomalee harbour. Their mortars were about

TAMIL WOMEN POUNDING RICE.

one foot six inches high, and the pestles were heavy bars of wood between three and four feet long. I regard my own muscular development as fully up to the average of Western women, but I could not wield these latter with anything like ease, even with both arms. Yet these women gave, single-handed, a really substantial blow to the grain, throwing the pestle from hand to hand alternately for each pounding stroke.

Specially interesting, after the attention which the recent Royal Commission of Inquiry has directed to the subject, is the great opium industry, and in this the women have their special parts. The "opium year" is considered to commence in September. As a rule, the poppy sowing follows a crop of Indian corn, the soil being prepared with the plough and *hingah* (*i.e.* clod-crusher), and the seed put in from the middle to the end of October. Only the white variety is grown, as, although it yields a smaller quantity of the juice, it suits the Indian climate best. By the end of January the silvery-white blossoms are out, and flowering continues till late in March, or even early in April. Then begins the women's share in the work, and this forms one of the greatest departments of female labour in the dependency, though it has never been brought into statistical shape. The corolla of the flower is formed of four finely textured petals, which are usually ready to fall on the third day. The women watch these, and as soon as fully matured, the forefinger and thumb are passed round them, and they detach themselves from the capsule. These petals are scarcely less important, as will be presently seen, than the juice itself, and great care is exercised concerning them. As soon as this work is done, that of extracting the drug begins, and is thus performed: "The capsule is lanced in the afternoon with an instrument known as a *nashtar*, consisting of four sharp blades tied together with cotton, which is passed between the blades to keep them about one-thirtieth of an inch apart. The incisions are made from below upwards in perpendicular lines, and much care and practice are necessary to ensure their being made of the right depth. A merely superficial scratch is of no use; but, on the other hand, the walls of the capsule must not be cut through. Each capsule is usually lanced in this manner three or four times, at intervals of two or three days; but sometimes a single incision exhausts the drug, while occasionally a productive capsule will give five, eight, or even ten discharges. The work is usually performed by the ryot and his family, and not by hired labour."

SORTING OPIUM TRASH.

Next day the juice which has exuded from the incisions is scraped off with a small trowel-shaped scoop of thin iron called a *setwah*, and taken to the hut, where it has to be carefully kept away from anything like tobacco or onions, which would impart an objectionable flavour to it, free from mould, and turned over from day to day. Meantime the women of the household, provided this be of a low caste, and accustomed to work in the fields, besides assisting in the collection of the drug, have been engaged in their special branch of the labour, which is in providing the "leaves" that are required later in putting up the drug in its export form. This is rather an interesting feature of the industry, and is one of the rare instances in which the sex in India has appropriated to itself a little perquisite. A handful of the gently gathered poppy petals are placed upon an earthenware plate set upon a slow fire, and are covered with a moist cloth. With another pad of damp linen they are kneaded until their resinous matter causes them to adhere into a leaf, varying from six to twelve inches in diameter, and from brown-paper up to cardboard in thickness. When well made the sheets have a peculiar haylike scent, which is supposed to give to Bengal opium something of the delicate aroma its connoisseurs appreciate, and they are a source of real profit to the women. Three qualities are recognized by Government, and are paid for at the rates of ten, seven, and five rupees a maund (82 lbs.). When the cultivator is a Brahman, Rajput, or of certain other high-castes, whose women may not participate in this source of profit, he must employ hired labour, as he is bound to supply a quantity of leaves proportionate to the crude opium collected, and this seriously diminishes the family gains.

To be allowed to visit either of the opium factories at Patna or Ghazipur is a very rarely accorded favour, and in my case was obtained personally for me by Lord Lansdowne. For various reasons I found it more convenient to go to the latter place, which is situated far up the main stream of the sacred Ganges river, about eighty miles above its juncture with the Gogra. To reach it from the main line of the East

Indian Railway, one changes at Dildanaggar Junction, and travels over about twelve miles of branch line to Tari Ghat, where the river must be crossed by steamer. The first sight of the place, with its crumbling old palaces, is extremely picturesque, while a sense of dignity is given to the factory by its protecting battery of two or three old twelve-pounder guns. Altogether, the factory covers some twenty-two acres, and in its busiest time, namely, from April to June, when the opium is being received in bulk from the sub-agencies, some four thousand hands are employed in it. Of this number about five hundred are women, and on the day that I saw it, during its comparatively slack season of packing, there were over four hundred of the sex engaged. I shall speak presently of the work specially done by them, for the first process in the preparation of a cake is to ascertain by chemical tests and assay the purity of the crude substance, and in that they take no part. Opium is good or bad according to the plants it is drawn from, but the temperature and state of the weather affect its subsequent conditions materially. When ready for storage, it is kept in thirteen huge vats, which will hold 19,140 maunds (1,569,480 lbs.), and for drying for Indian consumption about a maund and a half is placed in a shallow wooden vat, and laid in a huge flagged yard, where it is exposed to air and sun. Some hundreds of these vats or trays were there closely set in long rows, and containing the dark substance, which gave out a smell strangely pungent yet sickly to unaccustomed nostrils, and varying in thickness from a treacly syrup up to a paste dry enough to be handled with slightly oiled fingers. It occupies some days to bring it to this latter condition, the opium which has reached it all being together at the upper end of the yard, where stalwart coolies tread it to a yet firmer consistency, rolling and turning the heavy mass for some hours until it is sufficiently kneaded.

The opium is issued from the factory in differing shapes for Indian consumption and for export to China or the Straits. If for the former purpose it is run at a wax-like stiffness into an hydraulic press, which delivers it in square blocks of two pounds each, stamped with the crown of India, and bearing the words, "Benares: Akbari" (Customs). To be packed, each cake is wrapped in folds of a curiously tenacious tissue paper, made only in Nepaul from bamboo fibre. For the Chinese market, which absorbs by far the greater part of the entire output, the drug undergoes no drying process at all, and is made up in the form of balls, suggestive of a heavy artillery projectile in appearance, and weighing about four and a quarter pounds. To make these a brass cup, which constitutes half a perfect sphere, is necessary, and inside it a layer of the leaves of poppy petals before mentioned is neatly fitted in as a lining. This is laid on till a thickness of about one-third of an inch is obtained, and is rendered firm by brushing it with *lewa*, a thinner form of opium. A weighed lump of the drug of standard quality is pressed into the cup, more leaves and lewa are applied to cover any possible fractures between the joins, and the soft yet solid ball is put in the sun, standing in an earthenware cup, and continually turned every three days till dry. These earthen vessels form an important item in the factory economy, and fully 800,000 to 900,000 of them are required in the course of the year, while some 2500 a day are allowed as the average of breakages. When the balls have solidified as far as they ought to do, they are stored in enormous "go-downs," as any big shed is called in India, and in one of these alone—that moreover not being the largest of them

—were 83,150 in readiness for immediate issue, while the registered number in store on the day I was there was something over 240,000, that recorded for the year being 823,000 cakes.

According to official definition, "trash," which is a most important adjunct to the packing of the drug, consists of "the pounded leaves and stalks of the poppy plant." The plants are left standing in the fields until quite dry and withered, and all save the hardest stems are then collected and crushed, the nearest sub-agencies of the Ghazipur factory being called upon to supply a quantity rather more than proportionate to their delivery of opium. It is in dealing with this that by far the greater number of the women employed in the factory are concerned. The trash as it is brought in is very dirty, and mixed with sticks, small stones, and such irrelevant matter, and the first item of its preparation is to spread a quantity of it over coarse cotton cloths upon the ground. Nothing that I saw in the factory gave me a better idea of the vastness of its dealings than this scene, for in a long unbroken row from end to end of the enormous enclosure, were a hundred and forty women seated upon their heels in the characteristic Oriental fashion, with several yards behind them of the picked-over material, and moving slowly forward over the wider mass before. There was, of course, a certain amount of fine dust in the air, but as one saw them with their saris of coarse yet clean calico disposed over their heads, and the heavy barbaric ornaments on their wrists and ankles, one's mind irresistibly travelled back to the grimy unloveliness of a walled-in London dustyard, with its noisy sorters, in their tawdry feather hats or battered and rusty crape bonnets, and it was here that I first began to wonder whether the lot of the woman workers in the East is so immeasurably worse than that of her Western sister after all. At least these women, if their wages were only about twopence-halfpenny per day, were under a sunny sky, they could bring their babies with them, and were not disbursing for care of them any portion of their slender earnings to some old "day nurse" who would administer in a noxious form the very drug in whose preparation they were assisting.

A further process of cleaning has to be done with rather a ponderous form of the old-fashioned hand-winnowing machines similar to those formerly used in English homesteads, and all this work, including the carrying of the stuff in its half-sorted and fully cleaned forms, was done by the women, whose graceful carriage with the large baskets upon their heads was very noticeable. I asked Dr. Sedgefield, the superintendent of the factory, whether many of the women were consumers of the drug in any form, and he replied that scarcely one was. Indeed, throughout the factory, he stated that not more than about one per cent. of both sexes employed took it at all. It is about October that the cakes of opium begin to be dry enough to pack for export, and meantime the chests, which are made either of mango or salwood, with a good coating of pitch over any joint, have been seasoning well. The actual work of putting up is a noisy and a bustling scene. At the bottom of each box a layer of thoroughly dried trash is spread, and a frame of twenty compartments upon a larger scale than those used in England for sending eggs by post is laid in. Into each of these a cake of opium is placed, and more trash is shaken well down before a bamboo mat and another precisely similar frame is packed in, so that each case contains forty cakes. The strictest precautions are taken to insure that the opium

WINNOWING TRASH.

is not tampered with in any way before it leaves the factory, even to the despatch of a responsible official to Tari Ghat station to see it delivered safely to the railway company.

Another branch of female labour that I explored with exceeding interest were the colliery workers at Girideh. This is the principal coal-mining centre of all India, and, in fact, from these mines come fully three-quarters of the entire coal output (estimated to exceed 2,000,000 tons a year) of the dependency. The mines, which are directly under Government control, lie at the end of a short branch line of the East India Railway, and I arrived at this at the decidedly uncomfortable hour of three in the morning. But I think it was almost worth any small inconvenience to enjoy the crisp, almost frosty feel of a December morning in Bengal, until the spin of a dogcart's wheels and a cheery English voice of welcome rang out in pleasant greeting. Against the sky, as we drove for about a mile and a half, there was a yellowy-white glow of many distant coke furnaces; but, save for these, it was difficult to realize that one had reached the great coal-field of Bengal, for there were fine trees on all hands, and in the fresh night wind there was neither smoke nor black. The superintendent of these collieries is Dr. Walter Saise, a gentleman not only of great scientific attainments, but of unusual kindliness and sympathy in dealing with the curious peoples who go to make up the army of workers under his control, and as we went along he gave in brief summary a few details of the mines themselves. The property covers an area of about five and a half square miles, and its present yearly output, which is almost all absorbed by the railway company, approaches 1,500,000 tons. All told there are 11,560 souls associated with the working of the mines, of whom 8754 live actually upon the estate, forming one of the happiest working communities that one could find in any industrial centre. Schools and an hospital under the charge of a highly qualified native doctor have been established for the people; thrift has been inculcated in them in a fashion to be found but very unusually among natives, improved methods of cultivation have been shown them, and missionary effort among the aboriginal tribes has achieved a much higher degree of success than in many parts. The colliers themselves are especially interesting from the large proportion among them of the Kol and Santali aboriginal tribes, who still preserve most of their primitive customs and characteristics, though they have learnt to appreciate such civilized benefits as sick attendance and elementary education, even for the girls.

My first visit was to the hospital, an airy bungalow, containing three wards for men and one for women, in all of which were good iron bedsteads with mattresses, and due equipments of stretchers and appliances in case of accidents in the mines, which, though fortunately rare, have to be reckoned for in India as at home. Walking through the wards, however, the absence of any nursing staff struck me as curious, and I asked Dr. Saise if all the assistants were off duty. "Not at all," he replied, with a smile; "we have overcome two great difficulties in a very cheap and practical manner. The first is that of caste, where endless trouble would arise by the rigorous conventions which will not allow one to administer or receive food to or from another, and the second is that of home-sickness, which causes the patients to fret terribly to be back with their own kin. Well, when a man, say, is brought in, we send for his wife or daughter, allowing her full working pay, to come and nurse him. She cooks his food, and if he is on any special diet the assistant-surgeon sees that she gives him this, and she keeps him in touch with his own home. Thus he recovers far more quickly than he would under hands to which he was not accustomed, and we are saved the maintenance of a large nursing staff." This, as I have explained, is always a costly item in Indian hospital organization, through the prejudices of caste; while one must understand Indian working-class life to realize how easily a woman rolls up a cloth and a couple of cooking vessels and seats herself on the verandah outside to attend to her lord and master or her child under treatment. A benefit club is not a form of economy which commends itself as a rule to the native mind, but it has been adopted here remarkably well, and the small subscriptions are regularly and cheerfully paid up. The women are permitted to participate in its advantages, and receive monetary assistance for their confinements.

Factory legislation in India is likely some day to interfere with female labour underground, and already there are deep murmurs of dissatisfaction in the native community at the prospect. Let me therefore say emphatically and at once that there is nothing like the occasion for hasty steps that there were when the seventh Earl of Shaftesbury stirred British public opinion to its prohibition at home. I went down two of the principal mines, both of which were rather deep sinkings, and quite representative of the others near by. To descend, one stood upon a steel tray and held on to a bar of iron at a level about one's eyes, and as firedamp happily does not exist in these Bengal mines, naked lights could be carried with impunity. With these colliers, the earnings are reckoned rather by the family than by the individual, and the contributions of the women to the aggregate are well worth consideration in a land of low wages, as India is. The men's average earnings are four to five annas a day; the women's one and a half to two, and a little further help to the total is furnished by the boys. The cutting out and breaking away is done by the men, those of the Kol tribe being the strongest and quickest at this work, while the women pile it into the trollies, which

WOMEN IN THE GIRIDEH MINES.

they push to the points where they can be dragged on by ponies to the shaft, or if the distance to this is not very great, they take them all the way themselves. In these Girideh mines, the conditions of work are less irksome for women than they were in many of our own, for the cuttings are, as a rule, broad and high, and only in some of the remoter ones is it impracticable for a tall person to stand fully upright. The unpleasantness of standing in dirty water is very rarely encountered, and save in one or two of the very deepest sinkings the ventilation is remarkably good.

The women, in spite of their marriages at fourteen and fifteen years of age, were strong and well set up. Remembering, as one does, the terrible descriptions of the swearing, drunken, degraded disgraces to their sex that the north-country women workers underground used to be, the most remarkable point about them was their perfect gentleness and modesty. Each was dressed exactly as she would have been for any other occupation, though her cloth and sari were perhaps a little dirtier than they would have been in a less grimy one, and each wore a mass of bangles and anklets, some of them very interesting specimens of barbaric silver and bell-metal work. Save a little pause of curiosity to look at me and my own clothes, they worked steadily on, pushing forward the heavy trollies which, when laden, were a weight of eight hundredweight. One or two had requests to make of the foreman as he went on, in general these being trifling things, such as taking half a day's leave, or some little point about the land they held; but the general quiet, good order, discipline, and respect were all points that impressed me much. The few questions that I put to them about their hours, which only number eight per day at work, their food, and amusements, which seemed largely to centre in the big bazaar of Sunday, were straightforwardly and frankly answered, and as I left them to come up in the same fashion as I had gone down, I felt glad to think that I had the opportunity before me of seeing them, later in the day, in their own homes and domestic surroundings.

The Kols as coal-cutters excel over the other races with whom they work; while their predilection for agriculture gives them an advantage in tilling the plot of land which they can all hold, and which is one of the sources of the pleasant and manly independence one observes throughout the colliery. Their women are among the few native ones who indulge in any vagaries of fashion, and may sometimes be seen all wearing small black bead necklaces, while at another time large coloured ones will have come into vogue. They wear heavy armlets and bracelets of silver and bell-metal, and of the latter substance very large anklets are also made. These are of a very peculiar curved shape, and can only just be forced on with great violence. As wives, the Kol women are well treated, and as I saw them, they were a fine and healthy-looking community, so that I could well endorse Mr. Riseley's remarks upon them in his erudite dictionary of the tribes and castes of Bengal, in which he says, "A Kol makes a regular companion of his wife. She is consulted in all difficulties, and receives the fullest consideration due to her sex. Indeed, it is not uncommon in the Kolhan to see husbands so subject to the influence of their wives that they may be regarded as henpecked. Instances of infidelity in wives are very rare. I never heard of one, but I suppose that such things must occur, as there is a regulated penalty."

The Santali people, who divide the work of the mines with them, resemble them in most racial characteristics, though their women have to suffer one or two disabilities; but, on the other hand, if they are sufficiently Hinduized to venerate the goddess Kali, women may act as her *chetinis* or priestesses. One of these I saw—an aged creature who lived alone in a tiny hut of palm leaves adjoining the humble little temple in which she, whose name is the "Giver of Fortune," was worshipped. It did not require much persuasion to induce the old woman to show me something of her ceremonial, but the sight and touch of the little board studded closely with sharp upstanding steel points, upon which she sat down (though I fancy that she saved herself from any acute torture by raising herself upon her heels which were drawn under her), and a handful of steel chains with bits of jagged metal loosely attached, which she used as an instrument of flagellation, sent her in a very few minutes into a state of frenzy. During this she lashed herself furiously and foamed at the mouth, chanting the while a weird monotone till she fell back exhausted. Besides Kali, however, *Jair Era*, a kind of sylvan feminine deity, enjoys universal esteem among the Santals, and every village has a grove set apart in her honour, while every family has its *orak bonga*, or household god, and an *abge bonga*, or secret god, the name of which must on no account be divulged to the women of the establishment, but be kept with all care to the men.

Silk, both in its primitive native manufacture, and as one sees it in the Alliance Mills at Bombay—the one silk mill of all India—employs a large percentage of women. To speak first of this latter, which belongs to the Sassoons, one finds that it possesses machinery not surpassed in Leek or Lyons, and that among its chief out turn are very soft and fine saris in tones of colour delicate and pale, as well as in the stronger, cruder aniline violets, pinks, and greens which Western methods of dyeing have familiarized, the bright *glacé* satins which well-to-do women employ for the skin-tight little choli jackets they admire, and the *mashru* fabrics backed with cotton for Mahommedan wear in obedience to the ordinance of the Prophet which forbade for male wear the use of unmixed silk. There are 224 looms in this mill, and if all are fully at work they can turn out 2200 yards of woven silk a day. Raw silk from Bengal or Japan is used, and

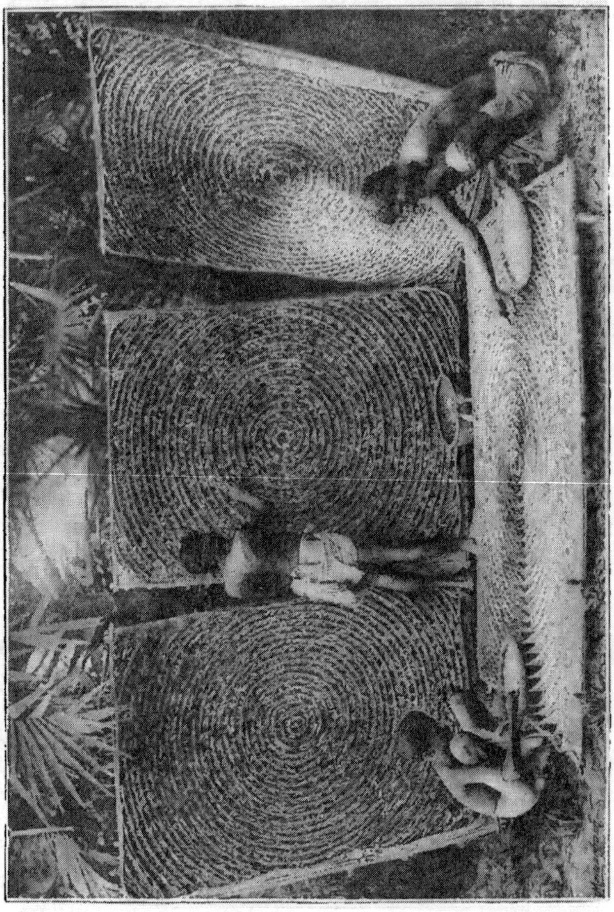

SORTING THE CATERPILLARS.

it is easy to tell at a glance which is which up to the dyeing process, as the Bengal is a clear canary yellow in colour and the Japan has all been bleached to a snowy whiteness. There are 350 women employed here, their work being, as well as winding the spun threads into hanks, to do what is technically known as folding the short-stapled filaments of silk after they have gone through the top dressing and carding processes. This is a branch of the

DRYING COCOONS.

industry requiring great neatness and dexterity of touch, and in it the women, who were almost unexceptionally Hindus, wearing a great amount of characteristic native jewellery, have developed a very high degree of skill. They are paid by the piece, a capable and industrious hand being able to earn from twelve to fourteen rupees a month.

I was fortunate while in Berhampore in being able to see the whole native series of processes, from the reeling of the

SPINNING.

silk from the cocoons up to the finished work upon the rough-looking looms. Of the first-named section of work by far the greater part is done by women. The cocoons are softened, and the thread is drawn out very rapidly on to a round frame of light bamboo or cane, which the spinster keeps in quick motion. When a number of skeins are spun they have to be sorted as to their strength and comparative fineness, and in this work delicacy of touch is the only guide.

SORTING SKEINS.

As the thread passes through the fingers, any variation in thickness is instantly detected; and it is then gathered on to the *latai*, as the whirling cage on which it is being wound is called, of its particular size, and so keenly is this sense of feeling developed that four or five latais are often used when it is desired to make a careful selection in comparative fineness. Like all the subsidiary mechanism employed, these latais are of the most primitive character, and the *polti*, or central reel from which the threads are worked off, is merely turned on its axis in a hole in the floor. For the throwsting or twisting of the silk the whole machinery does not cost more than two rupees to make, though the labour involved brings the price to a rupee per pound of twisted silk. It is difficult to make the process quite clear without a diagram, but four persons are engaged upon the work. A man sits before a rude frame, which supports the strands of silk. These strands have heavy weights on small pieces of stick attached to them, and pass over U-shaped canes, through glass rings (usually the cheap bangles favoured of the working women) set between horizontal pieces of bamboo nailed to poles stuck in the ground. Two more people, often boys or women, guide the strands in their course through the series of rings, and the twisting is due to the adroitness of the turn given by the man with his two hands to the weights attached to the threads of silk, which are wound by a fourth man on to a reel. Simple as this system is, it proves to answer well with the unevenness of native silk, which makes it always very difficult to manage in European throwsting machinery.

The women take a leading share in the several processes of dyeing, although this is performed in the simplest manner possible. Besides white, there are only five colours in general use. To produce a strong blue, pure indigo is employed, and with several successive dippings a black is obtained. For yellow there are three processes, each producing a full and rich tone, the first being with alum and kamela dust, the second with annatto flowers, and the third with lodh wood.

SILK WEAVING AT BERHAMPORE.

Tumeric and lac give red, and indigo and lac chocolate, while the green, which is the only non-permanent dye used in the district, is prepared with a decoction of bakosh (*adha*

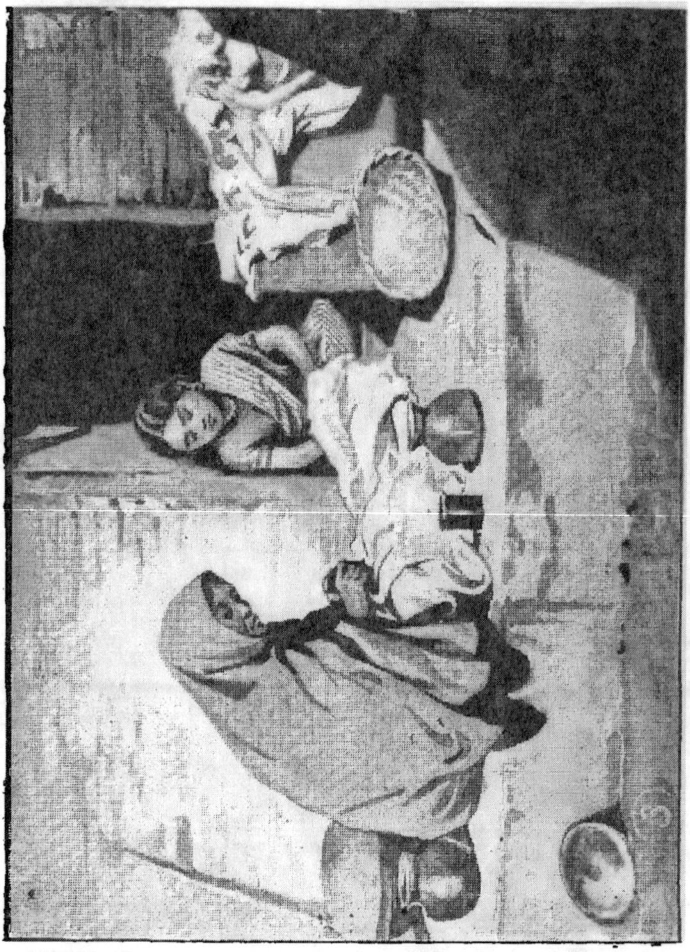

A WIDOW KNOTTING THE SILK FOR DYEING.

toda vasica) and sawdust of jackwood, the silk, before dipping, being steeped in alum.

Reeling is essentially a home and cottage industry, and one may often find the poorest old grandmother earning a few pice a day by winding the almost worthless silk of defective or pierced cocoons, though their produce can be used to make a coarse garment called a *matka*, which Mahratta women like to put on after morning bath. The women help also in making the pieces known as *banhus*, which are really spotted corahs, and find their chief sale among the women of

PRIMITIVE SPINNING.

the North-west Provinces and the Punjab. To produce the spots or rings of white upon a colour, the length of silk is taken, and the woman with a deftly-tied knot raises a series of tight little lumps upon its whole surface. The piece is then dyed, and when the spots are undone, regularly placed white spots are found to have been left. Very little silk printing is now done here, though, if it is executed, it is done in elementary primitiveness, and the parts to be left undyed are merely traced out in clay paste. Three colours are sometimes used in this way on the one piece.

Curiously enough, however, the sex is allowed very little share in the collection of the wild or "tasser" silk. These cocoons are mostly gathered and brought in by the Santals, who have learnt, with that curious habit of close observation which seems to be an heritage of all woodland folk, to note where the insects are spinning, while they are hunting bigger game or cutting fuel. The actual harvesting is attended by many superstitions, and the women may neither assist in the labour, nor even administer to the wants of their lords and masters at the time.

From official and technical information supplied to me, I learn that there are now something over a hundred and thirty cotton spinning and weaving mills, and in nearly all these the greater part of the winding of the yarn into hanks is done by women. They are to be found in all parts of the dependency, from Tinnevelly to the Punjab, from Bengal to Rajputana, though, of course, Bombay is the chief centre of the industry. Cawnpore is, however, making a big bid for commerce in this direction, and with her close-set columns of tall chimneys and heavy smoke-laden atmosphere is winning for herself the name of the "Manchester of India." Here spinning of the rather short-stapled Indian cotton is done by the Cawnpore Mills Company, while the Muir and Elgin Mills weave as well very useful qualities of cotton cloths for European as well as native purposes. From time immemorial cotton spinning has been one of the industries indigenous to the country, but there is a wide difference in the primitive methods one may still see employed by the remoter roadsides, and the huge mills, with their steam power and their thousands of mule, ring, and throstle spindles, and their hundreds of looms. Both here and at Delhi, where I went through the Delhi Cotton Mills, directed by Messrs. Thornton and Wilson, I had the opportunity of seeing the types of

A PRIMITIVE WHEEL.

women belonging to the sturdy and handsome races of the North-west Provinces who enter upon factory work. Yet neither in these nor in any others that I saw was there any evidence of the physical deterioration of the workers, out of which a good deal of agitational capital has been made; but I was warned that I would be more likely to note this in Bombay. Here, among others, I visited the huge Colaba Jubilee Mills, and through a sympathetic and reliable interpreter in Guzerati, quietly put a number of questions to the women as to their wages, hours, and wants. But I could hear of no grievance—nothing more than an admission that in the hot season a full day's labour was exhausting enough for an ordinary woman. As a fact, the work is all paid by the piece, and the Indian temperament is not in favour of too great a strain upon its energies. Even in Bombay the general standard of physique, taking into consideration the distinctive racial attributes, was by no means bad, and would have given decidedly better results than one would obtain by placing side by side average North Country mill hands with representatives of other English occupations.

Of course, it is said that it is too soon to observe depreciating effects to any marked degree, and that, at present, the higher wages to be earned at factory work are bringing in large reinforcements from the country. The facts are against both these assertions. The first mill started in India was in 1851, and by 1878 there were fifty-eight. The Indian peasant, born upon the soil, is extremely loth to leave it, and moreover, to quote from a high authority, "there is a certain degradation in working in either textiles or leathers, so that, as an outlet for the surplus population now thrown upon the land, the development of these industries cannot be regarded, save in very exceptional circumstances, as likely to benefit more than the lower labouring and menial classes." These, moreover, would find themselves at a disadvantage in labour requiring as much skill as weaving, and it is only to a very limited degree that they are to be found in the mills.

Several modifications concerning women were introduced into the Factory Act of India, in 1892, when the hours of labour were reduced to eleven, and in factories where a system of shifts is not in force, women are prohibited from working before 5 a.m., and after 8 p.m. No girl under fourteen may be employed, and it has strictly laid down how long the hours of labour shall be, stipulating that an hour's rest shall be allowed during the middle of the day. In this interval the women seldom go home, but sit in the nearest shade to the work-yard gates and chew betel or eat the cheap sweetmeats brought round to them by itinerant dealers. Their young children they generally bring with them to the mills, and, indeed, the stranger, going through the departments in which they are employed, has to walk warily between the podgy little brown lumps sleeping or crawling upon the floor.

Another phase of women's work that I noticed with interest was in connection with the preparation of coffee. Coming down the Malabar coast, I gained an insight into the many processes of cleaning and sorting through which the coffee-berry goes ere it appears in the grocers' window, and the most delicate and tedious of these—known to the trade as "garbling"—is all performed by women and girls. There is elaborate machinery to remove the husk of the berry, and a system of sieves of graduated sizes, not unlike those employed for the sizing of gun-shot, can be used to bring the various grades of the bean to the evenness which constitutes an important factor in its commercial value. But when all this has been done there remains an appreciable percentage of discoloured and unsightly berries which would lower much the standard of the samples, and such only can be removed by hand. In an enormous factory which I visited at Mangalore there were nearly two hundred women thus employed. They filled two immense sheds, the floors of which were of hard concrete. Each woman had her little mat of palm fibre, and two baskets before her, as well as a high heap of the grey-green berries. These she spread out before her, seeing instantly the defective grain or grains to

WORKING WOMEN AT MANGALORE.

be removed and placed in the smaller of the baskets, and gathering up with lightning activity handfuls of the beans, now cleaned and ready for packing. About two annas a day I found to be the usual wage to be earned at the work, though some, particularly expert themselves, and helped a little by one or two of their children, could make more than this.

On this coast also, where fishing forms a staple industry, the women do much of the work of drying and packing for export the enormous quantities of fish that goes inland, up country, to Ceylon, and to the Persian Gulf; and, of course, in the picking and preparation of tea an occupation is found for thousands. Time and great distances unfortunately prevented my going to Darjeeling and Assam, so that I am unable to speak from personal knowledge of this department of work. It is perhaps unnecessary, however, that I should adduce any further specific information, and to those who would turn upon me and say, "Yes, possibly in these material points the lot of the Indian working woman is less hard than it is often made out to be, but see how narrow are her ideas, and how much is sealed to her through her want of education," I would answer, that at home, with all our vaunted codes and standards, I very much doubt if relatively we have added much to the English working woman's range of thought, if one looks at the facts as they are. The London factory girl leaves school so soon as she has crammed enough knowledge to pass her fourth standard, or when she has turned fourteen years at the latest. Though cookery, and very lately laundry-work and housewifery, have been added to her curriculum, she is generally most lamentably ignorant of the domestic arts, while her utter incompetence with her needle is not one of the least factors in contributing to impose what Mr. Walter Besant calls the "inexorable law of eleven-pence halfpenny," and its provision of the cheapest shoddy and sweated labour upon us. Her reading is confined to halfpenny novelettes, save on the rare occasions that she takes up one of those hateful hotch-potches of vulgar jokes and irrelevant snipping which are served out in periodicals of the "bits" order. Of the movements of the world in politics, commerce, art, or literature she knows

UP-COUNTRY CARTS AT CALICUT.

and cares nought. Her recreations savour more of horse-play than of refinement; the inside of the public-house is not by any means a sealed book to her, and she marries with reckless improvidence. It is not a pretty picture, but it is a true one. Now in India the intense strength of the family tie and the hereditary traditions of woman's self-effacement seem to me to have imparted a kind of compensating mental attribute, that perhaps is not very much less valuable a possession than a power to read without the discriminating faculty what to read. According to modern "emancipated" lights, the answer of a poor Mahommedan woman in Calcutta to my question as to what she regarded as the chief happiness she would desire for herself might seem a contracted one. "To see my husband happy, and to know that what I have cooked and done for him has helped to make him so; to see my sons grow up as men, honest and strong, and to know that my daughters are well married"—is, in my view, a praiseworthy domestic ideal, enough even when set beside the possibilities of a bank holiday on Hampstead Heath. Thought may not be subtle, and talk may not rise much beyond pice and marriage, with these poor women; but relatively it does no more than that with their white sisters.

Moreover, it is to be remembered that the binding laws of caste, which have come down through the centuries, have induced an attitude of submission to things as they are, that it is difficult sometimes for the Western mind to grasp how complete the sentiment of resignation becomes. That a sweeper woman should always be a sweeper woman, and should marry a sweeper or some equivalently low-caste man, seems to them even as a decree of nature which it were useless to attempt to overthrow. Consequently there is a feeling of content which checks the wild yearnings of ambition, if indeed in the humbler castes this has not been wholly lost from the mental faculties, even as the body in time loses power in muscles or limbs never exercised. Traditions, unimpaired in strength, are handed on from mother to daughter, and thus, with her lack of aspiration and her simple standards of comfort and necessity, I do not think that the working woman of the East is in such bad case when set beside her European sisters.

This perhaps is not an inopportune place to interpolate a few facts as to the legal status of Mahommedan women, on which home views are especially hazy, but which, I venture to consider, are another point over which comparison continues rather in favour of the East. As with ourselves, as long as a girl is under age and remains unmarried under the paternal roof, her father or appointed guardian constitutes a controlling power. Directly, however, that she has attained her majority, the law, as laid down by the Muslim legists, recognizes fully her individual rights. She is entitled to a share in her father's or mother's property, not, it is true, in as large a proportion as her brothers, but still in a strictly defined and well-understood ratio. A woman *sui juris* can under no circumstances be married without her full and expressed consent.

Nor does she on her marriage lose her personal rights, or merge them in those of her husband. An ante-nuptial settlement in favour of the wife by the husband is a necessary condition among all save the very poorest; and, failing this, the law presumes one in accordance with the social position of the woman. A Muslim marriage is a civil act in itself, and all that is binding can be done with neither priest nor ceremonial. After it the man possesses no powers over the wife's person that the law does not define, and none whatever over her goods or property. The rights she possesses as a mother are, moreover, clearly laid down, and are not subject to individual caprice. Her person is protected against ill-treatment or brutality, while any earnings of her own belong strictly to herself, and cannot be touched by an extravagant husband.

In the courts she can sue a debtor or bring any civil action without cover of her husband's name, or the necessity of joining a next friend, and, in short, acts, if *sui juris,* absolutely as an individual. All these ordinances are plainly enjoined by the Muslim authorities on the law, who may be said to recognize no disabilities arising from sex.

I have alluded before to the conditions of divorce or separation; but unless the causes for demanding this were unusually grave, a woman usually has to sacrifice her dowry, or anything she brought into settlement. Should it, however, be the husband who seeks this, he has (except where the ground of complaint was proved infidelity) to make over to her the whole sum of money, with any jewels that he settled upon her at marriage. A woman, therefore, who works (for the Hindu rights are no less clear) does not do so as the mere chattel of her husband. If her earnings go, as they probably do, to swell the family purse, it is not because she has no other lawful method for their disposal, since they are her own to help her to broaden her horizon if she so willed. But instead of doing this, her own natural tendency is to narrow it. Our own example, our own education, has not yet touched the fringe of inner native life, and the first evidence of gratitude that the working-class mother will show for the good wages which the British raj, irrigation, and machinery, have given her, will be, not to send her daughter to school, but to keep her *purdah nashin,* and marry her as a child, as the first evidences of growing social importance. As a journalist, it is perhaps rather my instinct to record things as they are, and not as they should be; and to speak of womanhood in the East as satisfied under present conditions of life is always sufficient to send those of a certain school of thought into something like frenzy. But caste and the zenana system are closely interlocked, and together they are the two keystones of the whole fabric of Indian social life. The former teaches a pride or a humility, as the case may be; but, on either hand, an acceptance of that state of life to which they are called that is marvellously discouraging to restlessness and outside ambition. The latter possesses a prestige and a dignity that I scarcely know how to express adequately, but I think is sometimes, and in a measure, realized by the struggling shopkeeping class when they attain to a competency, or receive an unexpected legacy, which enables them henceforth to "live independent" among their working neighbours, or in a higher circle when knighthood is won. While these two forces are the dominant influences in the life, there can be no appreciable change, even with education and European example. For to abolish them would be to effect a revolution so sweeping and so vast that the India of Hinduism, Buddhism, Islamism, and history would have disappeared, and a new nation would have arisen upon the face of the earth. But the tinkering meddlers who would graft a lot of Europeanized excrescences on to Eastern habits and beliefs seem unable to grasp this as a truth.

CHAPTER VII.

DRESS.

> 'Ενθ' ἐνὶ πέπλοι
> Λεπτοὶ εὔνητοι βεβλήατο, ἔργα γυναικῶν.
>
> *Odyssey*, H. 95, 96 (Homer).

It is not the traveller who races through India, and then comes back to talk with vague enthusiasm about the beauties of draping and colour of dress in the East, who can tell the variety and charm that there is about it; nor is it she, on earnest purpose of inquiry bent, who would convey a true idea of it from the inspection of schools, seminaries, and institutions. For it might happen to her, as it did to me on more than one occasion, that my visit was expected, and the children had been bidden to put on their "best" clothes. Horror of horrors upon Hindu heads, these included about a dozen bonnets as turned out in the native bazaar in a kind of travesty of the styles favoured at home some six or eight years ago! They were worn turbanwise upon the very top of the head, and one that lingers in my mind was of flimsiest sky-blue satin with black velvet strings, and a cluster in front, formed of three ill-conditioned ostrich feathers and some vivid magenta flowers. Two pretty little sisters appeared in frocks founded upon English ideas, and of brilliant blue and yellow, with alarming bonnets of yellow satin and green leaves, and yet one more uncommendable innovation remains to be chronicled in light cotton stockings with coloured stripes passing round the leg. These worn with German made shoes much ornamented with white stitching and pearl buttons, with the native heavy silver anklets duly put on also, are only laughable till one thinks what the change may portend.

I have, however, almost as bad a quarrel with the missionary element in India concerning clothes as I have over embroidery and needlework, and there is something of cause and effect between them. With that extraordinary inability to recognize anything that is admirable unless it be of the most conventional and villa-residential character, which seems a peculiarity of the Englishman, and even more particularly the Englishwoman abroad, many of them profess to find the native dress "unseemly," "indecorous," or, as I have even frankly heard it called, "indecent." Now, in Bengal and other parts of India, the tiny *choli*, or short jacket, which fits very closely over the shoulders, is of fine net, and the women have a very charming way of working and darning it in fine silks of delicate hues, which might have been borrowed in idea, save for the addition of colouring from our own needle-run laces. There is an artistic and laudable vanity about these among the girls, but, alas! for readily offended and pious susceptibilities, these dainty little garments are not sufficiently opaque! Their production is discouraged in favour of Berlin woolwork tigers seated beside baskets of flowers, or the manufacture of comforters in stripes of violet and scarlet. And then we get a draggled skirt and battered bonnet in place of the sari—one of which I saw in Calcutta which was merely of fine white cotton, with a narrow dark blue border, and had cost only six rupees to buy. But upon it had been expended twenty rupees' worth of silver and silver-gilt wire thread and spangles; and some idea of the quantity used may be gathered from the fact that at Bombay there are wire drawers who can produce 800 yards of metallic thread from two shillings' worth of silver. This was worked into a close and elaborate design at the end, while all over were dotted the queerest little stars and sprigs, and the whole effect was one of delicate richness.

One may admit that it is a little startling at Mangalore, Tellicherry, and Calicut, on the West Coast, when one meets the Nayar and Tiyar women wearing no more than a single white cloth between their waists and knees. Only on a damp or chilly day do they throw anything over their shoulders and bosoms, for by a strange reversal of ideas it indicates immodesty to be covered above the waist, as well as being distinctive of low caste. But one grows accustomed to it, and soon realizes that they are simply doing what has been customary with them through the centuries; while, moreover, it is perfectly evident that to themselves it suggests nothing that is improper or immodest. This, however, is the only part of India in which one sees anything that could bring a blush to the cheek of easily shocked British matronhood, and even this need never do so to any save those who seem to find prurient suggestiveness in everything that is natural.

Of course the garment that is characteristic and representative of Indian womanhood from Cape Comorin to Quetta is the cloth, or *sari*. It is common to ranee and basket-weaver—lowest among the castes. It is worn by Hindu and Mahommedan, by Parsee and by Sikh. It may be of brocade stiff with gold, such as is made on the looms of Benares and Umritsur, or it may be a hideous travesty of a Scotch plaid turned out from Manchester, and costing but a few pence in the native bazaar. It may be a lovely China *crêpe*, a Dacca *malmal* (silk muslin), *kattha* (the stout country cloth of the Punjab), or a gold-figured *mashru* (silk and cotton fabric) from Trichinopoly; but it is the same in its various forms, and is always managed with the same perfect grace of draping. Let the unpractised hand try to arrange one on herself, and her wonder at the security, the comfort, and the elegance with which an Indian woman wears it will be not a little enhanced!

Beneath it a well-to-do woman generally wears a smaller cloth round her waist, while over her shoulders she has one of the tiny *cholis*, or jackets, to which I have referred before. According to fashionable ideas these should be cut from one piece of stuff, and only shaped by the shoulder seams. They always fit literally skin tight—far, far closer than we Englishwomen could endure for an hour—and are tied frequently with a cross-over string knotted between the shoulder-blades, but they vary very much in different localities, and indicate the wearer's status. The working women, for instance, have them of cheap printed or gay self-coloured cotton during the greater part of the year, while in the cold season or the rains it is a protection and a comfort to them to obtain one of flannel or woollen material. Richer women, in Bengal especially, affect embroidered muslins and clear nets, while in Gujerat and the west, and indeed almost throughout India, a very bright *glacé* satin, in almost every shade of colours, finds high favour. They are often embroidered and trimmed, especially upon the right sleeve, and are sometimes edged down the front and at the end with what we should here term a *guimpe* or *passementeric*. For full dress wear they are always selected to harmonize well with the *sari*. The Parsees of the upper classes, who have accepted most of our European habits and fashions, now generally wear a petticoat of white lawn or batiste, or even of silk all frilled and laced, and a bodice of silk or material cut after the English or French patterns, though without any extravagances of exaggerated sleeves or high and stiff collars.

A full-sized sari should be about five and a half yards long, and from thirty-six to forty inches wide. To put it on, a woman makes a few pleats at one end in her hand, which she draws through in front of a band or string already round her waist. The length of the material is then carried round her figure towards the left, and when it has been brought completely round, the end is taken over the shoulder and draped over the head. It is only of course from long practice that the perfect art of disposing it is reached, but one sees tiny girls of three or four emulating the examples of their mothers with pieces of calico about as large as a pocket-handkerchief; for the Indian girl longs as keenly to leave the shapeless *sacque*, which is the first garment of her baby years, and attain to the dignity of a sari quite as eagerly as her sister of the West desires a long skirt and its attendant privileges.

Certain districts have specially favoured colours, however, and throughout Gujerat this is a very warm, deep crimson, enriched with delightful embroidery. On the West Coast the women of caste generally wear white; while those of the lowest orders have small checks or stripes in various mixtures, a dull yellow and red being much affected. In Calcutta scarlet divides favour with lilac and white, while indigo-dyed blue is more or less general everywhere. *Bandhna*, or "tie and dye" cloth, in cotton as well as silk, is much used in the central provinces and native states. The design, which generally takes the form of flowing lines, squares, and circles, is traced out by a draughtsman. The woman then takes the cloth, and picks up a tiny piece of it, round which she deftly and tightly binds a piece of cotton thread. It is then sent to the dyer, and when the knots are unwound, small white rings appear all over the surface. This method, primitive as it is, is used very successfully throughout Bengal and the north-west, and silks thus ornamented in Berhampore find their way alike to the furthermost frontiers of the Punjab and to the heights of Assam. By means of certain coloured threads for the knotting process, a variety in the colours of the rings is imparted. These *bandhna* fabrics are also much used for turbans, and in Jeypore, where the work is nearly always done by the wives of the dyers, I was assured that there are no less than a hundred and eight kinds of knot in use.

Very poetic and pretty are the names by which some of the designs and colourings in favourite use for silk are known. These have come down from the sixteenth century at least, for Sir George Birdwood tells how in 1577 three shiploads of Berhampore silks were despatched by way of the Persian Gulf to Russia, and that among them were patterns described as "ripples of silver," "nightingale's eyes," "peacock's neck," and "sunshine and shade." Such names survive still, for fashion alters practically not at all, and a girl desires to include in her trousseau exactly what her mother had before her. In fact, the only instance in the varied inquiries that I made upon the subject in which I found that any whims of fashion existed was among the Kols, who are very capricious about their ornaments, and may sometimes be seen all wearing small necklaces of fine metallic threads, while at another time large beads or lacquered devices will have come into vogue.

A girl of the upper classes takes a long time to gather her wedding outfit together, and this always includes as

The chief distinction between Hindu and Mahommedan clothing is that the latter wears much more actually made-up raiment than the former. There are strong Hindu traditions against cut-out and sewn garments, and though these are dying out, especially where the two great races are much thrown together, it is by no means difficult to trace prejudices undefined yet existent in the prevailing fashions of everyday wear. Indeed, it is believed by Captain Meadows Taylor, and many other high authorities, that, before the Mahommedan invasion of India, anything like a shaped coat or bodice was entirely unknown, and the use of the needle in the making of wearing apparel was entirely a Muslim introduction.

It is not necessary to enter upon a detailed description of the various classes of cotton goods from heavy unbleached calicos to fine and soft muslins, that are produced in all parts of India; but, from an artistic point of view, it is satisfactory to find that there is no very marked deterioration in designs to be noted as a result of European influences. The stripes and checks employed, though commonplace enough, are seldom if ever offensive, while the repeated washings they have to go through soon tone down early crudities of hue. Patterns remain small and unostentatious, and nowhere did I find that large or staring or gaudy ornamentation were favoured. The native taste retains its inherent purity in this direction, and rejects unerringly the vulgar and the ugly. In colour, unfortunately, one cannot speak so reassuringly. Brilliant tones appeal strongly to the Oriental mind, and the vividness of the aniline dyes of the laboratory has proved irresistible. In the great Alliance silk mills of Bombay no pretence whatever is made on the subject, and one is shown the dyeing vats filled with the most dazzling of the coal-tar combinations. It is the gaudiness of rose-pink, of emerald-green, of royal-blue, or amber-yellow which constitutes a leading attraction of our European piece goods, and commends them to native purchasers when they are displayed in the native bazaars. On their mere merits of quality they would be less dangerous rivals to the indigenous manufactures, whose softer, deeper, richer tones, drawn from vegetable sources, are quite eclipsed by the staring, shouting hues of the imported article.

As one wends through the crowded alleys of the great bustling cloth fair of Bombay, with its tons and tons of Manchester—ay, and German also—cotton fabrics, this fact is pressingly borne in. It explains one of the grievances which have led to so much friction and ill-will upon the question of the cotton duties, for the Indian weaver cannot command the resources, even if he wished to do so, of the scientific chemist, and thus indigenous products are handicapped beside the brilliant attractiveness of imported shoddy, to please the manufacturers of which the Home Government has not hesitated to offend alike the native capitalists and workers. It explains too, I think, in a measure that impression of widespread poverty which the superficial traveller dilates upon as evidence of "something wrong" officially, for these wrappings lose their fugitive brilliancy in a very few days under the glare of the sun, and after a washing or two are reduced to a miserably ill-favoured appearance of faded shabbiness. One point that helps to convey the sense of general prosperity in Katthiawar and Bhaunagar is the dark blue and dark red county-woven cloths worn by both men and women down to the very poorest. These keep their warm full colouring to the last, and look therefore always well and fresh. It is perhaps rather deplorable that the merely novel and gay should replace the old and the sober; but when was it not thus? It is even as when the cheap adulterated silks of foreign looms drove the unsurpassable British brocades and moirés, tabinets and damasks, out of the field.

CHAPTER VIII.

EMBROIDERY AND NEEDLECRAFT.

"Them hath He filled with wisdom of heart, to work all manner of work, of the engraver, and of the cunning workman, and of the embroiderer, in blue, and in purple, and in scarlet, and in fine linen, and of the weaver, even of them that do any work, and of those that devise cunning work."—EXODUS xxxv. 35.

EMBROIDERY, in India, is by no means as distinctively a woman's art as it is in the West. In fact, down the picturesque Chandni Chowk of Delhi, where the European sightseer is pressed to buy examples of its famous gold and silver embroideries upon satin, it is the men who are to be seen sitting at large frames and working with infinite patience in glistering metallic thread, it may be one of the immortal designs of the knop and flower, or pomegranate variations. Again, at Bombay, where the wealthy Parsee ladies do not hesitate to pay ten or twelve pounds sterling for a gold and silver worked border for their *saris*, it will be men's fingers that will execute the order. More than probably, too, the cap with its elaborate gold and silver lace, that the Mahommedan gentleman of the north-west wears in the house, will have been adorned by a Hindu man.

Sir George Birdwood, greatest of all authorities on Indian domestic art, wrote in connection with an exhibition of needlework arranged in London, in 1893, by Mrs. David Carmichael and the Society for the Preservation of Indian

Art, "I have myself seen women weaving in India, but never, save for domestic purposes, embroidering. . . . I did not know of any needlework being produced by the women of India for sale, excepting the *phul-kāri* (*i.e.* flower-work) of the sub-Alpine Himalayan region of the Tarai." The collection Sir George pronounced of especial interest, and remarked further, that "its public exhibition in this country was not unlikely to mark a distinct step in the advancement of the education of Indian women, in a direction for once happily in complete consonancy with their inherited indigenous culture. Unfortunately the collection, judged by its merits, was very disappointing. It demonstrated, indeed, the presence of widespread accomplishment—in the conventional, not the etymological meaning of the word—but also in the widest absence of that absolute artistic achievement which imparts even to a scrap of needlework a beauty moth and rust cannot corrupt, nor thieves break through and steal, for, once its fair idea, or Divine archetype, as a Platonist would say, is realized, it lives for ever, a heavenly treasure, in the memories of men."

When I saw that display, however, I did not grasp what I have since, and that is, that in no branch of Indian art has British influence been so mischievously detrimental as in needlecraft. The native women are quick to seize upon a small novelty that can be passed on from one to another, and the vulgar showiness and easy accomplishment of our Western woolwork, in all the worst hideousness of Berlin cross-stitch and crewels, seems to have pleased some innate sentiment in them, for, unfortunately, they have adopted and perpetrated these in the vilest form. The mission schools are to be held responsible for most of the evil that has been wrought in this direction. Drawn, as so large a percentage of their teachers are, from the lower middle classes, and imbued with the worst philistinism of their order, these instructors from outside were equally utterly unable to appreciate the wondrous beauties of form and colouring of indigenous embroidery, or to impart a knowledge of anything better than the decorative tastes of the back parlour.

It is bad enough to find a table laid out with such monstrosities on exhibition when one goes to visit a school, but it is a thousandfold worse to find that a wholesale acceptance of their horrors has run like a bad plague into the women's domestic life in the large towns. One may go into a middle-class zenana and find a young wife crocheting an abomination in violet and yellow for her husband, who is employed on night railway duty, which he will wrap about his pate and speak of in the vernacular as a "head comfort." In fact, to take an Indian journey by night in mid-winter suggests nothing so much as that a violent epidemic of acute toothache has broken out, so many are the heads swathed up in these woollen marvels of ugliness. One may go into the women's quarters of a palace, and find an exquisite silver bottle all chased or *repoussée,* and filled with rose-water or some fragrant scent which will be sprinkled over the inevitable bouquet presented on leaving, and standing upon a mat of magenta and sky blue. For under such circumstances one realizes the painful truth that ugliness in these forms has become an everyday fact. Moreover, it is also true that girls come to school purposely to learn how to do crewel-work or how to make "water-lily" mats, an illustration that would be comic, if it were not also very sad, of the perverse instinct of human nature to learn what it had better not know.

I naturally expressed myself with some vigour on this

question, alike to educational authorities and school teachers, as well as in one or two of the leading Anglo-Indian newspapers. The excuse invariably put forward was, the official recognition of needlework as a code subject was next to nothing, and that funds for the purchase of good designs and materials were seldom available. But these difficulties are far from insuperable where any sense of artistic purpose exists; for in the Hobart (Mahommedan) girls' school at Madras I saw a delightful phulkari embroidered in shades of rich orange silk, upon deep red *dungaree* (a native cloth), that was altogether an artistic delight in its rich yet subdued tones and even stitching. Some of the table-cloths here were also quite harmonious and pleasing. Again, at the opposite corner of the dependency, in the native state of Bhaunagar, where Miss Brooke is to all intents and purposes directress of female education, the needlework was deserving of all commendation. Fashionable young ladies in the Gujerat district affect a lavish amount of embroidery upon the right—the uncovered sleeve of their *cholis*, and have another odd little taste in placing a tiny square or oval device upon the right breast. Miss Brooke, therefore, set herself to obtain some of the best native designs favoured for these uses, and encourages the girls to exercise their own wonderful—when not perverted by Western models—taste for colouring, and the results at the Mahjiraj school, both in made-up *cholis* and decorative work, were nothing short of charming. When I visited this institution, Princess Kesaba, the daughter of the enlightened and cultured gentleman who is the Maharajah of the State, had just completed, according to her own design and taste, one of the daintiest pairs of slippers ever seen outside Cinderella's fairy ball, in pearl white velvet with gold and silver thread, and so delicately pretty were some of the lawn handkerchiefs embroidered in white flax in the well-raised chikan stitch, that I perforce begged one or two to bring home.

From the purely utilitarian point of view even, the folly of fostering the production of so much ugly and useless work should be apparent. Nobody will buy it, for if any appreciable native demand arose for it for "decorative" uses, the machinery of Switzerland and Germany would promptly glut the bazaars with d'oylys and antimacassars of the lowest and cheapest grades of mechanical production. Europe certainly does not want it, as our own "depôts for poor ladies' work" can tell; but, on the other hand, Europe will purchase good and characteristically native work to an almost unlimited extent. Since my return to England, however, I learn with great satisfaction that the Society for the Encouragement and Preservation of Indian Art has taken the matter up, for if once there comes a suspension in the sequence of teaching as mother has passed it on to daughter, the beautiful arts of stitchery and taste of colour may be lost, and that would in truth be a loss to India herself as well as art-loving Europe.

It is on the Bombay side, throughout Gujerat and Katthiawar, that one finds the most interesting and uncontaminated indigenous needle-craft. How old, as an art, it is in this district one may judge from Marco Polo, who referred to the "beautiful mats in red and blue leather, exquisitely inlaid with figures of birds and beasts, and skilfully embroidered with gold and silver wyre. They are marvellously beautiful things; they are used by the Saracens to sleep upon, and capital are they for that purpose."

Roughly speaking, the embroidery for household uses and personal wear is done by the women of Gujerat, Kutch, and Katthiawar, while that for commercial purposes is mostly wrought by men. It is by no means easy to obtain good pieces of the former character, for the women are loth to part with what has cost them so much and such tedious labour. For general wear they affect cotton cloth of hand-loom native manufacture, and dyed to a rich deep shade of red with, I believe, cochineal and *narsingar*, the honey-scented flower of *Nyctanthes arbor tristis.* The designs are of primitive character, and include rude geometric patterns, squares, stars, cones, pyramids, and sometimes uncouth animal forms. Silk and cotton is often used side by side, and one often finds, as in a petticoat border that I have, green cotton and yellow silk pyramids alternating. The green chosen is usually a warm myrtle, the yellow leans to strong orange, blue is a deep royal shade, and crimson decided though bright. The effect of these embroideries is enhanced by small bits of mirrored glass which are worked in in a curious stitch uniting a little of both button-holing and cross-stitching in itself.

The stitches themselves are all somewhat difficult to classify exactly, as one seldom finds them practised precisely as with ourselves. The chain and feather stitches are employed, however, without much modification, and the satin stitch is also used for careful and ornamental effects. Darning is often very cleverly utilized to produce small and regular patterns upon large surfaces, and cross-stitch both in its primitive simplicity as well as in the greater complexity of its Persian form one meets with frequently. "Couching" or "laid" embroidery is also general, this being the technical term that is used to define all such patterns as are worked by threads, whether of gold, silver, silk, cotton, or crewels stretched flatly upon the ground material, and fastened into position by small stitches brought from the back at intervals. This is employed in many variations, including one very much like the basket stitch, which, in its representation of plaited openwork, is usually reckoned very difficult of deft execution.

Not alone for work upon silk, cotton, or cloth is the Bombay side famous. With the emancipation from *purdah*, that the Parsee women have secured for themselves, they have also thrown off many of their former conventions concerning dress, though they wisely retain the *sari* in its graceful and becoming drapings as their principal garment. But the style of these has changed enormously during the past thirty years, as I realized when one of the leading Parsee ladies in Bombay showed me what had been her mother's most costly and valued wardrobe, and her own, according to the newer idea prevailing among the more fashionable of her community. The older draperies were generally of native manufacture in heavy silks and in characteristic native or somewhat Persianized design and colouring. Rich and highly decorative as examples of the weaver's craft they undoubtedly were; but somehow, even to me, with all my admiration of the native art, they seemed a trifle heavy and antiquated for personal wear. Nowadays it is Japan and Paris that are supplying the Parsee society women with their materials, the former sending in a very fine and clinging silk, made about thirty-four inches wide, and in the most exquisite shades. Parsee ladies, I should mention, now favour very delicate colouring, and shell-pinks, straw, peach; mauve of the tint of the palest Parma violets, pale sky and twig-green, are among their favourite tints. This the Japanese have learnt, and these silks constitute a very appreciable item in the shipping business that is monthly developing in importance between Bombay and Japan. Paris supplies gauzes and *crêpes de chine* in similarly well selected colouring, as well as the rainbow and serpentine effects, lately favoured of European fashion, which are also meeting with approval from Eastern buyers.

But none of these can be regarded as made up saris until a border has been put to them. For everyday and morning wear the girls and women embroider these for themselves upon ribbon, and I noted with great pleasure in the Parsee schools in Bombay, that the students are rather encouraged to do this, to them really useful work, than to waste time over hideous woolwork and mat making. For greater occasions and full dress-wear, at, say, official dinners or dances, these borders are much more elaborate, and are usually worked in gold or silver wire upon the best ribbon velvet. It is obvious that for such a purpose, where the folds must be the softest and most graceful, none but the most flexible metallic thread can be employed, and this, which is known as *kullabatoon*, is thus prepared: "For gold thread, a piece of silver, about the length and thickness of a man's forefinger, is gilded at least three times heavily with the purest gold, all alloy being previously most carefully discharged from the silver. This piece of gilt silver is beaten out to the size of a stout wire, and is then drawn through successive holes in a steel plate until it is literally as fine as a hair. The gilding is not disturbed by this process, and the wire finally appears as if of fine gold. It is then flattened in an extremely delicate and skilful manner. The workman is seated before a small and highly polished steel anvil, about two inches broad, with a steel plate in which there are two or three holes set opposite to him and perpendicular to the anvil, and draws through these holes as many wires—two or three as it may be—by a motion of the finger and thumb of his left hand, striking them rapidly but firmly with a steel hammer, the face of which is also polished like that of the anvil. This flattens the wire perfectly, and such is the skill of manipulation, that no portion of the wire escapes the blow of the hammer, the action of drawing the wire, rapid as it is, being adjusted to the length which will be covered by the face of the hammer in its descent. No system of rollers or other machinery could probably ensure the same effect, whether of extreme thinness of the flattened wire or its softness and ductility.

"To wind the wire upon silk thread, the silk is very slightly twisted, and is rolled upon a winder. The end is then passed over a polished steel hook fixed to a beam in the ceiling of the workshop, and to it is suspended a spindle with a long bamboo shank, slightly weighted to keep it steady, which nearly touches the floor. The workman gives the shank of the spindle a sharp turn upon his thigh which sets it spinning with rapidity. The gold wire, which has been wound upon a reel as it passes behind the maker, is then applied to the bottom of the silk thread near the spindle, and twists itself upwards, being guided by the workman as high as he can conveniently reach, or nearly his own height upon the thread, but it is impossible to describe in exact terms the curiously dexterous and rapid process of this manipulation. The spindle is then stopped, the thread, now covered with wire, is wound upon it and fastened in a notch of the shank, when the silk thread is drawn down, and the spindle is again set running with the same result as before.

"On examination of the *kullabatoon*, the extreme thinness and flexibility of the flattened wire, and its delicacy and beauty, will at once be apparent in comparison with attempts made in Europe with rolling machinery. It is remarkable that the gold and silver alike never tarnish, but retain their lustre and colours even though washed. This is the result of the absolute purity both of, the gold and silver employed. There is, of course, no doubt but that *kullabatoon*, with considerable alloy in the wire, is also made and used in India, but it never enters into the higher classes of manufactures."

Surat is a great centre for Western India of embroidery work, though it is mostly done by men, of whom it is estimated that about seven hundred are fully occupied by it. The gold or silver thread is supplied to them by native and local merchants, who employ them to do the embroidery at rates varying from 7*d*. to 1*s*. 3*d*. a day, according to their skill and proficiency, and their average earnings are estimated at from fifteen to twenty-five rupees a month. The designs, which are generally very simple in character, are printed in gum and chalk by means of little wooden blocks, and the ribbon or material to be worked upon is kept taut over a primitive wooden frame, while ordinary needles are used.

From Delhi, too, comes a great quantity of this gold and silver work, and at Bombay a very large firm of embroiderers from here are settled. In Delhi and Agra, also, considerable skill has been shown in adapting native designs and work to European uses, and that on the whole with a creditable freedom from vulgarization of design. Very charming are satin slippers, unmade up, but suitable for evening wear; and I also saw good work applied to Zouave jackets, and many other accessories of European dress. Here, indeed, it forms one of the staple industries, and in an old report of 1881–82, that I chanced to turn up while at Delhi, it is noted that in the Punjab, with the old Muslim capital and Agra as chief centres, some 50,000 are employed in this craft, and it was then estimated that 328,000 miles of silver and silver gilt wire were produced here for use in the province and export to other places.

More recent official information says the purity of the metals used, which in former times, especially at Lahore, was the subject of stringent regulation and surveillance both on the part of Governments and the guilds of wire-drawers, is now necessarily left to the exigencies of a trade in which cheapness is yearly growing a more essential condition. A sort of assay, however, is consequent on the demand of the municipality for octroi duty. Mr. Stogden, speaking with the authority of official knowledge, thus describes this part of the business: "The Municipal Committee have established an octroi station in Delhi. To this station the dealers bring their raw material to be melted down, and the amount of duty payable by them depends on the quality of the ingot they intend to turn out. The scale is as follows: Gold kandala, Re. 1-8 per ingot of 75 tolas; silver kandala, Re. 1-4 ditto; sham gold, 8 annas per ingot of 75 tolas; ditto silver, 4 annas; *kandala mel* (half silver, half copper) 12 annas per ingot; silver wire, three pice per tola. The dealer presents his silver and copper to be weighed, and on payment of the duty a receipt is granted to him. He then takes his metal into the station and melts it down in an earthen crucible, called *kathála,* in one of the numerous compartments set aside for the purpose. From the crucible he pours it into an iron mould called *reya.* The bar or ingot of silver and copper when thus melted down is called *gulli.* If it is intended to work gold leaf into it, it is about 8 inches long by 1¼ inches square. The *gulli* is then made over to the *kandala kash,* or wire-drawer."

I was shown an enormous *portière* at Delhi, worked to

give a veritable needle-picture of the Taj, and for the description of the way in which such pieces are wrought, though few are now undertaken, I may be permitted to borrow a few lines from an article by Mr. Kipling, C.I.E., on the industries of the Punjab.

"In cases where the whole of the field is to be covered with gold work, a stout cotton cloth is stretched on the frame. On this the design is drawn by the draughtsman, and the parts to be raised are worked over with thick, soft cotton, dyed yellow, passed on the surface from a reel, and stitched down at each passing with ordinary sewing thread. The centre veins of leaves and other forms are marked with stitching, and a kind of modelled surface is thus produced in thick cotton thread. Over these forms the gold and silver thread is laid, their lines following sometimes those of the cotton underlay and sometimes going in opposite directions. For the grounds, varieties of basket-work and herring-bone stitches are adopted; spangles and lines of twisted wire are introduced to mark and relieve the leading lines of the pattern. Several men work at once on these fabrics, and they are not so long in execution as this description may seem to indicate. The sheen of the gold threads, interlaced in different directions as they cross over raised surfaces, produces a brilliant and, in large pieces, a splendid effect. In cases where coloured silk velvet is bordered with raised gold embroidery of this kind, the velvet is sewn on strong cotton cloth, and during the work the parts to be left plain are kept carefully covered up. In the same way caps, cushions, tea-cosies and other trifles are wrought; but as relief is not always necessary, as in large throne cloths, elephant housings, and the like, the forms are not always embossed in cotton."

Another famous centre of embroidery was and still is

Dacca, where the art is chiefly in the hands of the Fantis, an off-shoot from the weaver caste, which was supposed to possess the secret of making muslins of such filmy fineness, that Sir George Birdwood tells us, in the days of Shah Jehangir a piece fifteen yards long and one yard wide weighed only nine hundred grains, while if such were laid upon damp grass it became almost invisible. Thus it had the name of *shabnam*, or "dew of evening," and another description was known as *ab rawan*, or "the running water," because it was quite indistinguishable in water. Their inherited tastes are therefore towards embroidery upon cotton, and this they do with great skill, varying it often with drawn-thread effects, rivalling those of Sicily and Crete. In India this is known as *chikan kari*, or *chikan dozi*, and for the best classes of it a frame is always used. But although one finds Hindus thus working, in spite of the exceedingly stringent rules of caste which obtain among them, embroidery generally is far more done by poor Muslims. From Dacca still a considerable trade is done with Jedda and Bushire in worked cotton or mixed silk and cotton cloths for Mahommedan wear. Though sketchy in design, and rough in execution, many of these pieces are decoratively effective, but better perhaps is not to be expected for the low rates which are paid for them. It is done almost exclusively by the women of poor though respectable Mahommedan families, and is rather a curious instance of the "pocket-money" wage, as I am assured that only a rupee to a rupee and a half a month is given for it, which is accepted, much as the worker at home, assured of her bread and butter by father or husband, undersells the necessitous wage-earner merely to obtain enough to buy the finery she covets.

I was unable to extend my travels into Cashmere, but

in all the towns of the north-west one sees ample example of the splendid boldly designed and coloured work that comes down from its distant hills and plains. As to the embroidered burnouses, caps, and dressing-gowns, upon its exquisitely soft native woollen fabrics, they are familiar enough, but it is a wonder to me that no enterprising dealer in artistic carpets has ever placed upon the London market the worked rugs that the shops of Delhi and Agra display in fascinating temptation. These are of two sorts, one of which is a very thick and soft felt, made usually about six feet long, and three feet six inches wide. They are generally of a beautifully subdued turquoise blue, a natural cedar brown, or bleached white, and are embroidered all over in a running conventionalized floral design, in the most delightfully harmonized colours, both vivid and dull. I have seen them in a dark indigo, and a rich orange ground, but these shades are not so general. For the other description a heavy diagonally woven material, somewhat resembling a rougher form of the European so-called "art" serge, is employed. A stout lining of cotton is given to this, and the stitches of the embroidery are carried right through. These are often made as much as ten feet long, and the shades I have seen most generally used are a rich deep crimson, or a delightful sage green, but it is usual to add to them a black border, which is also worked over.

Wool, very much like crewels in texture, is the medium of embroidery, and a great variety of colours is generally employed, but always with the artist's eye for blending. The stitch used is simply the chain, looped round the needle, with an occasional employment of that known as the stem, but with these, usually so stiff and rigid in Western needlework, these Cashmeri women-workers obtain not only the most gracefully running curves and sweeps, but a very good filled-in effect for impossible flowers and foliage. They are not a luxury that the economical traveller must perforce forego, as in Delhi the prices for such pieces are from five to ten rupees each, while in Bombay they are only very slightly dearer.

In Southern India, where mission effort has been longest at work, and imported ideas have perhaps taken their firmest hold, very creditable copies of Maltese, Torchon, and other laces are made in the schools and homes of the people. Quilon and Alleppy are both well known for their work of this description, which is bought at very low prices of the women makers, and taken round to the European and Eurasian inhabitants of the towns. The average European resident has, however, very little conscience as to fair prices for even hand work, which she expects and bargains to buy for the same price as the products of the Nottingham looms, and really choice work, for which the delicate native fingers would be pre-eminently suited, does not receive the encouragement it deserves. But in this respect lace stands no worse than any other art product of the East. The curse of cheapness has fallen upon all that is popular, degrading design, vulgarizing execution, and I came to the conclusion that the only way to bring back what was covetable and desirable was to look for such things as Guzerati petticoats, the silk, or the brass ware of native use, and the rugs not discovered yet by the "art furnishers," in order to escape the workings of that inexorable law, as it works out in the Calcutta or the Bombay store, "one rupee, fifteen annas, five pice."

CHAPTER IX.

JEWELLERY AND ORNAMENT.

"The bravery of their tinkling ornaments, and the cauls, and the round tires like the moon, the chains, and the bracelets, and the mufflers, the anklets, and the headbands, and the perfume boxes, and the amulets, the earrings and the nose jewels."—ISAIAH iii. 18-21. Literal rendering.

FROM the poorest sweeper woman of the towns, who puts half a dozen glass bangles upon her wrists, or the Kol coal-cutter girl who painfully forces heavy curved anklets of bell-metal over her feet, to the wealthy begum of a native state, or the "emancipated" ranee who has broken her *purdah* and goes to the Government House receptions, the love of jewellery is to be found among the entire female population of the East. It forms an appreciable factor in her dowry, it is a fruitful source of troubles in jealousy and quarrels, and it is a perpetual anxiety from the temptations it affords to robbery; but it is a woman's most precious belonging, and nothing, not even fine clothes, affords any compensation for its absence. The taste exists universally, and though forms and patterns differ with almost every province, or even district, it is as characteristic a feature of the sex at Madras as Lahore, in Bhaunagar as at Calcutta.

The very lowest form of all is, of course, the cheap glass bangles. There is a common belief that these are supplied by the continent of Europe, but so far as my own efforts at tracing them to their source went, I found that a large proportion were Chinese. I bought numbers of them in the original half-dozen sets in blue, green, and amber glass, paying on an average a halfpenny each bracelet for them, and in every instance the cards to which they were fastened bore Chinese characters, and in some cases the words "from China" as well. There is a still lower grade, however, made with waved lines, and in a size so tiny that I could not pass it over my own 6½ glove-size and very flexible hand. These, I believe, are manufactured in the north-west; and at Delhi one sees them in great quantities in the native bazaar.

Of only slightly higher importance are the lacquered bracelets, and the process by which these are made gives a good idea of the exceeding cheapness of labour when this allows of their being sold at less than a penny each. A chief centre of their manufacture is in the Panch Mahal district of Gujerat, and the lac used in making them is gathered by the Bhils, a woodland people of Upper Western India. They exchange this for grain with the Banya trading community, who in turn retail it to the actual makers. The lac is softened, and rings of it are formed round the well-oiled top of a rice-pounder, which is about the size of a woman's wrist. Twenty-five of these are thus made, and are just sufficiently heated again to cause them to stick together. They are then rubbed with powdered brick-dust, and polished with blue, red, or yellow-coloured copal varnish. Mr. H. A. Acworth, who has devoted much attention to this industry, states that in the next step, which is to print a pattern upon the bracelet, a whole day is occupied in pounding together two ounces of tin with a small lump of glue, till they form a grey metallic paste, which is afterwards boiled in a copper pot, and then strained. Meanwhile a piece of cotton wool is bound upon a stick, and is wetted and pressed till it is firm enough to retain an impression drawn upon it with an iron point. When this primitive stamp is dipped into the tin solution it brings out a modicum of it, which is pressed on to the ornament in the design. This turns to a bright golden colour on the application of varnish, while specks and points of white or red, produced by the admixture of chalk or vermilion with the tin solution, are dropped on to heighten the effect. These *choories*, as they are called, are immensely popular in feminine estimation, and one may often find a rich lady wearing two or three of them among her gold and silver bracelets, while the poorer woman puts on ten or twelve. The same composition is used in the central provinces and Upper India to make the *sithi* or *bindi*, a head ornament, which has a centre point to fall back upon the hair, and large bosses for the ear.

Until one makes a good deal of direct inquiry, one is unaware that bracelets vary in name according to the position in which they are worn upon the arm. The Hindu women, for instance, have the *guyra*, the *kukna*, and the *punchi*, which are worn next the hand, and which generally have some further descriptive appellation to denote whether they are supposed to represent teeth, seeds, flowers, or beads. Then come the *choories*, but there is a certain *chun*, usually a simple band of silver or metal, which may be put on among them. Beyond these last, and towards the elbow, are the *kuttri*, *panch-luri*, *puchna*, and other forms, while above the elbow several forms of armlets may be worn, a favourite one being the *nao nugger*, or "nine gems," and occasionally one sees in these a very pretty and uncommon blending of stones. In the marvellous collection of Indian peasant jewellery made by Mrs. Rivett Carnac there is a pair formed of large and pale yellow topaz, surrounded with turquoise, and the delicate charm of this combination is scarcely to be imagined.

The next step up from the cheap glass and lacquer ornaments are those made from bell-metal, this being of various alloys, and often containing, as in the particular manufacture for which Berhampore is celebrated, an appreciable admixture of silver. Where bell-metal is employed, it is usually in the form of very heavy armlets and anklets, and it is rather a characteristic of the non-Aryan tribes. Many of the Kols of Bengal wear enormous masses of what one may almost call ironmongery, and I have seen them as much as five inches deep and an inch thick, and perfectly solid. From six to eight pounds in weight is by no means unusual, and in exceptional instances they are still heavier. The hammered ornamentation is simple but effective, and they are worn with great pride. Indeed, it is often a matter of severe pain to put these huge things on, and unless it be done while a girl is still very young, it would be impossible to force them over the heel. Even then, as in the case of some that are slightly curved in shape, the process is one of real torture, which would not be borne save at the command of female vanity, and one sees girls with their feet swollen and chafed after it, smiling over the addition made to their beauty. The armlets are generally furnished with some form of clasp. Some of the very low-caste women, as Doms and Dhobies, wear a graduated series of thick brass or bell-metal bangles, almost covering the arm from wrist to elbow.

There is an immense amount of imitation jewellery worn among the poorer classes, and mock pearls and stones abound in the native bazaars. The favourite designs of *jumka,* "the shaking," or pendent for the ear, and the *bala bijli,* or "the lightning" from the flash and shimmer of its light fringe, and many others are freely copied and adapted, and little girls spend their earliest pice in buying gilt and glitter of this sort.

Head-dresses vary greatly in different parts of India. The Mahratta women have the *kaituck*, which is composed of three separate pieces, a round boss being worn in the centre of the hair, with leaf-shaped or crescent ornaments extending forward towards the brow. In Madras, however, the side pieces disappear, and a number of smaller circles or brooches are fixed in the hair; and here I may mention the curious fact that no native woman uses hair-pins. The general method of disposing of her tresses, which she is fond of oiling and scenting, is to twist it into a close knot at the back of her head, and I have never seen this "come down" under any exercise or exertion, or look other than neat and smooth. The prettiest and most artistic hair-dressing that I know is among the Nayar and Canarese women of the west coast. They possess this "crowning glory" in abundance, and it is soft and fine. It is all gathered into a mass towards the top of the left side of the head, and with one or two deft twists they throw it round in a perfectly charming coil. Against this, however, the Canarese women are guilty of a hideous practice in wearing the huge earrings with which they distort the lobe of the ear. A small bar of metal is first inserted, and gradually larger pieces are introduced till they can wear a disc of as much as two and a half inches in diameter. With the poorer women this is often only of dark polished wood or bone, but the richer ones have them of gold or silver.

The rings form an important item in the parure, and are worn equally on all fingers of the hand except the second. Indeed, even the thumb is adorned, and in this one often finds a small piece of mirror, or else it has a tiny receptacle to contain a piece of cotton wool steeped in some strong aromatic oil or perfume. There is no special characteristic about native rings, unless they are signets, which though occasionally worn by women, are more particularly a man's ornament. These often bear interesting devices or anagrams, intelligible only to the initiated.

Some of the boxes in which a native woman keeps her betel and areca nut, cardamoms, spices, the soorma to darken her eyelashes and eyebrows, and other cosmetics, are very curious, especially in Southern India. One of these that I brought home was of bell-metal, circular in shape, and divided into nine compartments. Each of these had a separate cover on its own hinge, while to fasten all down in the centre was a screw, finished on the top with a conventionally modelled peacock.

The Mahommedan woman of the north-west and the Punjab does not differ markedly from the Hindu in the ornaments characteristic to her outfit of jewellery. First there is the *tika*, or adornment for the head, which is generally of flexible workmanship, or composed of closely interlocked links. The two parts forming this pass one on either side of the brow and face to the ear, and are generally finished with a pendent but very close-set fringe of tiny devices, which may be balls, stars, lozenges, ovals, circles, or crescents. From the centre, over the parting of the hair, there falls on to the forehead an ornament, round, square, or crescent-shaped, and matching in finish the bordering of the rest of the article. At the lobe of the ear, where the broad strips join it, another large boss appears, but from this further eardrops, which may be quite different in design, are often added. Such an adornment naturally only belongs to the comparatively wealthy, and I have never seen these of anything less valuable than silver. I should add that in the case of such heavy earrings as these usually are, and many more like them, that besides being supported in the pierced lobe, there is generally a wire which passes right round the ear to keep them in position. Except by the Canarese women, just alluded to, it is regarded as a deformity to spoil the natural contour of the organ of sound.

Then comes the nose-ring, which the Muslim women as a rule do not wear so large as the Hindus, and with the former is often no more than a small and inconspicuous jewel.

The necklace has many names and many varieties, as *mala*, *luchcha*, *do-lari*, according to design. It is often a broad *collier*, shaped to fit the neck and shoulders, of interlinked rings or cables, and finished, like the *tika*, with a thick but loosely set border of tiny metallic devices. The bracelets usually correspond exactly. Longer necklets, reaching sometimes to below the waist, made of beads, often very beautifully cut or chased, and occasionally of exceedingly quaint oval form, are also worn, and are generally finished with some medallion or pendant. A glance at this will tell one instantly to which of the two great races the wearer belongs, as the Hindu is almost certain to exhibit upon hers one of the many deities of her Pantheon; but the Mahommedan, forbidden to make any "graven image or the likeness of anything that is in the heaven above or the earth beneath," falls back upon the presentment of conventional figures and geometric patterns. Necklets, like girdles, are also made of squares linked together, and I have seen many really covetable examples of these in silver, delightfully enamelled in shades of turquoise blue. One of the really prettiest of the Delhi patterns which are most worn in the north-west is the twisted or *babul* setting for large amethysts, turquoises, topaz, or garnets, which are often employed for costly necklets. Each stone is set in a separate little square, and surrounded by fine gold work, based in treatment upon the suggestion of the soft yellow filaments of the flower of *Acacia Arabica*, and the separate pieces are fastened together with small chains. A woman's possessions may begin with quite a short necklet, but as time and prosperity goes on another and another square will be added, until it reaches at last a handsome length.

It is considered right that the bridegroom, wherever practicable, should present the bride with a gold ornament, but a ring is not used to denote the wedded state as with ourselves. A small iron bangle, with no visible juncture, is one of the most usual symbols of marriage, as it is supposed to indicate the strength and indissolubleness of the bond. Certain castes also wear a bead necklet, and it is regarded as an extremely inauspicious omen should this accidentally break, though no harm arises from re-stringing it. I found less superstition, however, concerning jewellery than I expected. There are certain talismanic charms accredited to the diamond, and the *nava ratna*, or *nos ratan* of nine gems, is supposed to bring good fortune. The jewels composing this are the coral, topaz, sapphire, ruby, a flat diamond and a cut diamond, emerald, jacinth, and carbuncle. Another form substitutes for some of these the pearl, ruby, and lapis lazuli. There is nothing, however, as greatly prized for its direct influence with the gods as the salagram, which is a kind of ammonite found in one or two of the tributaries of the Ganges. The most precious are perfectly black, and they then belong to the symbolism of Vishnu and Krishna. If they are violet they are associated with one of the more angry incarnations, but are nevertheless of great value. In the Vishnuite temples, where one is generally kept, they are washed and oiled with exceeding care; but almost every true Brahman endeavours to possess at least one in the house.

Of indigenous gold ornaments, the most interesting specimens perhaps are furnished from Southern India. From Bangalore come large raised discs with crescents attached, worn as earrings, and often remarkable for beautiful beaten work; and Mysore, Vizianagram, and Tanjore all send out the large but very light ornaments for the head that are worn on festal occasions throughout the Madras Presidency, and very widely also in the native States. The Swami ornaments of this district, with their representations of Vishnu and his ten incarnations or *avataras*, in one of which he is found, besides his consort Lakshmi; Rambha, the type of womanly loveliness and amiability; Siva, "the omnipresent, but especially in twelve forms and places," and others in which Krishna appear, are universally popular; while in the Bombay Presidency, and throughout Gujerat, one finds very pretty bracelets and necklets of gold beads threaded on string. They are marvellously thin and light, yet they are beaten into beautiful and always appropriate designs. Some of the fine gold wire jewellery is also exceedingly charming, and bracelets so soft and flexible are made of it as to be almost crushable in the hand.

To European eyes the gemmed ornaments of the women are wont to seem rather gaudy and tawdry, besides rough in setting. The heterogeneous mixtures of stones, which will place a turquoise, an emerald, and a garnet in close juxtaposition, seems strange after the reserve shown in the West as to jewel combinations, and undoubtedly our own styles of cutting show precious stones to greater advantage than the native methods. Mr. Kipling, whose knowledge of the inner workings of the jewellery trade of Delhi is not to be gainsaid, points out that European forms are, however, growing in favour, and that articles made for wealthy natives, even where indigenous designs are retained, are growing noticeably neater. Moreover, many of the richer native ladies of the large towns are beginning to wear genuine Bond Street ornaments. Two very strictly *purdah* brides, with whom I had tea at Bombay, showed me their presents, and among these were dainty watch bracelets of a well-known London house, safety-pin brooches with quaint little sporting devices, and other things which seemed characteristic rather of a fashionable wedding in town. As to the trade in jewels, Mr. Kipling remarks, in the official Punjab Gazetteer—

"The telegraph and the modern facilities for travel have brought the precious-stone trade of the world together in a way that is surprising to those unfamiliar with its workings. It is now, as always, a somewhat secret branch of commerce. German Jews, trained in Paris, are perhaps the most prominent and leading dealers. There is scarcely a wedding or an accession affording an opportunity for the sale of precious stones that is not telegraphed to Paris, London, St. Petersburg, Amsterdam, Berlin and Vienna. Delhi and the rest of India are now included in this secret syndicate, and are periodically visited by dealers who come and go unnoticed; so that Tavernier was but the forerunner of a succession of jewel merchants. For pearls, Bombay is a great market; but even there, one of the leaders of the trade, the late Panniah Lall, was a Delhi man. In coloured stones this city has still a considerable trade, and the greater part of the valuable find of sapphires in the Cashmere territory has been absorbed by the Delhi jewellers. Most of these men are in the hands of bankers, or, perhaps more correctly, they are the agents of bankers."

Especially noticeable, too, is the Europeanization of design and purpose that has come over the filagree work of Trichinopoly and Cuttack. It is exceedingly fine still in execution, but all that was primitive and simple has gone out of it. The most horrible degradation, however, that I saw was at Cochin, which possessed once a very good little school of silver filagree workers, who produced stronger and bolder work than that of the two other seats of the industry. I wanted an example or two to bring home, and eventually secured one or two that did not offend me, but I was offered —take note, O Society for the Encouragement and Preservation of Indian Art—brooches in the form of banjoes, tennis-racquets, and parasols! Even so far have the horrors of Birmingham designs wrought their mischievous effects!

CHAPTER X.

AMUSEMENTS AND PLEASURES.

> "Therefore the ways were swept,
> Rose odours sprinkled in the streets, the streets
> Were hung with lamps and flags, while merry crowds
> Gaped on the sword-players and posturers,
> The jugglers, charmers, swingers, rope-walkers,
> The Nautch girls in their spangled skirts and bells,
> That chime light laughter round their restless feet;
> The masquers wrapped in skins of bear and deer,
> The tiger-tamers, wrestlers, quail-fighters,
> Beaters of drum and twanglers of the wire,
> Who make the people happy by command."
> "The Light of Asia" (Sir Edwin Arnold, K.C.S.I.).

INDIAN girls have a few games that are peculiar to themselves, and very pretty and graceful some of these are. As mere children they join of course with their little brothers and cousins in various pastimes, and generally find their first toys in tiny clay models. There are also rude musical instruments which are given to them, and, save in form, the contents of the *bibi ghar* nursery are not so very widely removed from our own. The *jhuta-jhulna*, or swing, is invariably a part of its fittings, and a taste for this exercise survives when the girls are grown up. Indeed, I have seen a portly grandmamma sitting in the seat, which resembled a small cot, and realizing apparently a beatific sense of restfulness with the regular backward and forward sway.

The doll, however, is the delight of all others of a little Indian girl's life. It matters to her very little whether it has been dressed by her mother or aunts—a mere rude rag presentment—or is a waxen triumph from France or Germany, brought by a kindly father from some big European stores in the nearest town, it is a treasured possession, valued with a personal affection that I think her little Western prototype in these days of high schools does not attain unto. The dramatic sense, so strong in the natural child, comes uppermost in these little Hindu and Mahommedan maidens, and the "marriage" of their dolls with those of cousins or playmates is celebrated with pretty travesties of *mangni* and *shadi* rites, of which they hear so much talk from the women by whom they are surrounded. Up to the age of twelve or fourteen years the boys can play with the girls, but whenever these marriage games are gone through, the lads have to act their parts with the same submissiveness which they will have to affect in seeking their own brides later on. These action games are played in all seriousness, the elder girls enacting the parts of mothers and aunts, and finishing up with the cooking of imitations, as nearly as they can manage, of the special wedding dishes.

And the taste for playing with dolls does not end with childhood. Big girls, who have done well in the school examinations, are more pleased with a doll as a prize than almost anything that can be given to them, and I have seen those whom I may fairly call young women show real disappointment at a distribution to find that their first prize was a new sari, while a third or fourth received some showily attired *guryen*, as they will call them, and I am assured that even after they have children of their own the dolls remain a joy. Perhaps the wife of Ibsen's "Master Builder" had hereditary Oriental tastes in the affection that she lavished upon the much-discussed "nine beauties."

In Madras the girls have two extremely pretty and graceful games, which have been systematized for use as physical exercises in the schools. One of these is called *kollatum*, and in idea resembles an English maypole dance, with the substitution of gaily-coloured strings or flower garlands for the ribbons. Each girl, however, carries two

GIRLS' GAMES IN BHAUNAGAR—ARDOGARDO.

short rods in her hands, and goes through the plaiting of the streamers to a soft chant, to which accentuation is given at intervals by short strokes from the sticks, and as certain points in the plaited design are reached, each one slowly sinks to her knees. *Kummi*, the other game, is almost a figure-dance, performed by groups of four, and this

I found in almost precisely similar detail to be a favourite pastime in Bhaunagar, where it goes by the name of *ardogardo*. It was beautifully rendered for me here in the Wadwha working-class school, the little exponents assuming the most picturesque poses with an ease that the London pantomime child would find a positive fortune. Here, too, they showed

GIRLS' GAMES IN BHAUNAGAR—PHESPHEDHODI.

me *phesphedhodi*, in which the little performers cross hands, and whirl round in a giddy crescendo of speed till one expects to see them drop. Not so; when it is finished, each couple is eager to begin again.

Another game which I saw here for the first time was *rhasado*. In this one girl stands in the centre of a circle of her companions, and chants a rhythmic poem on what good girls ought to know, the others taking it up and accentuating each period as they glide around her by a whole turn of the body performed with exceeding grace.

Subsequently I saw this at Bombay, played both by middle-class Parsees and poor Hindus, but in a somewhat different form. Here the girls placed a stool in the middle of the room, and in honour of my visit were allowed to add to the effect by obtaining a brazier full of burning coals. Round this they circled, invoking, in curiously airless strains, Saraswati, the consort of Brahma, who is the goddess of speech, song, and music, as well as of all covetable learning. The words they repeated were curious, and ran thus: "Sisters, let us in the beginning remember Saraswati for the sake of blessings. She will take from us all unhappiness. Sisters, she who has inherited of the spirit of Saraswati alone knows true joy. An educated lady need not be at a loss for pleasure. In knowledge she will find happiness. An educated wife is the greatest pride of her husband."

As a bride in the zenana of her husband, a girl-wife in her new dignity must to some extent forego her games, and the worst feature in the life to an outsider seems its unvarying monotony. I have visited dozens of houses, literally of all sorts and conditions, from slums in Madras and Calcutta up to the palatial houses where ranees and begums live, and the want of broadening interest in the day's continual routine constitutes to European minds at least a terrible blank. There is not even the pleasant fuss of pretty surroundings or artistic furniture to gratify the eye, and I well remember how this deficiency struck me, calling on the wife of a wealthy *zamindar* at Berhampore. I was shown into an apartment absolutely void save for a common *charpoy*, or bed, and judging from the delay in its arrival the whole house must have been searched to find a rickety three-legged stool for me to sit upon. Conversation seemed rather halting, till one of the ladies began to examine the gold bangles I was wearing, and I asked her whether she would show me her own jewellery. This she was quite ready to do, and must have spread out over a thousand pounds' worth of really lovely gold work and gems for me to admire, but the contrast between her costly possessions and the bare chamber in which she set them out seemed curiously sharp.

Of course the ordinary visitor who goes to a well-to-do native house, or a ruler's palace, is received in the public reception rooms, which are generally furnished according to the "regardless of expense" style of Tottenham Court Road, and susceptibly artistic eyes are grieved over flower-patterned carpets, rosewood chairs and tables *en suite*, and rep curtains, such as obtained in the earlier decades of the reign. Only one bright exception do I know to this, and that is the palace of the Nawabs of Murshedabad, where there is an authentic Rembrandt of great price, and a Cuyp, a Teniers, and other pictures worth going to see, with a fascinating collection of early native arms, and a library in which are Korans of untold value, which the non-believer may not touch even with a gloved hand.

But a lady's visit to the ladies of a family shows a very different sight of the home life. One that I paid in Calcutta to a titular ranee, whose state, though by no means as imposing as before family feuds had weakened the heritage, is still upheld with great dignity, was characteristic of many others. In visiting ladies of this rank, it is thought a mark of courtesy to give notice of one's intention to call some hours at least before, and all, therefore, was in readiness for my reception. The house in which this lady lived was enormous.

As seen from outside it would be little exaggeration to call it a palace, for indeed within its walls were lodged the whole eighty (besides servants) who make up the total—brothers, their wives and children—which at present constitutes the chief branch of the family. I entered under a massive stone gateway, surmounted by lions carved in stone, and at the door stood the ranee's little daughter of about eight, clad in much festal bravery of yellow satin underdress and a sari of soft olive silk embroidered in yellow, and wearing some handsome gold ornaments. The child, who was accompanied by several of her cousins, gave us a pretty salaam, and took me by the hand to escort me to her mother. This was evidently a point of etiquette to which she attached much importance. She never let go her hold, though she had sometimes to move from one side to the other, for never have I gone along such a winding intricacy of small chambers, passages, and stairs as that which we had to pass to reach the zenana from the entrance hall.

In this instance the ranee paid me the honour of receiving me in the best room of the zenana, and I took particular notice of its equipment. On the right on entering, through a door which was guiltless of new paint for many years, was a large double bed, at the head and foot of which was some bold wood carving. On this was a flock mattress and sheet, several bolsters, large and small, and a wool-stuffed coverlet of printed moreen. There was a large press, something like an old-fashioned dresser, and another one with glass doors, in which were the oddest jumble of "curios" imaginable, from penny china dogs to dainty little cups in damascened silver, from indiarubber dolls in knitted raiment to the engraved talc handscreens of Madras. On the walls were a portrait of her father-in-law (by a native artist, who had given due prominence to the jewelled aigrette of his turban and handle of his scimitar), a German oleograph of the Repentant Magdalene, a photogravure of Lord Ripon, and a "Christmas number" presentation coloured plate. Chairs were put for us round a small table, on which, in the centre of a beaded mat, was the inevitable scent to be sprinkled on one on leaving. The ranee, followed in a minute or so by her sisters-in-law, entered.

She was not one who would be classed as "educated," for I do not think she could read a word, but she possessed intelligence, as well as good breeding, and as a hostess was certainly successful. She was simply dressed, and was not wearing much of her jewellery, for, as she subsequently explained, there was great anxiety in the house as to the illness of one of her brothers-in-law—which she described very much as an English lady would—mentioning that the high temperature, of 102 degrees, at which he remained caused them much uneasiness. Several questions about the Queen and the Royal Family were put to me by all the ladies, who spoke in a vein of respectful loyalty most pleasant to hear; and they asked, also with intelligent interest, about my voyage and what I had seen in Madras, especially what native ladies I had called on there. We remained about a quarter of an hour, and before we left a plate of fruit and sweets—these latter mainly made of cocoa-nut paste, and cloyingly sweet—were put before us, and we duly tasted them. Salaams over, I came to the conclusion that, so far as talk was concerned, I had paid many far less interesting visits in London.

As a rule in a native house one has to traverse a stone passage, opening upon a tiny bricked court, where two or three servants will be cooking, amid a litter of vegetable refuse; some stairs to climb, a balcony with small and dark rooms, in which the only furniture is a bed; and when the lady is reached she will be found in a chamber similarly poverty stricken in appearance.

Mahommedan houses are wont to be, in Calcutta, less alluring, if possible, to European tastes even than Hindu ones, and in one instance that I saw the narrow passage which we crossed was dirty in the extreme, and littered with orange-peel, while in the yard were the female attendants slicing vegetables on a large blade set in a block of wood, and crushing the curry spices upon a stone with a heavy roller. We had to climb some steep and broken brick and cement steps to reach our hostess, whose young daughter, being strictly purdah, was taught reading and writing by ladies of the Church of England Zenana Mission at her own house; and both, who were not expecting any call of the kind, received us in morning *deshabille* of no jewellery and simple cotton saris.

In this case the girl was the wife of a young man coming over to one of the English universities, and her education was being continued at his desire. She showed me her exercise-books and promising English handwriting, and evidently felt some interest in her studies; but when I asked her if she would like to accompany her husband to England, she smiled rather hopelessly at the idea, and gently said that native women did not take long journeys, and she thought she would be afraid to go on the sea.

Flowers of course play an important part in the daily life of the people, but the pleasure of their arrangement does not belong to the women of the household. Caste here gives a monopoly to the Malakars, who make up the bouquets and chaplets required for wedding festivities. For a bride the orthodox floral headdress are white bela flowers, arranged with jack leaves and a single bright red rose. But flowers possess so much and such deep symbolism among the Hindus that it was perhaps inevitable that their disposal should have become a profession in itself. Certain things, for instance, must never be offered to particular deities, and it would be considered most inauspicious to present the Java or China rose in wedding ceremonials, or to any other than Kali, to whom is also dedicated the aparajita (*Clitonéa ternatea*). The sacred blossom of Siva is the dhatúrá, and that of Saraswati is bákas (*Justicia adhadota*). For temple garlands and decorations the powerfully scented champak, so lovely in its clear waxy white just tipped with lemon yellow, is almost invariably admissible, as are the various jasmins, gardenias, and pink and white oleanders. The narsingars, like immense marigolds, in shades both of lemon and orange, are also much used, and in the Benares temples they are offered for sale by basketfuls. One point in the manufacture of these flower-chains is that under no circumstances may they be tied with string, and dried fibre of the plantain stem is invariably employed. I found this to be the case in every district that I visited.

In calling on a native lady, there are two or three marks of courtesy that she never fails to show. She will present a small bouquet of flowers, often really tastefully arranged, and generally sprinkled with rose-water. She will offer scent, and it is good manners to receive this upon an unfolded pocket-handkerchief. It is not always to be accepted with unreserved gratitude, for native perfumes have a clinging and penetrative quality derived from the essential oils which are their basis, which far surpasses any European product, nor can one feel whole-hearted thankfulness at being copiously sprinkled with patchouli, for which the only consolation is that it will quickly lose its objectionable aggressiveness; but all these are signs of respect, and as such must be borne. If the visit has been a formal one by appointment, flower-garlands will be placed round one's neck on leaving, and probably a dish of sweets will be offered. I own that these are not always enticing to the European palate. Fortunately, however, it suffices, to show that the gift is accepted in the spirit that is meant, to touch the lips with it, for where *ghi* (oiled butter), cocoa-nut, honey, and saffron are blended into large lumps, it is a little fearsome to the unaccustomed.

Of dancing I saw little, and the loss did not greatly concern me, as this can hardly be reckoned among the amusements of the women. Lucknow has the repute of training the best dancers, and here there are schools for the purpose of teaching them the simpering, posturing, and manipulation of draperies which seem the chief features of the art according to its native exponents. But the tendency to the adoption of European education among the rajahs and the wealthy men, formerly the best patrons of the dancing-girl and her calling, is changing taste in this direction. The faddist and the crank is even stepping in, and though at present he has not much influence wherewith to boast, it is a little instructive as well as amusing to find that in Madras has been founded, with all formality and importance, a "Society for the Suppression of Nautch parties," from whose propaganda it is urged that it is a short step from the nautch-party to the nautch-girl's home. And, further, nautch-parties are a sort of advertisement to these women, while the inevitable missionary has delivered his soul upon the subject by saying, "If the rich had money they could thus waste, it would be far better to use it in relieving the poor and the distressed than to squander it to give expensive presents to those who did not need it, and to fill the pockets of bad women who are hired at enormous cost to divert the crowd with unseemly gestures in dancing, which only tended to feed the flame of passion." The reverend gentleman's ire on the subject, it may be added, appeared from the context of this pronouncement to be principally due to the fact that as much as a hundred rupees a night are sometimes paid to a popular dancer.

I was naturally anxious to witness a native play, but it was not until I reached Bombay that the opportunity to do this afforded itself. A native actress is, however, a great rarity at all times, and in Western India she practically does not exist. There is, however, excuse enough to include an account of the drama in Gujerati, in a book devoted to "Woman in India," on the ground that the sex when it enjoys the chance is as fond in the East as in the West of seeing a play. The space immediately before the footlights, which in a European theatre belongs to the orchestra, is given over to the female spectators, who, if they are Parsees or anything but the most rigorously purdah of Hindus, can attend and enjoy the spectacle with little fear of being seen, as the seats are sunk a trifle below those of the first rows in the auditorium, and a high screen of wood is interposed.

The theatre that I visited is the largest and most important in the native quarter of the city, and its manager, Mr. Kussonji, prides himself upon his enterprise and liberal spirit towards his patrons. It was, however, a somewhat embarrassing experience, as I found that the visit of an English lady was decidedly rare, and in honour of the event new yellow satin-covered chairs had been placed in the front row for my own and my friends' accommodation, while the manager himself was in waiting to receive me with a very thick garland of white jessamine and pink oleander, which he placed round my neck, and I had thus to wear something like a sweetly scented boa of natural flowers all the evening. The theatre itself is a large one, and holds about fifteen hundred people. In construction it may be compared to one vast pit and large gallery, and in the matter of decoration it cannot be called extravagant, as, except for a little painting on the walls, decoration is non-existent. Though the play had been running for some weeks, the house was well filled in all parts, and the drama, which began at nine o'clock and lasted till nearly two in the morning, was followed with close, but not demonstrative, attention throughout. As in mediæval times with ourselves, all the female characters were personified by men, but in some cases the counterfeit, in make up, voice, and dress, was so good that I own that until the curtain had fallen on the first act I was not sure that the performers were not of the sex they were representing.

The title of the drama, which was borrowed from one of the old legends, and had been written up to the more modern conditions which even the native playgoer is beginning to demand, was "Mansing and Abhazasing," these being the names of the two sons of a great king. When the curtain rose the lads were seen at play, when to the well in the garden come some girls to draw water. The boys tease the girls, one of whom gets her chattie upset or broken, and though she herself is neither harmed nor hurt, she is indicated as a revengeful little minx, and goes off, promising that the lads, princes even as they are, will find themselves punished. She is married to a foolish youth, who has not sense or authority to bid her look on the affair as merely a joke, and is the son of a rich and influential man, who chooses to feel aggrieved at the "insult" to his daughter-in-law. Accordingly the father-in-law resolves to seek redress from the father of the boys, who enjoys the reputation of being an unflinchingly just and wise ruler—a reputation which he maintains in this instance by ordering the lads, despite all their mother's tears and prayers, into exile.

These incidents, told in several scenes, with a gorgeous stage picture of the king receiving his subjects and pronouncing his decision, formed the first act, and in the second the young princes, habited now in sober sable and stripped of nearly all their rich jewels, were seen halting for the night in a dreary jungle. Both are very tired and lie down to rest, but though an angry tiger (which was very cleverly worked, by the way) comes snarling across the stage, one of the deities of the Hindu Pantheon accords a protection to them. Against a wriggling serpent, however, this beneficent protection does not extend, and the younger boy is stung. From the effects of this he dies, bestowing his little bundle of possessions on his brother, and bidding him not trouble about his dead body. This injunction Mansing obeys, and goes on his journey; but presently come on to the scene a party of wealthy travellers apparently making a pilgrimage. The daughter of one of these, seeing the dead body of the beautiful young prince, declares that no other lover will ever satisfy her, and she is quite ready to sacrifice herself in suti for him. Such devotion, however, brings its own reward, for the opportune appearance of a holy Brahmin upon the scene results in a miracle of healing, and on the restoration of the youth to life, the couple are united in marriage on the spot.

Meantime the older boy had found his way to some hospitable kingdom, where his grace and good looks secured him the hand of its heiress-apparent, and in time the younger one, in the guise of a poor messenger, arrives there after having endured great hardships. The story of his resuscitation becomes known, and a wealthy *bunnia*—a term which I should explain is used equally to express a merchant or money-lender, a shopkeeper or a Shylock—has him shipped by crafty means on a vessel bound for

THE DRAMA IN GUJERATI—A SCENE FROM "MANSING AND ABHAZASING."

Java, on account of the superstition, that one like him, who has been restored from the dead, can secure safety to the boat and its cargo. Here he and the princess of the place, who possesses boundless riches, become enamoured of one another and marry, and the *bunnia* induces him to take a passage with his wife and her waiting-maid back to their native country. The *bunnia*, however, looks with envious eyes upon the wealth that the princess has brought to her husband, and resolves to possess himself of it by poisoning the young man. This design is frustrated by the waiting-maid, who learns the plot and conceals her master safely. The princess is led to imagine herself a widow, and on reaching the kingdom of her brother-in-law is offered to him in marriage. Again the faithful servant comes to the rescue, and at the wedding ceremony saves her mistress from dishonour by substituting herself, and meantime the father and mother of the two princes, Mansing and Abhazasing, have arrived with a great retinue of relations and retainers. The chambermaid tells her secret, the younger son is brought forward, and there is a general family reconciliation and joy all round, even the wicked *bunnia* and his myrmidons sharing in the universal good will.

Such is the story which occupied some half-dozen acts and hours to unfold. As I have said before, all the female parts were taken by young men, who occasionally acted with a degree of feeling and vigour that one would hardly have expected from them. Notably well played, for instance, was the scene between the queen-mother and her husband, when she was trying to induce him to modify the sentence of banishment passed upon the two boys; and very touching, even to ears like my own, which could not follow the sense of the Gujerati words, was her subsequent farewell and parting advice to them, while in her dark sari and handsome jewels she quite realized the picture of what the senior ranee often is. The parts of the princesses as brides were merely such as at home we should classify as *ingénues*, and required very little subtlety of acting, and all that was demanded of their exponents was to look pretty, according to native canons, be modest and retiring as a Hindu maiden ought to be, and wear rich clothes and showy ornaments with matter-of-fact ease. The lads entrusted with these parts fulfilled these requirements remarkably well, carrying their chatties on their heads with the same erect grace that the girls acquire, and indicating cleverly the half-shy reserve with which young women in the East listen to the conversation or move about in the presence of their elders. Very much in earnest were the two actors representing the two princes, and the one who took the part of the older and less tried exile worked hard to convey the proper sense of Oriental regal repose, while the other bore his manifold troubles with curiously characteristic quiet and even stoicism.

Proportionately the dresses would have borne comparison with those of the average theatre at home. The kings and princes wore kinkhabs of splendidly hued violet, orange, or crimson silks, stiff with golden brocading, and turbans with stripes of metallic threads. Ministers, *bunnias*, and Brahmins were all correctly habited, servants had liveries, and even the supernumeraries were very well dressed. For the female characters some of the cloths and saris were very rich and costly, and the colouring had been chosen with a remarkably good sense of stage effect. There was a constant change of scenery, and the transformations were effected rapidly and smoothly. Many of the "sets" were, indeed, very pretty, and notably among these might be mentioned the jungle scene by moonlight, with the two sleeping boys; and the revels and dances that are held when the older prince arrives in the palace of the princess whom he subsequently marries. From a strictly realistic point of view, however, much of the effect is marred by the custom which obtains of allowing the orchestra—composed, as it is, of weird and shrill wind and stringed instruments and tom-toms, which are played with monotonously vigorous rhythm—to have their places on the sides of the stage within the proscenium.

The managerial room was not unlike that of a London theatre manager. It was simply furnished with a desk, table, and stools, and over all lay a business-like confusion of papers and correspondence. Several "books of the words," in Gujerati, a luxury cheaply supplied to the theatre-goers, representing the present and previous productions, were there, as well as cuttings from vernacular papers, not merely, I was told, of "notices," but of new poems and dramas of whose existence it was well to be aware, and of writers whose names might possibly be worth bearing in mind. The bookshelves contained various volumes of reference, as well as of plays, among which were the renderings of Shakespeare's dramas which have been made into Gujerati; and on the wall were several photographs of former stars and present members of the company. It was, perhaps, more curious than discreet, taking into consideration the sex of the "actresses," to accept Mr. Kussonji's next offer of a sight of the dressing-rooms. Here I was initiated into several of the secrets of the men's successful make-up as women. The little *cholis*, or bodices of bright satin or embroidered net, had a little padding discreetly introduced, which imparted to them the due effect of exceeding tightness which the conditions of Oriental good fit demand. For the hair there were wigs or false tresses, which could be easily fastened on under the heavy jewelled head ornaments so dear to Hindu women; and paints and powders there were in abundance that would not look mean beside those of a Western actor or actress. For raising and lowering the curtain, and shifting the scenery, the manager had availed himself of the best machinery he could get; and the crowd of native carpenters and shifters had been admirably drilled to their work. I remained in the wings during a scene or two, watching the guardian deity of the wandering boys—a sufficiently awesome presentment, with gilded face and much weaponed in half a dozen hands, riding upon a lion—taken by invisible wires across the stage; and I noticed that the trees and a small bank were remarkably solidly constructed. Then I was taken below the stage that I might judge of the property resources that were stored there, and had pointed out to me with great pride the mahogany counter, with gilded rail and network, which had figured in a previous drama in which was a great bank robbery scene. Thus has realism and modernity reached even the drama in Gujerati.

Of course the wonderful in juggling and acrobatics are always popular, and when an entertainment of these is given, the purdah ladies generally manage to witness it from some gallery or behind a screen. The ordinary tricks, which begin from Port Said, when a clever conjurer comes on board the steamer and wears eggs as eye-glasses, while he produces kittens from his spectators' hair, or finds live chickens on the arms of a deck-chair, follow one more or less round the whole way, and the oft-described basket and mango tree tricks seem to be known to all "who make the people happy by command." These, moreover, are generally performed with dexterity, and even the closest attention fails to reveal "how it's done." Though in each case the performers were Indian, the newest (to European eyes) and neatest feats I witnessed were in Ceylon. Sitting in the verandah of the Queen's Hotel, Kandy, I saw a scantily clad and attenuated individual, who laconically said, "Good show, *ek* rupee." I had read all the newspapers of comparatively recent date, and a rupee for at least half an hour's amusement, till it should be cool enough to drive out, did not seem exorbitant. So I ordered the performance, and saw yards of coloured paper produced from his angular elbow, and after realistic contortions as of great internal pain, a heterogeneous collection of stones, knives, pieces of cloth, and small bottles were taken from his mouth and laid at my feet. Presently he

A CONJURER AT PORT SAID.

brought out a snake-skin, which he offered me to handle and examine, and though I must admit that I possess all the antipathy of my sex to touching anything snake-like, I took this, and it undoubtedly was what it purported to be. As I returned it to him, he apparently laid it on the ground, and touched the gaping mouth with some liquid. Almost instantly it appeared to come to life, and in a few seconds a hissing cobra with hood erect was in its place. It was a most clever bit of sleight of hand, for the live snake was substituted in the same position as that in which the dead skin had lain, and again when, after a few passes, he had brought back the empty skin, the illusion was extremely well performed.

It was at Trincomalee that I witnessed the most brilliant feats of balancing and acrobatics of my tour on the part of a travelling troupe. One item was almost gruesome, and was certainly startling. A man stood upon his head, and gradually lowered his body, keeping it quite rigid till it was only twelve or fifteen inches off the ground. He then moved it round, his head being all the while an immovable pivot, till the idea forced itself upon the spectator that he was bound to twist himself off his own neck.

One must plunge far into the native states to see quail or cock-fighting, which are both extremely popular masculine pastimes, and at the fairs held once or twice a year in the big towns of the feudal territories they always flourish prominently.

Music is not, save with the Parsees, a feminine enjoyment, for it is considered, like dancing, to be an exclusive prerogative of low caste or bad women. The Parsees, however, to their credit, have raised it from this degraded view, and many of them are accomplished performers and highly trained vocalists. By special invitation, while in Bombay, I was able to attend a concert given in honour of Mr. Naoroji, M.P., with a programme of strictly national airs and songs. It had been organized by Mr. Kabraji, a gentleman whose name is honourably known to English musicians by his really scholarly rendering into Gujerati of the words of the National Anthem with musical adaptation. This was

PARSEE CONCERT.

sung by one of his daughters, as solo with chorus, and may certainly be pronounced successful. I do not profess to understand the intricacies of the Hindu scale, which recognizes quarter-tones, and of course to European ears there is a certain airless monotony at first. But in due time one begins to detect that it has subtle harmonies, which are far from unpleasant when well performed.

Whenever sympathy is expressed for the want of amusement or outside interest of the Indian woman's life, I think few have any idea how fully her aspirations in these directions are supplied by her religion, which satisfies so well the cravings of the feminine nature towards the romantic and the dramatic. It so happened that I understood this from the first, for soon after I reached Trincomalee, where I first stayed in the East, and where the native population are for the most part devout Sivaites, I found the great festival of Kali—known in Bengal as the Durga Puja, and in Western India as the Dasara, when her victory over the demon Mahihasura vested Siva with a little brief authority—in full celebration. For nearly a week the quaint little temple was decorated outside with pendent chains of the exquisite "temple flower," and the *jasminum undulatum*, with its strong perfume, while night after night a stream of men, women, and children, in considerable bravery of holiday attire and jewels, passed up to witness in material and tangible performance the episodes of the legend. On the last night but one, Kali, in her aspect of the destroyer, was brought out with all her panoply of upraised trident, coloured flags, and red-and-white flowers, seated upon a lion, the demon first appearing with the head of an elephant. Both were carried upon large wooden platforms, the bearers of which were a number of stalwart and bronzed natives; but while the goddess moved forward with slow and dignified advances, Mahihasura's porters were bidden by peremptory words of command to surge hither and thither, to part the crowd, or to career round the temple. The demon was armed first with a bow, but after a sufficient rushing about on the part of his energetic bearers, a slight movement forward on the part of the awesome "propeller of the chief of weapons," caused the diabolic assailant to drop his arms amid the shouts of the crowd. This proceeding was repeated as the demon reappeared with a sword, a trident, and a club, and was gone through again in same order after he had assumed other disguises, for fully two hours, under the glare of torches kindled with cocoa-nut oil. For the concluding scene processions came up from other temples of Kali, and all met upon an expanse of green which lies outside of Fort Frederick, to take part in the final destruction of Mahihasura; when, after fruit and flowers had been offered, the impersonator of the demon, followed by torch-bearers and a noisy crowd, rushed down to the seashore and cast his garments and masks to the waves, and was carried back prostrate and comatose after the excitement and exertion.

Then again at Berhampore I was fortunate enough to arrive just in time for the Ras Lila festival, which, through the generosity of the Maharanee Surnomoyee, is celebrated there with more than usual pomp. Krishna, as is familiar to those who know the story of the puranic gods, was changed at birth for the female child of a cowherd's wife to rescue him from the wrath of his uncle, Kansa, to whom it had been predicted that a boy would wrest his kingdom from him. Kansa, hearing of the fraud, tried to kill this lad, sending the demons Arishta in the form of a bull, and Kesin as a horse, for this purpose, but he evaded them; and at last Kansa invited his nephew to a boxing-match with him, in which Krishna slew his uncle. In this festival this episode was commemorated by a marvellously dramatic presentment in almost life-sized clay figures, modelled by the famous artificers of Krishnagar. Five or six tiers of seats were ranged round three sides of an enormous marquee. In the centre, at the top, sat Radha,

FIGURES IN THE RAS LILA CELEBRATION AT BERHAMPORE.

Krishna's favourite wife, while all the rest were filled with nobles and importancies invited to witness the contest. No two—and there were some hundreds of them—were alike in features, expression, position, or dress, and it was extraordinary how the sense of fear, awe, satisfaction, or contempt was expressed upon their faces as Krishna, having freed himself of his persecutor, whose corpse lies on the ground, is bending humbly to perform the meritorious penance of washing a holy Brahman's feet.

Owing to the association of the god's early days with things pastoral, the cow generally finds a prominent place in any observances connected with him. On this occasion, there was a herd of about forty of them, presented with a fidelity and variety no less astonishing than that of the human models. It was just such a herd as one sees daily in Bengal, some comparatively sleek and well-conditioned, others mere skin and skeleton. There were cows with calves beside them; some were snatching a hasty bite of grass; some were pushing to the front; one was licking a leg in realistic fashion. There were draft-weary bullocks, and the ugly water buffaloes, with their immense down-curving horns, and all shown nearly life-size.

Crowds came and went all day, and outside a fair was in full swing. It was a really interesting glimpse to me of the inner enjoyments of the people to whom this mud Madame Tussauds', if I may so speak of it without offence, was not only a wonder and a delight, but was also a religious ceremonial of high importance.

CHAPTER XI.

FEMALE CRIMES AND CRIMINALS.

"Vindicta
Nemo magis, gaudet quam fœmina."
JUVENAL, *Sat.* xiii.

"IT can hardly be said that crime entailing incarceration is otherwise than stationary among the women of India," is a line that I cull from the last-issued official report as to the gaol and criminal statistics of the dependency. The very small ratio of female to male malefactors is, however, one of the most remarkable and interesting aspects of the whole social system of the East from whatever point of view one regards it; while favourable to women as even the mere figures are, their statistical morality is placed even higher when certain facts concerning those who are classified as offenders are taken into consideration. First, however, it should be pointed out that crime among men shows a marked tendency to increase. In 1881, the number of male prisoners in gaol was 402,823, and ten years later those figures had jumped to 526,804, though better administration in Burmah may be held responsible for an appreciable percentage of this very large increase. In the corresponding years, of this number, only 23,718 and 24,933 were women; while in the intervening decade the total never exceeded the latter figure, nor sank below 21,794. This, for all practical purposes, places women convicts to men convicts in the proportion of 1 to 20·5.

Comparing this with our own ratio, I find in the corresponding British judicial statistics, that during 1891 the ratio of female to male offenders sentenced to penal servitude was 9·2 to 90·8, which is nearly double. It is true that 1892 saw these figures standing at 6·3 to 93·7; but the fluctuations in them during the past twenty years or so have been so marked that I fear, for the credit of my sex, the lower proportion is hardly likely to be maintained. The classification of the various headings of crime show a wider range to the Englishwoman's breaches of the law to that of her Indian cousin, and it is instructive to note the following table concerning those convicted in England during 1891 :—

	Proportion for each class of Offences.	Proportion of Males.	Proportion of Females.
Offences against the person	18·8	92·2	7·8
" " property, with violence	24·7	95·7	4·3
" " " without violence	46·5	87·4	12·6
Malicious offences against property	2·4	94·4	5·6
Offences against the currency	6·0	88·9	11·1
" not included in the above	1·6	100·0	—

These proportions were somewhat diminished in 1892; but as I am unable to give the equivalent Indian statistics for that year, comparison cannot be instituted.

Recommittal is very rare among the Indian women, and with all save petty depredators the punishment of imprisonment exercises a deterrent effect. It is not so with ourselves, where the higher proportionate numbers of females frequently recommitted is always very noticeable. In 1892, I find that the males recommitted to English gaols were 41·7 per cent. of the total number of males committed (exclusive of debtors

R

and naval and military offenders); and the recommitted females (exclusive of debtors) formed 60·3 of the whole. In the preceding year the proportions were 42 per cent. with respect to males, and 54·6 per cent. with respect to females.

Now the first fact that tends to reduce the proportion of offenders among the average female population of India, is the existence of a thieving and begging caste. This is perfectly well recognized by those responsible for the administration of the law, and when I went through Agra gaol, where against 1900 men, there were only 66 women, no less than 11 belonged to this order, which is more or less nomadic, and goes by different names in different parts of India.

Secondly to be considered is the point, that an extraordinarily large number of the female offenders are in prison for receiving stolen goods. In this it is but just that the woman should be leniently dealt with, as in almost every case concerning which I made inquiries I found that she was more or less the tool of her husband or the men of her family. The stolen property was brought to her, and she was ordered to conceal it, a command which, with the submissiveness to those she has been taught are her lords and masters, as well as the possibility of *force majeure* if she had declined, she naturally obeyed. But surely, in such instance, it is fairer to judge her as a victim to her circumstances than as a lawbreaker on her own account.

The Indian female thief is as a rule guilty only of petty larceny, and minor depredations, such as a handful of rice from the grain-seller, or wood or charcoal from some wealthier neighbour's stores, or she may obtain possession by fraud of a kinswoman's jewellery; but she lacks the nerve, the readiness, and the resource for bolder efforts. Cases of assault are comparatively rare, and I think indeed nothing shows more pointedly how thorough have been her life's lessons of discipline than this, when one takes into account the numbers of sisters and sisters-in-law, both married and single, who are to be found living in the one house, with a mother-in-law over them in supreme command and control.

The crime to be set down as the characteristic one of Indian women is infanticide. Not, be it understood, as it is with us, when it is generally the last desperate, piteous effort of a betrayed girl-mother to hide her shame from the world, but as an angry wife's most furious form of vengeance for a husband's coldness, neglect, or infidelity. Eliminating the female convicts under punishment for the offences I have named, it will always be found that fully four-fifths of the remaining prisoners are undergoing sentence for this crime. The unfortunate infants may be strangled, deserted, poisoned, or thrown down wells; and the bitterness of the revenge is always enhanced tenfold if it be a little son whose life is taken. In one case that I saw at Benares, the woman, who was awaiting trial, was accused of having left the baby upon the public highway to the endangering of its life. Her defence, however, was that she had only done it to bring her husband to a sense of his duty, as he was withholding adequate support from her. In the Agra prison I saw no less than ten women under life sentences for infanticide, and in two or three of the cases it had been done for what seemed absurdly trivial reasons, such as that a husband had commended the cooking he had seen at another house.

Murder among the women is very rare, and the only notable instance of it that I saw in the many gaols that I visited was at Madras, and it struck me as a rather tragic illustration of the way in which at times these women of the

East view the domestic arrangements sanctioned by long custom in their land. This was the case of a young woman under sentence of ten years' "rigorous" imprisonment. She was unusually handsome, with a low broad brow, a wealth of coal-black hair, flashing brown eyes, and a tall lithe figure that would have served for a Venus in bronze. In a moment of mad jealousy she had murdered her sister, who was married to the same husband as herself. It was impossible to withhold a glance of pitying sympathy as her keen eyes rested upon mine while she grasped the fact that the wardress was conveying to me, in the little English at her command, the stormy story of her passionate love.

Madras was quite characteristic of all the other gaols that I saw, and though its male and female departments are actually within the same enclosing walls, and under the equal supervision of Mr. Macready, its kindly and courteous superintendent, the women's quarters are quite isolated, and under no circumstances whatever do the prisoners of the one sex see or meet with those of the other. A high wall and heavy iron-studded gates, similar to those characteristic of such establishments in England, have to be passed to gain admission; but, once inside, the gorgeous sunshine and the luxuriant ever-present flowering plants, which thrive in all corners and crannies, give a far less sombre appearance to the well-kept place than that of the grey, granite-flagged yards associated at home with prison life. Considerable enlargements and improvements were being carried out in the men's workshops, and when these are complete the prison will as a whole be one of the best equipped in the whole dependency.

On the day that I visited the Madras prison it contained 870 prisoners, of whom only 33 were women. This, Mr.

Macready informed me, was slightly below the average number, which is about 40; a total rarely exceeded by more than two or three. A European matron and a native wardress—a remarkably intelligent young woman, who seemed not only to have the power of commanding respect and discipline, but also to feel a gentle feminine sympathy with her unfortunate charges—formed the whole staff necessary for the maintenance of good order, though over the prisoners themselves was appointed from their number a maestry, who was responsible to the matron for the execution of the tasks allotted to the prisoners. The woman in this position was a Hindu of the weaver caste, and was undergoing a sentence of seven years for infanticide, but her good conduct since her conviction had won for her marks enough to secure the remission of nearly a year of her time. The women sleep in a large dormitory, to each one being allotted a stone *piall*, or bed, the equivalent of our plank bed at home, a sleeping suit, a mat to lie upon, two blankets to cover her, and a pillow. This chamber is light, and particularly well ventilated—a very important point in any institution in the tropics. The dietary is the same as that of the men, only a little reduced in quantity, and gives them rice twice a week and raggi the remaining days, with curry, and a small quantity of meat or vegetable daily. Raggi, though highly nutritious, is not greatly enjoyed, and its use may be regarded as equivalent to that of oatmeal porridge in a London house of correction. It is a small grain, not unlike rape seed in appearance, and when ground fine produces a greyish flour. This is boiled with water and salt to a very thick batter, and is poured out into pound moulds, when it looks like a rather stodgy chocolate pudding, and is served with about a third of a pint of thick and very savoury-smelling curry. All the cooking is done by prisoners of caste, so that no outrage is done to inherent prejudices on this point; and certainly in quantity and quality it seemed all that the most advanced humanitarian could desire. There is a small hospital set apart for the women, where iron pallet beds and mattresses are provided, while the food given them is according to medical orders. Two cases of slight fever were in it under treatment on the day that I was there, but as a whole the health throughout the prison—unless Madras should be visited by an outbreak of cholera, when it suffers proportionately—is very good. A kindly concession to maternal feelings allows any woman to keep her baby, whether born before or after conviction, with her until it reaches the age of two years, and a sufficient quantity of milk over and above the prison fare is allowed the mother for the baby's use.

All the jewellery, which is such a treasured evidence of social position to Hindu women, is of course taken off them when they pass behind the prison walls, and the only things they are permitted to retain are the symbols of marriage—usually a small gold charm worn suspended round the neck by a cord or beads, or the iron bangle, and the sacred cord which indicates certain Brahmin castes. The prison dress consists of a strong cotton unbleached or coloured cloth, which they drape round them in the manner they have been accustomed to wear it, covering the breast and left shoulder. Their hair is not cut off, and they twist it into a knot low down at the back of their heads.

The women, like the men, are put to varying employments in different prisons. One almost invariably, however, finds them set to clean and sort the grain, and afterwards pound it for the staple food of the gaol, this of course being labour to which they are quite accustomed at home. In many of the prisons, too, where carpet or other weaving is carried on, they are set to wind yarn, and in others basket and mat-making provides occupation for many more. In Madras the female prisoners themselves weave a broad webbing tape, which is almost all supplied to the army, who use it for tent fastenings and girthings, on account of its reliable strength and quality.

CLEANING GRAIN IN MADRAS GAOL.

"Rigorous" confinement is the equivalent of our own hard labour; but I believe that women are not subjected to the additional punishments of "close" or "solitary" confinement. As one often hears exaggerated statements concerning the frequency and severity of this extra correction, I went at some detail into this question, and learnt that "close" punishment, which consists in keeping the prisoner alone in a cell, save for his daily exercise in company with other prisoners, can only be imposed at the following ratio to sentence: "Habitual convicts, if sentenced to less than two years, three months; two, and less than three years, four months; three, and less than four years, six months; four, and less than eight years, eight months; over eight years, twelve months; which must be served in two periods of six months, with an interval between of two months." The terms of "close" imprisonment for first or second time offenders are less in proportion. There are two grades also of "solitary" confinement which, under no circumstances, can be inflicted for more than seven consecutive days in a month, and which, with its accompaniment of lessened diet, is only resorted to in the extremest cases of refractoriness, insubordination, or violence to warders or fellow-prisoners.

Once in a way even now, there are instances in which settled law has failed to satisfy the instincts of the people, and since my return to England, I have had sent me the details of a luridly tragic story, which is surely one of the most notable instances of wrong-headed heroism and supreme self-sacrifice of modern days. It comes from Katthiawar, and to understand it, one must know that before law and order were introduced by us, *dharna* was a recognized mood of obtaining redress or compelling the payment of a debt. In this process the injured individual simply took up a position before his debtor's house and abstained from food, and religious ordinances compelled the debtor to do the same, and also to forego his usual amusements and pleasures. If the fast were continued until the suitor died, the debtor was held responsible for the death.

From this custom there grew up a caste of heralds known as *charans*, who made themselves responsible with their own lives for the fulfilment of public engagements or bonds, or important family contracts and bargains. The sign of their office was a dagger, which, in the event of their failure to carry out what they had undertaken, they would plunge into their own hearts. This form of duress was called *traga,* and if a herald feared that, in spite of the shocking odium which it brought upon a defaulter to have caused a herald's death, his own self-sacrifice would not suffice to overawe the wrong-doer, he would add to its weight by claiming also the lives of wife, children, or leading members of his caste. And in all these years the *charan* and *traga* have survived, and even yet vindicate sometimes their existence and principles.

In this particular instance, a banker had made a loan to a landholder in one of the native states, and took the precaution of securing the sign manual of the herald's dagger as a guarantee. When the time for discharging the debt came, the *charan* went and demanded payment, but the debtor was supercilious about old methods, and with a contemptuous laugh, referred his creditor to the machinery of the civil courts.

For these the *charan* had no particular respect, but his own honour and the fair fame of his caste he held very dear. He went home and talked the matter over with his aged mother and his brother, and the decision was taken. She would be the sacrifice to the solemn obligations of her race, and her life should be laid down in confirmation of her son's sacred bond. A last *sraddh* was performed, and the brave mother set out with her two sons to the defaulter's house. Again the demand was made, "Wilt thou pay or not?" and this time the debtor was not sneering, but rather conciliatory. The mother unfalteringly knelt, and bared her head and neck of the draping sari. The debtor understood the grave reality now before him, and said, "I will pay as soon as the wheat is in-gathered," while the old woman's head was unflinchingly bent. Once more the request was peremptorily repeated for instant discharge of the loan, and in abject terror and confusion the debtor made some too-prevaricating reply. Then the stalwart herald's heavy Rajput sword fell, and with one sweeping cut his mother's head rolled in the dust at his feet. The brothers then inflicted wounds upon the awe-stricken defaulter, for the formal purpose of having his blood to blend with that of their own sacrificed victim to sprinkle upon the doorposts of his hated house. The police were quickly brought, and the prosaic procedure of ordinary justice was invoked to finish this fierce, chivalrous, barbaric drama; and the son, for whose pledged word his mother had given her own life, was sent into transportation over seas for life. But the debtor, knowing full well the withering infamy in which public opinion would henceforth hold him, starved himself to death for very shame.

And yet there are English people who will assure one that truth, honour, and heroism are not to be reckoned among the attributes of Indian women!

CHAPTER XII.

DEATH AND FUNERAL CUSTOMS.

"A band
Of waiting people: foremost one who swung
An Eastern bowl with lighted coals; behind
The kinsmen shorn, with mourning marks, ungirt,
Crying aloud, 'O Rama, Rama, hear!
Call upon Rama, brothers;' next the bier,
Knit of four poles with bamboos interlaced,
Whereon lay stark and stiff, feet foremost, lean,
Chapfallen, sightless, hollow flanked, a-grin,
Sprinkled with red and yellow dust—the Dead,
Whom at the four went ways they turned head first,
And crying, 'Rama, Rama!' carried on
To where a pile was reared behind the stream.
Thereon they laid him, building fuel up.
Good sleep hath one that slumbers on that bed!
He shall not wake for cold, albeit he lies
Naked to all the airs—for soon they set
The red flame to the corners four, which crept
And licked and flickered, finding out his flesh,
And feeding on it with swift, hissing tongues,
And crackle of parched skin and snap of joint,
Till the fat smoke thinned, and the ashes sank
Scarlet and gray, with here and there a bone
White midst the grey—the total of the man."

SIR EDWIN ARNOLD, "The Light of Asia."

OVER marriage, with its joyous symbolism of new life, the Hindu lavishes all the ceremonial and rejoicing that he can command; over death, with its solemn mysteriousness, he is restrained and simple. In the Indian funeral customs there are scarcely any survivals of barbaric forms, and indeed the

Rig Veda itself inculcates ideas by no means distant from those of Christianity, and sings—

"Depart thou, depart thou to the place whither our fathers have departed. Meet with the ancient ones: meet with the Lord of death. Throwing off thine imperfections, go to thine Home. . . . Let him depart to those for whom flow the rivers of nectar. Let him depart to those who, through meditation, have obtained the victory, who, by fixing their thoughts on the unseen, have gone to heaven. Let him depart to the mighty in battle, to the heroes who have laid down their lives for others, to those who have bestowed their goods on the poor;" while a somewhat later canticle in the "Atharva Veda" carries on the idea with, "May the water-shedding spirits bear thee upwards, cooling thee with their swift motion through the air, and sprinkling thee with dew. Bear him, carry him; let him, with all his faculties complete, go to the world of the righteous. Crossing the dark valley which spreadeth boundless around him, let the unborn soul ascend to heaven. Wash the feet of him who is stained with sin; let him go upwards with cleansed feet. Crossing the gloom, gazing with wonder in many directions, let the unborn soul go up to heaven."

Speaking generally, it may be said that the Hindus of the Brahman and higher castes dispose of their dead by burning, while the Mahommedans and Hinduized aborigines and the non-Aryan tribes resort to burial. The funeral observances of the Hindus are simple, and there is very little to be added in description of them to Sir Edwin Arnold's lines with which this chapter is prefaced. Before the corpse is taken out of the house a *sraddh* or ceremony of offering and propitiation of departed ancestors takes place, and rice, oil, spice, and the usual objects of sacrifice are presented. Among the

Rajputs this *sraddh* is performed on the thirteenth day after death, and another, known as the *barki sraddh*, takes place on the anniversary. The extremely orthodox of these people impose upon the sons a daily offering of water, but if there were no boys in the family, the *sraddh* and *barki* do not lose efficacy if carried out by the daughters, and I may mention that the Rajput women have what is known as a *Tihi Puja* (held on the 15th day of Asin, at the end of December), when they make offerings of cakes and oil to the souls of their mother-in-law, grandmother-in-law, and great-grandmother-in-law, in gratitude, it is averred, for the good husbands with which they are blessed.

The Rautias of Chota Nagpore are particular that the body of a married woman should be bathed, anointed with oil, and dressed in a new sari, the two latter details being omitted in the case of a widow. When the corpse is laid upon the pile, the head must be to the north, and the nearest relation takes a torch, which must be made of five dry twigs of bel soaked in *ghi*, walks seven times round the pyre, and touches the mouth of the corpse with the torch before setting the wood alight. Before this, however, a small piece of clothing is taken from the body, and in it a knife or bit of iron is wrapped. For ten days this must be carried about by the chief mourner and placed beside him when he sleeps, while he must also daily make libations of water or milk during the same period to the ashes which have been collected and placed in a new *ghauti* or earthen vessel.

To the strict Brahman, and all who are truly orthodox, burning on the shores of the Ganges is the most desirable method of disposal. Like the majority of travellers, I had a somewhat morbid desire to see the much-talked-of burning ghats of Benares; but I am bound to say that there is nothing particularly gruesome about the place of incineration itself, unless perchance one sees the unceremonious manner in which

THE BURNING GHAT AT BENARES.

the body is doubled and crushed up to fit upon the pile of wood. The bodies, tightly swathed in cotton cloth, which must be white for a man and red for a woman, lie for one hour upon the water's edge, where they are just lapped by the stream, and the pyre is lighted by a near male relation from a sacred fire, the monopoly of which is held by a man of the servile dom caste. The scene is neither impressive nor repulsive, and as a spectacle may take rank among one's disappointments of travel. One may see as many as three or four fires alight at once, and unless the breeze happens to puff a smoky heavy odour of burnt fat in the direction of the boat, which may be moored as closely up to the scene as desired, there is absolutely nothing to tell one that the cremation of human remains is going on.

It is of course only the wealthy who can take their dead to Benares, or the almost equally sacred Gya, to be burned, and so the scene may be witnessed in any town or village that one looks for it. Indeed the Malabari Brahmans have an axiom that the corpse of a man or woman should always be burnt in their own compounds. But it may be possible even to the poorest to be able in time to cast the ashes upon the broad bosom of Mother Ganga, or in the sanctified branches of the Kaveri at Birunelli in the Wynaad, and Perur in Coimbatore, and, until opportunity offers, the remains can be piously preserved in an urn at home. The advantage, according to Brahmanical ideas, of casting the ashes upon a sacred stream, is that a body, provided all orthodox prayers have been recited, passes into the keeping of Radra (one of Siva's many forms), and his cares cease when the burning is complete. All that is left after the incineration is pure, and therefore belongs of right to another of Siva's incarnation, Paramesvaran, who is reached through the holy waters. I heard in Calcutta of a curious instance of the way in which the orthodox are beginning to adapt the resources of Western innovation to the assistance of their religious rites in a carefully elaborated plan which a Brahman laid, in all seriousness, before the Postmaster-General for a system by which the ashes of the holy might be sent by parcels post, to be thrown upon the regenerating flood at the specially desirable seasons. Thus, at Calcutta or Bombay, and in fact wherever Hinduism flourishes, from Cape Cormorin to Beloochistan, there the place of burning will also be. And the widows go to make lamentation with their bereaved friends, and one of the most dolorous spectacles of which I have the recollection, was the sight of some five and twenty of them seated upon their heels and clad in dull ashen grey, which was not far removed from black, in a dreary upper room in one of the many-storied houses of Bombay, and monotoning the while a wailing, melancholy dirge.

Among the non-Aryan, but wholly or partially Hinduized races there are a few interesting survivals in burial customs, but, as a rule, a woman's remains are disposed of with less ceremony than those of a man. Some of the Mahilis, for instance, bury their dead face downwards, while the Paús, Malés, Bagdis of Orissa, the poorer Goraits of Bengal, and the Koras, among many more, are careful that the head should be towards the north. Burial customs of certain castes often differ in localities, but the Jugis, who rank among the very lowest, are invariable in their methods of interment. They make a circular grave, often as much as eight feet deep, and a niche is made to receive the corpse in a sitting posture, the face being to the north-east, the quarter of the Sivaite paradise. A new cloth is wrapped round the body, and in a bag over the shoulder four cowries are placed to pay, as in pagan mythology, for the ferry across the gloomy waters of Vaitarani. When the grave is filled up, food of various sorts is placed upon it to appease the wandering spirits, and a few cowries are left as offering to the earth-god, whose space has thus been taken up.

Money again enters into the funeral observances of the Mangars, a fighting tribe of Nepal. Almost as soon as the breath has left the body, the corpse is tied to a bamboo pole and taken to the grave, where it is dressed in a new cloth, and sectarial marks are put upon the face. The money, however, is put by the Mangars into the mouth of the dead, together with a piece of coral, to which all sorts of talismanic virtues are ascribed. Then, a near relation, who should be a maternal uncle of the deceased if possible, after sundry minor rites of touching the lips with fire have been performed, lets down a piece of board in which nine steps or notches have been cut, the idea of this being a ladder to help the spirit to the regions above, while every one present also cuts a nick in another similar length of wood, which is afterwards broken in two. These people have another oddly reasoned custom, in that of placing a barrier of close-set thorn bushes across the path leading to the house of the dead. Beside this stands one of the chief mourners with a censer filled with an aromatic incense. Each one must step over the hedge and through the smoke, as the spirit then could not force its way through the thorns, nor could it be carried over on any one's shoulders, as smoke is anti-pathetic to it. Thus it is prevented from annoying the living in its former haunts.

With the Oraons—who usually burn and not bury their dead—the women of the village are expected to do the chief part in the outward evidences of mourning. They first loosen their hair, and then by their loud lamentations let their kinsfolk and acquaintance know that the sad event has occurred. In an Oraon family the task of laying out the body devolves solely upon the women, and a wife is expected to set alight the funeral pyre of her husband, her female friends uttering piteous dirges the while.

Every separate tribe and caste has its distinctive days for feasting, purification, and *sraddh*, or propitiatory offering to deceased ancestors. These details occur earlier with some than with others, but I know of none who dispense with them entirely, nor of any who do not at one period or another consider a banquet as essential. Still, the true Hindu, orthodox or not, does not spend anything like the money upon funerals that he does upon weddings; and in that respect, as well as in a good many others, he sets our own working classes an example worth imitation, for "a gude solid burying" seems hardly to recommend itself as a popular recreation on sanitary or æsthetic grounds. But that is the light in which the British middle and lower orders regard it.

There is very little variation in the Mahommedan observances, and it is only in minor details that a woman's burial differs at all from that of a man. In theory, hope is never abandoned, however certain death appears, as a good Muslim argues that to count upon the end is reckoning that the Omnipotent could not, were He so willed, perform a miracle of saving. Therefore, though the house may be filled with the near and the distant relations, no preliminary steps may be taken towards funeral necessities, and the *rafan*, or shroud, may never be ordered until life is undoubtedly extinct. The *rafan* must never be cut with knife or scissors, nor may it be touched with a needle.

The corpse is washed, and laid in the new cloth, which is tied at the head and feet with slips torn off it. When the grave is nearly complete, the *janāza*, as the bier is called, is brought to the house, and the women, if *purdah*, look upon their relative's face for the last time, which they do with every sign of deep grief, and the recitation to one another of the good and womanly qualities she possessed.

If a bier is not obtainable, then an ordinary *charpai*, or bed, can be used to convey the body to the cemetery, to which it is carried at the usual walking pace on men's shoulders, and it is an Islamic command that if the number of bearers appears insufficient, or they show the slightest signs of fatigue, any passer-by, even though a complete stranger, must lend his aid. This task, wherever possible, and especially for a woman, should be done by the nearest relations, and there are a few small signs by which the members of the faith know whether the corpse is that of a married or unmarried woman. The *kalima*, or confession, is repeated by all as the procession moves along.

There is almost invariably a mosque, small and humble as it may be, within every cemetery, and to this the body is taken, and *namaz-i-janāza*, or the funeral office, consisting of portions from the Koran, is recited. As soon as the body has been lowered into the grave itself, all the relations present repeat a short but important chapter, called *Kul-hawallah*, from the same sacred book thrice, and cast earth upon the remains. Then the face is uncovered, and a last look taken, and it is the final tribute of respect to the strictly kept *purdah* of a well-born lady, that no man except her father, brothers, husband, sons, or the few more distantly removed relatives who could see her in life, should look upon her after death. It is a touching little proof, I always think, of how intensely strongly is the theory of a woman's non-existence for any save her own kept up in tradition and practice.

Boards are then laid above the corpse, and the grave is

filled with a tenacious mud, and if the family is wealthy enough to command such a religious luxury, a *hafiz-i-Koran*, *i.e.* one who can repeat the whole book by heart, is appointed to recite this at the grave for the benefit of the dead. It is an invariable rule that liberal alms shall be given to the poor after a funeral has taken place.

Muslim hospitality in India commands that all who attend the funeral shall be received at the house of the deceased for at least three days afterwards. At the end of that time *tija* or *suam*, a gathering of friends from different parts, is held in the family mosque early in the morning, and prayers for the souls of all the faithful departed are offered, and there follows a distribution of a particular form of confectionery known as *chani*, and *batashi*, a sweetmeat into whose composition sugar and dates enter largely. This does not, however, end the funeral feasting, as on the tenth and fortieth days after the death numerous dishes, for which special and costly ingredients are required, are prepared, and are sent to all who were present at the previous ceremonies. Commemorations of the departed one also take place six months and a year after death, and the same dishes are again served at these.

A Mahommedan woman's tomb is easily distinguishable from that of a man by having a small semi-circular elevation upon it. This is soon learnt after a sight of the Taj at Agra, in which I was prepared to be disappointed, for one has high expectations where almost all men speak well. But surely one's eyes would be wanting in some quality of artistic appreciation did not one submit from the first moment to its unutterable charm of form and brilliancy. My first view of it was under the waning sun, when a soft rosy glow lay upon its glistening whiteness, and there was a quiet hush upon its gardens, deserted save for two or three native students who looked at it with reverence and almost awe. No photograph does it justice, for this cannot convey the marvellous charm of colour of its inlay work, where choice stones have been lavished with unsparing hand, or the delicate fineness of the marble carvings outside, assuming now, under the hand of age, which is dealing very gently with the whole, the creamy richness of old ivory. The screen round the tomb and the doorways conveyed the idea to my mind of petrified lace, while the quotations from the Koran are engraved in black marble with a grace of curve and flourish that our stiffer letters could never possess. There are some who profess to find a "weakness of femininity," as they are pleased to express it, about the Taj. I would rather see in it Shah Jehan's discriminating sense of what his loved wife, Urjumand Banu, to whom it is the memorial, would herself have admired most, and respect him for having given to a woman the most beautiful monument in the world.

Curious in contrast is the simple grave at Delhi to Jehanara, the good and beautiful and virtuous daughter of Shah Jehan, which is a plain headstone, bearing at the top the words, in Arabic, "God is the life and the resurrection;" while over the grave itself grass, always kept green and fresh, is growing, in obedience to her wish, recorded in Persian, upon the stone:—

> "Save the green herb, place naught above my head,
> Such pall alone befits the lowly dead.
> The fleeting, poor Jehanara lies here.
> Her sire was Shah Jehan. . . ."

It might indeed be a grave in a country churchyard; and strange in truth is it that the daughter of her over whom one of the wonders of the world has been reared should thus have chosen so modest a memorial.

Lastly I come to the funeral rites and ceremonies of the Parsees, which are perhaps the most curious in all India. The Parsees have no reticence whatever about their strange customs, but explanations to understand them thoroughly are long, and few, I think, trouble themselves to do more than look at the "Towers of Silence" of Bombay and other places in Western India.

Precisely the same observances are carried out for a Parsee woman as for a man, and indeed the equal rights of women are put forward in the Zoroastrian books with considerable insistency. The death preparations begin, unlike the Muslim practices, from the moment that the case is pronounced hopeless, and priests are sent for to recite the *patet*, which is a prayer of repentance, and a complete robe of white, in which the dead body is to be clad, is washed by a near relation. The *kusti*, or sacred thread, which every adult Parsee wears, is tied after death round the waist by a relative, and after that the care of the corpse passes to the professional watchers by the dead.

Then is performed the *sag dīd*, or "seeing of the dog," an office that I do not attempt to explain, nor in truth do the Zoroastrian authorities agree in offering any solution of the idea. A dog, however, at certain intervals of the day, is brought to where the body is lying, but whether with any belief that it will indicate whether life be really extinct, or as the symbol of the destroyer of the sensual passions, avarice and pride, it is impossible to say. A brazier filled with sandal-wood, frankincense, and other aromatic substances is then kindled in the room, this being solely based upon reasons of sanitation, which is a guiding principle of all these special funeral rites. Meanwhile a priest sits beside the flame and recites portions of the Zend Avesta till the body is removed, which *must* be done in full daylight.

About an hour before the time fixed for the removal of the body to the tower, two corpse-bearers, clad in pure white, come to the house. They bring with them an iron bier, called *gehan*, on which to carry the corpse, and it is a curious fact that every detail of a Parsee funeral must be done by people in couples. Even the mourners must come in pairs, and walk holding a white handkerchief, or *painand*, between them, the idea being that mutual assistance and consolation is derived from company. After certain offices have again been said, the friends and relations take a last look at the deceased, and the procession sets out. The mourners are enjoined to walk at least thirty paces behind the bier, and the men must be clothed in white.

The Bombay towers occupy the loveliest site on the very crest of the Malabar Hill, commanding a marvellous bird's-eye view of the great busy city, with its tall factory chimneys, its streets, churches, and public buildings, while southward lies the open sea of sapphire blue. There are five towers, the oldest of them having been built in 1669, and the newest only a few years back. They are surrounded by all the gorgeous luxuriance of splendidly kept tropical vegetation, and flaming crotons in their metallic glories of gold and bronze, purple and crimson, lovely waxy oleanders, pink and white, and feathery palms; and the simple structures themselves would not attract much notice, perhaps, but for what Professor Monier Williams has aptly described as "an extraordinary coping, which instantly attracts and fascinates the gaze. It is a coping formed, not of dead stone, but of living vultures. These birds, on the occasion of my visit, had settled themselves side by side in perfect order, and in a

A TOWER OF SILENCE, BOMBAY.

complete circle, around the parapets of the towers, with their heads pointed inwards; and so lazily did they sit there, and so motionless was their whole mien, that, except for their colour, they might have been carved out of the stone-work." But with the exception of the corpse-bearers, who form a class apart, none may see more. Even the priest may not approach within thirty yards; and the body, according to the directions of the Zend Avesta, is carried in naked, and laid upon clay bricks, stone, and mortar. What the formation is we know from official description, and this I give in the words that were furnished to me.

"The circular platform inside the tower, about three hundred feet in circumference, is entirely paved with large stone slabs well cemented, and divided into three rows of shallow open receptacles, corresponding with the three moral precepts of the Zoroastrian religion—'good deeds,' 'good words,' 'good thoughts.'

"First row for corpses of males.

"Second row for corpses of females.

"Third row for corpses of children.

"Footpaths for corpse-bearers to move about.

A deep central well in the tower, about 150 feet in circumference (the sides and bottom of which are also paved with stone slabs), is used for depositing the dry bones. The corpse is completely stripped of its flesh by vultures within an hour or two, and the bones of the denuded skeleton, when perfectly dried up by atmospheric influences and the powerful heat of the tropical sun, are thrown into this well, where they gradually crumble to dust, chiefly consisting of lime and phosphorus. Thus the rich and the poor meet together on one level of equality after death.

"There are holes in the inner sides of the well through which the rain-water is carried into four underground drains at the base of the tower. These drains are connected with four underground wells, the bottoms of which are covered with a thick layer of sand. Pieces of charcoal and sandstone are also placed at the end of each drain, which are renewed from time to time. These double sets of filters are provided for purifying the rain-water passing over the bones, before it enters the ground—thus observing one of the tenets of the Zoroastrian religion that 'The mother earth shall not be defiled.'"

To Western ideas the system seems repugnant, and yet the most prejudiced leaves with a feeling that nothing to be seen outrages in any way the dignity and solemnity of death. There is nothing at all revolting or repulsive in the quiet scene, and the ill-favoured birds are merely performing nature's purpose in nature's own manner. They nest within the grounds, and scarcely ever take a circling flight of wider sweep than that enclosed within the boundary walls.

A Parsee woman's prayers are sixfold. While she is a girl she is taught that she may ask for a good and a worthy husband—no unfitting thing surely, even though a European mother might forbid it among that "little hoard of maxims preaching down a daughter's heart"—and on engagement she asks to be permitted to retain her husband's full love, confidence, and respect. On marriage she beseeches the inestimable joy of maternity, and at the prospect of this her prayers are for safe delivery, to which she couples a formula begging that the child may be naturally intelligent, healthy, strong, one that shall grow up to lead a virtuous life, able to enter into the deliberations of men, and "one that shall add to the glory of his family, to the glory of his street, to the glory of his city, and to the glory of his country." Lastly, her prayer is for milk at her breasts to nurse her child, for a woman who is unequal in this respect is, according to Zoroastrian tenets, to be classed as a maternal failure, who has not done her duty in preserving the purity of her own and her husband's race.

All these facts bear upon the Parsee doctrines as to the future state, in which for the first three days after dissolution the woman's soul remains within the limits of this world in the care of the angel Srosh, but on the third night it goes to the gates of the Great Bridge. There stands the grim judge, Meher, with the angels Astad and Rashné, who symbolize Truth and Justice. Meher weighs the actions good and bad against one another in his scales, and the woman who can throw in obedience to her husband, and the meritorious act of having thrice daily experienced the desire to be one with him in thoughts, words, and deeds, has a heavy weight of virtue to cast on the side of her own advantage. For if the good deeds outweigh the evil ones, even by the smallest particle, the soul may cross the bridge to the paradise beyond; but if the balance is on the other side, the erring soul is hurled into the yawning abyss of hell below. For those whose virtues and vices make a perfectly level scale, there is a place called Hamast Gehan, which appears to offer a refuge for all too bad for heaven and too good for hell.

Nothing, I think, is a more impressive evidence of the immense diversity of racial modes of thought and custom than the variations in burial rites. The conditions of soil and atmosphere, important considerations in the disposal of the dead, are common to all, yet each great race, nay, rather each tribe, caste, and subsect, has observances peculiar to itself. So far, English rule has been to allow all liberty and freedom in matters of domestic habit, and the result has been that the Hindu has not interfered with the Parsee, the

Mahommedan has not troubled the non-Aryan, and all has worked well. How long this will continue, if every officious busybody who scampers across in three weeks from Bombay to Calcutta is permitted to dictate what he (or, worse, she) thinks should be done, it would be rash to predict. In following the Indian woman's life along its successive stages and concerns, I have tried to show that its present conditions are the result of countless generations of hereditary influences, and that the separate elements which go to form the vast empire are only to be welded together by the most judicious handling. The policy of interference and innovation only introduces further items of discord which, under the existing order, it should be our utmost care to avoid.

We bestow a great deal of pity upon the Indian woman. We might give it where it would be more useful and more appreciated. The tone we have adopted towards her and her prejudices, customs, and theories of life, derived, be it remembered, from a civilization that was old when our own began, has savoured too much of patronage, and a forgetfulness of that eternal truth, *Ce que femme veut, Dieu le veut.* She has now before her all the possibilities of education, though truly she shows no exuberant enthusiasm to accept them. Having laid these within her easy reach, let us now leave the situation to its own development, helping, as with medical aid, to those things which without us she could not enjoy, but not forcing upon diverse races and peoples one stock pattern of conventional European ideas. It will be, perhaps, to some a lamentable suggestion of non-progressiveness to venture to remind the rough and ready exponents of new methods, new views, new woman, and much more that is rash and crude, that social systems which have endured through the centuries, and survived in face of political revolutions and changes, cannot be without recommendations to their particular needs and environments, even though the Western mind fails to grasp what these may be. It is part of the charter by which we rule India that private freedom in matters of faith and conscience shall be fully respected, and we are only fulfilling this while we recognize that any demands for change in the domestic conditions of the people must come from within, rather than forcing upon them artificial reforms from without.

THE MARCHIONESS OF LANSDOWNE, C.I.

CHAPTER XIII.

ANGLO-INDIAN SOCIETY.

"It is silly to imagine it possible to save India without having anything to do with natives, without native troops, and with contempt for all national prejudices and feelings."—VISCOUNTESS CANNING.

"NOT quite *Truth*, but something Simla," is said to have been a smart Anglo-Indian criticism of certain Plain Tales, and the same might be said of a good many of the efforts that have been made to depict society as it is in India. In its broad outlines, it is after all very much as it is here. Hard work under enervating conditions may make play when it comes a little more exuberant than with ourselves; little social shortcomings are perhaps more leniently dealt with where each has a kind of feeling of fraternity among aliens; a few nice old-fashioned prejudices as to the correct line of demarcation between friendliness and flirtation with the sexes are perhaps ignored, but on the whole, the presidency towns would not come off so very badly in the statistics of comparative morality with London, Edinburgh, or Dublin, nor would hill stations look very bad beside an average season at Brighton or on the moors.

In India one may belong to the official or non-official set, but one is nowhere unless one can visit at Government House. Officially, therefore, society is guided precisely as it is at the Court of St. James's, and the ladies who represent the Queen in the East may be very well trusted to maintain all the traditions and conventions which the majority of well-bred people have no desire to see overthrown.

If I were an old Anglo-Indian I should begin with a lament over the more middle-class wave that has come across society since competitive examination swept aside the

THE THRONE ROOM, GOVERNMENT HOUSE, CALCUTTA.

privileges of birth or association. But I am not this, and I am recording simply a few impressions, chief among which perhaps is that I am certain, in the palmiest and most renowned of John Company's days, India enjoyed no more cultured and sympathetic administrators than those who now fill the highest positions. For the affection and the prestige that the British raj enjoys in the East, far more credit is due to the individual men and women who have carried out the loftiest conceptions of English truth, virtue, and gentleness, than to the collective wisdom of the office in Downing Street.

This book professes only to deal with women, so that I am under no obligations to discuss the whys and wherefores of recent policy shown by Lord Lansdowne, Lord Wenlock,

THE DINING-ROOM, GOVERNMENT HOUSE, CALCUTTA.

and Lord Harris. Lord and Lady Elgin only took up the reins of office a few days before I left Bombay and India altogether, and beyond formal presentation to them at the great evening party given by Lord and Lady Harris in honour of their arrival, I know nothing personally of them. But to follow the Marchioness of Lansdowne as the leader of society in India is a course of difficulty from which the most finished woman of the world might well shrink. The Marchioness of Dufferin and Ava, gracious and gentle and considerate, yet withal so regal and so essentially the *grande dame de la haute politique*, had won every heart by her sweet sympathy, and had maintained a stately dignity impressive alike to natives and English. The example was a splendid one, but to come worthily after it was what few women could have done. The Marchioness of Lansdowne was, however, one of the very few able not merely to do as well as her predecessor, but to do it in her own individual way.

Like Lady Dufferin, Lady Lansdowne came to her position of vicereine with an already immense previous experience of official life, and a certain knowledge already acquired of Indian affairs from the fact that Lord Lansdowne had held office as Under Secretary of State for India. Lady Elgin does not enjoy the advantages that come from a long and varied association with foreign governments and colonial bureaux, and in dealing with races so diverse as those which go to make up the Indian Empire, this deficiency must be a serious handicap that no amount of good intention can quite overcome.

The hospitality of the government houses of the three Presidency towns is proverbial, and the fortunate stranger who brings out a sufficient personal introduction is assured of a pleasant reception. Invitations to dinners, balls, or receptions, are of course issued by the aides-de-camp in waiting, and the drawing-room cards pass through the hands of the military secretary, who is therefore a kind of minor lord chamberlain. Lord William Beresford had filled this onerous post with tact as well as firmness, and bitter, very bitter were the regrets at his departure. Colonel Durand, of Gilgit and Nilt celebrity, however, succeeded him, and as he comes of a family who have contributed no small part to the making of Indian history, as well as enjoying a great social repute, there was a small crumb of consolation in the matter. The calling hours at Calcutta are peculiar, and are rigidly fixed between twelve and two, during which time the "book" lies upon the hall table, and the names of those entitled to the privilege of placing them there must be set down at the

THE DRAWING-ROOM, GOVERNMENT HOUSE, CALCUTTA.

beginning cf the season, and after a dinner or dance. The etiquette of a vicereine's drawing-room, which takes place in the throne-room, is precisely similar to that observed for presentation to the Queen, with the exception that court trains are not worn.

For home life, in the narrower sense of the word, a vicereine has but little time, and Lady Lansdowne's great popularity seldom allowed her an afternoon free from bazaar or exhibition opening, prize distribution or hospital inspection. She tells of a funny experience that she had in this last connection, when she went to visit a large institution for *purdah* women in Southern India. She was a little surprised at first to see every bed occupied, while apparent

THE BALL ROOM, GOVERNMENT HOUSE, CALCUTTA.

patients were squatting on mats on the floor. On closer inspection she saw that there did not appear much the matter with any of them, and asked why so many were under treatment. It was then explained that the women had come, hearing of her intended visit, telling the most piteous tales of non-existing maladies and sufferings, simply that they might enjoy a sight of the great lady whose name they held in affection, and perhaps some wondering awe. The authorities of the institution lent themselves to the little fraud to show that any who entered the hospital would be treated well, and a good deal of prejudice was thus met.

It did not fall to Lady Lansdowne's lot to initiate a great movement as Lady Dufferin did, but I am not sure that the task which devolved upon her was a less difficult one. For she took the scheme of medical aid into her hands at a critical moment, and under circumstances at which wreck and disaster would have followed any error of judgment, while she had also to formulate those alterations of detail which only the experience gained in actual working could suggest. The whole question, however, of medical aid for the Indian women occupied close attention on her part, and I have good reason for knowing that her interest in the subject has not ceased with her departure from the East. There was no phase of philanthropic work, whether missionary or educational, with which she was not familiar, and did not know with more than a superficial acquaintance. It was not enough for her to formally "visit" an institution or school, but she would go into the details of its management, and seldom left without making a really useful or practical suggestion.

As a hostess her tact and grace were unbounded, and under her *régime* it was a pleasure as well as an honour to dine at Government House. As a type of the aristocratic society woman she was perfect, but no less decisively could this word be employed concerning the two other great ladies of the dependency in their respective and differing directions. Lady Wenlock at Madras represents the poetic and artistic order in the trio, but it is only very few who are privileged to hear the sweet verse into which she has poured her heart with feeling, made the deeper by the constant ill-health which often precludes her presiding over the stately dinners and

THE LADY WENLOCK, C.I.

dances of Guindy or the banqueting hall—the handsome

annexe to Government House, Madras. Of her talent in painting she is less chary in revealing herself, and once or twice she has exhibited her strong and unconventional work at the smaller shows in London. She has caught, as few ever can, the subtle charm of the brief after-glow of an Indian sunset, and has read aright the mystery of the heat-

GOVERNMENT HOUSE, MADRAS.

hazy landscape, where perhaps others would only have seen a few straggling palms and a common-place village tank.

Very thoughtful for others, very ready to encourage well-directed charity, Lady Wenlock is popular throughout the southernmost Presidency, though her tastes in the directions of art and literature are hardly those to commend her to the more rollicking ideas of enjoyment which generally obtain upon a hill station. There are not many in India to give this little leavening to it, and perhaps it will not be among the least of her claims to a social remembrance when she returns to England.

Lastly, the perfect embodiment of the bright, cheery, natural, English country gentlewoman is Lady Harris. Native society could not, and even now does not, understand her complete absence of formality, which would stop her

GOVERNMENT HOUSE, GUINDY.

carriage in the bazaar to talk to a couple of poor children, could speak kindly to her servants, and show a personal interest in her *ménage* and horses. But they have learnt to recognize that she is gifted with a singular depth of sympathy as well as a remarkable fund of downright common sense. She will spend days of real exertion organizing simple theatricals to give pleasure to *purdah* ladies, whom she frequently invites to Government House; but if any ill-advised enthusiast comes to her with a mission to teach the

THE LADY HARRIS, C.I.

same ladies the elements of biology, or to recommend them to become lady journalists, she has a most beautifully chilling method of throwing critical cold water down. She is one of the best and wisest friends that the cause of female education has ever had in India, though she does not write articles for magazines or make speeches on the subject, for she has seen that it by no means follows that what is the perfect code for the Western girl is of necessity to be slavishly followed for her of the East. Just as Lord Harris has done far more for the Indian boy in introducing him to cricket, as a much more healthy form of amusement than gambling for pice in a sordid back court, than half the noisy agitators who have led him to wear English dress and seek an English wife, so has Lady Harris, by lending her influence to diffusing general and useful knowledge among the girls, rather than encouraging a handful from among them to effect a few showy sensations in the examination rooms, helped to lay a much more solid foundation for future results than those who do not know how quietly she works are ready to believe.

She is a keen sportswoman, a fearless cross-country rider, and one of the best cricketers of her sex to be met. European society in Bombay, though it is surprised sometimes that she is not more fettered by forms and ceremony, is devoted to her; and the girls, who often find themselves in India as of small importance beside the young married women, are never overlooked by her. She is an artist of considerable skill, and has a very neat turn for writing pungent *vers de societé*. Of her thoughtful tact I may mention in this connection one little episode. She was writing a few of these "up to," as they say in illustrated journalism, some clever pictures to be sold in the "post office" of her annual fancy fair, on behalf of one or other of the Bombay charities. A momentary loss for a happy rhyme led one in the group to suggest a line in which the word "nigger" occurred.

"That will not do," she said decisively. "It is a word we never employ at Government House."

And here I strike off at a tangent to the really interesting aspect of the position of the European community towards the natives by whom it is surrounded. As long as one remain in the uppermost administrative circles, with governors, lieutenant-governors, residents, high-court judges, commanding officers, and district superintendents of police, all is well. The educated native, holding, it may be, some high civil appointment, and able by manners and breeding (for a native gentleman does exist, and not very rarely either) to conform to the usages of society, is made welcome, treated with courtesy, which it does not lower the proud ruling race to show, and there is a kindly consideration evinced towards what we may regard as mere caste prejudices, but which to him are matters of religious life or death. Shopkeepers, servants, lower native officials, are spoken to with civility, and not summoned by some opprobrious nickname of abuse. The natural good manners, in short, of the English gentleman or gentlewoman, which are extended at home to any inoffensive fellow-citizen, whether he be cabman, or costermonger, or shop-assistant, not to mention social equals, are not wholly forgotten, and one owns on seeing it to the little thrill of satisfaction as to the invariable *savoir faire* of well-bred people.

It is a satisfaction, however, that does not last if one steps down to the average middle-class Briton filling subordinate posts in the departments of the State, and as a rule, though I know many exceptions here, the mercantile order, with the large aggregate who have come out to take posts as machinists, foremen, managers in the vast factories springing up on all hands. Little Mrs. Drye-Goodes, whose heart is yearning for the joys of the Peckham masonic ball, and whose drawing-room is decked with the fourpenny-halfpenny fans and the "art furniture" of Westbourne Grove, to whom the story of India is not of half the interest of a quarrel between two families in the street at home that she left, tells one with a giggle that "she hates these beastly niggers," and thinks it something commendable to add, "we don't let any of them come to our club." She cuts her servants' wages down to the last anna piece, and if she ascertains that they have not let her benefit to the uttermost pice of their bazaar bargainings, storms at them as pick-pockets, and launches forth on the thievish propensities of the dependency. Early and late they must be at the beck and call of her sharp tongue, and if she dares she will call her cane into requisition.

To try to learn something of the inner mysteries of the life around them, to collect the queer artistic trifles that every district has of its own, to ascertain the conditions of labour around them—it would seem to such people an evidence of a wholly unaccountable aberration of mind to be interested in such things. It would be regrettable if this detestable insular "side" only had the effect of making them personally disliked in their neighbourhoods, but it has a further effect than that. It tends to discredit the English reputation, and with peoples of the Oriental temperament, to whom flowery courtesy is one of the fine arts of existence, it is bitterly resented at heart. Mrs. Drye-Goodes thinks no doubt that she has effectively admonished her bearer when for some small offence she hisses out the hateful word *sowar* (pig), but he does not forget, and it may be the spark that kindles not his own only, but his tribe's hatred for the over-bearing and altogether unnecessarily insulting demeanour adopted concerning them.

It is not a pretty phase of English manners towards inferiors, but I think few grasp how obnoxiously ill-bred such people can and do show themselves to those who are their social equals. In Bombay one may sometimes hear of a "scene" that disturbed its social circles considerably in Lord and Lady Reay's period of office. It was a big dinner at Government House, and a certain English "lady" was introduced by the aide-de-camp to a much-respected Mahommedan high court judge—a gentleman, be it said, of the highest intelligence and learning, and well known throughout India. The English female showed him not the slightest recognition, but turned to the aide-de-camp and said excitedly, "You don't suppose I'm going in to dinner with a native?" The aide-de-camp quietly said that it had been her Excellency's pleasure thus to assign her, whereat she said, "Then the list must be altered, or I leave." There was some further talk, the irate dame insisting that her grievance should be referred to Lady Reay direct; but she, wise as well as dignified, properly refused to allow ill-breeding to dictate to her, and the insulted one therefore took her offended self away.

The people of whose sympathies this pleasant tale is completely characteristic have a funny little cant excuse which they repeat till one first grows weary of it, and afterwards laughs at. It is always said quite gravely, and as they think is crushingly convincing. "They don't let us know their wives. And until they do that we really must, you know, decline to admit them to society." One softly suggests that their present *purdah* customs are the result of some centuries, and ventures to ask what special effort towards civility the ladies who are volubly assuring one of the "impossibility" of showing courtesy towards native neighbours have ever attempted. "Oh, let them come out and call on us, and let us take our husbands to see them!" say these summary reformers; and it would be comic if it were not sad. For this is the comprehension shown of the characters and peoples over whom our sway is one of moral influence rather than physical force!

No one dared to say it in the recent anxieties concerning the tree-smearing in Behar, but the province contains a more than average proportion of the planting and non-official element, and knowing how objectionable this can be in its dealings with the natives, I have very little doubt that the mysterious marks were a sign of the angry resentment felt towards the alien race. Had the smouldering spark broken out into open flame, British bad manners and want of generous treatment would have been responsible for very much.

The attitude is not a new one. Viscountess Canning, in those shrewd, sympathetic, far-seeing letters contained in "The Story of Two Noble Lives," makes many references to it, especially deploring the ignorance and prejudice of the Anglo-Indian Press, which then embodied the middle-class sentiments far more than it now does, and when all were demanding mere blind cruel revenge for the atrocities of the mutiny, she was, with her husband, among the few who could show a sane judgment and write, "Strict stern justice, we all agree, is a *necessity*, but I cannot see the wisdom or righteousness of injustice, and these rules* were only to prevent very various punishments and cases of injustice. I do not think the objects of 'Canning's Clemency' will very much delight in it; it is not at all in the style of mercy, and

* Ordering civilians not to execute summary punishment upon Sepoys, taken unarmed, but to hand them over to the military authorities, and for checking the burning of villages.

very like the hardest and strictest justice. People here would like every Sepoy to be hanged at least, whether for his deeds or for his thoughts. If one mildly observes that the men at Barrackpore, who have never been out of our sight, did not share in the massacres five or six hundred miles off, people say, 'Oh, but in their hearts they approved and would like to do the same by us!' That is the sort of speech one often hears." And, I may add, is precisely the line of defence for dislike that is still adopted!

One is inclined to ask who or what is responsible for the bad form shown in this direction by middle-class and minor society in India. It is certainly not in imitation of their betters, whose conduct in the matter is perfect, but while it exists it is a little inconsistent to hear them blaming caste because this interferes with the bearer undertaking the cook's work. The fact did not escape Mr. Clement Scott, in his rapid scamper across the dependency, who speaks with pardonable sarcasm and warmth about it. "These highly educated, extremely intelligent Parsee ladies and gentlemen constitute the race," he remarks, "whose lavish hospitality is accepted by Europeans, but by some mysterious unsigned order must never be returned. Thus, you may play cricket with a Parsee gentleman, but you must not bring him back to dinner. You may attend the *soirée* of a Parsee lady, but you may not ask her to drink tea at sunset on the terrace of the Bombay Yacht Club. You may beg for subscriptions from a Parsee capitalist to start a gymnasium, but it is etiquette to turn his children from the doors. You may meet the *élite* of Parsee society at the Government House reception on Malabar Hill, but if you asked exactly the same people to your breakfast-table you would be cut by English society." The only qualification to be made concerning this latter sentence is, "English society of sorts." I am glad to be able to say that in the English society it was mostly my good fortune to keep, native ladies and gentlemen associated on equal terms, but the existence of the other aspect is none the less a fact, and is often bitterly commented upon by those whose pedigrees may go back to nobles loyal to the British crown under Clive and Hastings, when the forebears of the insolent and arrogant snobs who snub them were probably sweeping warehouses or packing parcels.

I have tried hard to understand the cause of complaint against the native, for it is always instructive to know how the mental altitude of others has been reached. The conclusion that I have come to is that it largely rests upon the differing standpoint from which the two races view dancing. The native, as we know, fails to see why he should exert himself in this direction, when he can pay others to do it for him, and the professional ladies who accept a wage for their performances are not, as a rule, exponents of the most elevated codes of feminine morality. Being aware that this view obtains, Western people are secretly a little humiliated in their innermost selves at the ideas that they know that dancing suggests to the native mind. I know instances, indeed, in which tickets have been refused to native gentlemen for charitable entertainments in which skirt dancing has been in the programme, on account of the different light in which it is regarded by performer and spectator. Thereupon Mrs. Drye-Goodes and her class blaze up at the "disgusting tone" of prevailing native opinion round her, quite oblivious of the fact that this with equal warmth feels that the "tone" of women who dance in public leaves something to be desired. This is the most tangible grievance, ludicrous as it is, that I have been able to discover, for the others are merely shadowy abstractions and vague expressions of dislike.

Incidental reference has been made to the Anglo-Indian Press, and this, from my own journalistic associations, was a source of considerable interest to me. Of the general tone and stamp of the half-dozen or so great papers of the dependency, the *Pioneer*, the *Statesman*, the *Englishman*, the *Indian Daily News*, the *Times of India*, the *Bombay Gazette*, the *Madras Mail*, the *Madras Times*, and the *Morning Post* of Allahabad, it is impossible to speak too highly. Their politics differ widely, but each in their several directions loyally supports the crown primarily, though the details of how they do so vary according to conservative or liberal tendencies. I use the word "liberal" advisedly, for rampant radicalism soon tones down in India, and, with the exception of a few publications of small moment and chiefly circulating among "advanced" natives, this phase of politics has very scant journalistic countenance. One finds perfectly fair examination of native views and opinions, and no effort is made to belittle their claims socially or politically. In fact, in the matter of even-handed justice and impartiality, I think the leaders of the Indian press stand very well beside their *confrères* at home. The papers are well edited, well turned out, and are enterprising as to new fields of interest.

Only in one or two cases is the language degraded and our prestige as rulers lowered. In one instance it is through a so-called "comic" weekly publication, which in vulgar impudence and blackguardly obscenity would not be tolerated under Lord Campbell's Act. In the other it is a professedly "religious" organ, which seems to have been called into existence by a desire to show to any natives who may take it up how irreligious all English professing Christians are. Will it be credited that in its columns, the usual courtesy prefix to the names of gentlemen who are members of Council is invariably written in inverted commas, as the "Honourable" Mr. ——; that such objectionable remarks about Lady Harris were made in it as to compel Lord Harris to demand, and obtain, a public apology; that the occasion of unveiling Sir George Birdwood's statue in Bombay was made the excuse for penning one of the most blasphemous libels ever composed upon a public man; and that if an unfortunate missionary reciprocates much kindly hospitality by asking a few friends to his bungalow, and allows his guests a mild "peg" before leaving, he is held up to obloquy by name and accused of carrying on drunken orgies? Such mischievous and scandalous prints are not calculated to command respect for ourselves.

Women, who rarely in the East find the same amount of interest and occupation for their lives as their fathers or husbands, are wont to complain of its tedium and monotony. Even the active aspect of housekeeping is lessened by the fact that the hausfrau herself can take so little real part in it, after giving directions and checking accounts. Long custom has decreed that all marketing and almost all ordering and shopping shall be done by the servants, whose assumption of extreme dignity of demeanour makes the youthful mistress feel herself to be lessening her own importance in their eyes if she exercises too close a personal supervision in minor details. Anglo-Indian hostesses often make loud lamentation about the laziness and incompetency of their servants, but I imagine that the majority of them on their return must think regretfully of the deft, obliging, willing, resourceful fellows they have left behind, and must find marked difference in the attention and quality of the service they can command at home. It is only a really energetic character, in fact, that does not become demoralized into flabbiness and inertia under the combined influences of heat, laziness, and servants at command.

The first sign of deterioration is when a woman omits her corsets from her toilette, and begins lolling about in a sloppy and tumbled tea-gown in the mornings. Then the downward course is rapid, and she soon joins that large army of her sisters in the East, who, save "for company," or in calling hours, or when she goes out, is never to be found trim and neat. If the habit is once permitted to begin, it will develop other forms of laxity, and the slackness and indolence that characterizes so many Anglo-Indian women will become a second nature, requiring all the awakening that busy English folks can give it.

It is not of course those who live in the Presidency or larger cities upon whose hands time hangs heavy. There they have society of their own order, be this middle-class or more exalted; they have theatricals, amateur and professional at intervals, flower-shows, races, balls, and dinners, no less than at home. In the season they go to the hills, and picnics, lawn-tennis, riding, and outdoor amusement they can enjoy to any extent. The less fortunate ones are they who by appointment or necessity must live in up-country stations or the minor towns. Here, where European society is limited perhaps to two or three families, diversion and society is not much varied, and unless a woman can develop some strong interest in art, archæology, botany, or natural history, the days may seem unutterably long. This is the duller side of Indian life, which fills the homeward-bound steamers with dissatisfied, peevish creatures, who have not had the courage or the ability to find out how to make it, if not a gay and lively, at least an interesting existence. These, however, form the class that would shriek the loudest at the idea of cultivating the confidence and friendship of their native women neighbours.

It is said by those who remember the India of some four or five decades back, that hospitality is waning, and that the splendid generosity which used to impress English travellers so strongly is rarely met with now. But the diminished rupee accounts for much, and, however sociable instincts may be, it is surely impossible to gratify them when the rate of exchange is at a fraction over a shilling and a penny. Then, too, the cheapness and facility of travel sends out increasing numbers of the "T. G." element, as the *argot* of official Calcutta designates the "travelling gents" of a cold-season trip; and even the most hospitably inclined limits his or her welcome after a long course of experiences of friends' friends. But for all this, the kind, warm-hearted spirit exists still, even if it cannot show itself in some of the extravagantly lavish forms of bygone days, and the moment that it becomes recognized that one has any good reason for being in India, the help and the invitations that one receives claim gratitude that it is difficult to put into words. Even the possibility of entertaining unawares another "Padgett, M.P.," does not seem to act as any deterrent to a gracious reception. As to the friendly lunches and dinners that I used to be invited to at the coast ports, and the pleasant drives to places and people that I used to find arranged for me within a few minutes even of the ship's having dropped anchor, I can only tell those who did so much for me that I shall always remember gratefully their considerate attention.

The strictness of etiquette as to precedence in Anglo-Indian society always excites the cheap derision of those who want to pose on their return as smart observers, who fail to see that this has a perfectly sound reason. In official circles, as we all know, the order is all carefully laid down, and money or display gives no advantage. There is in Indian society so enormous a preponderance of the strictly military and official element, that possibly to the outsider, who at home does not care whether Mr. A. or Mr. B. goes in to dinner before him, since neither can claim a social precedence of the other, it may appear that the rigid Eastern code is often a mere affectation. But this it is not, and by making its observance an unswerving law, it not only keeps a continual object lesson as to each one's true position with regard to administrative discipline before his eyes, but is, in the long run, the best safeguard against personal jealousies and piques.

It is the outsider, however, who magnifies any trifling weaknesses and foibles. In itself, Anglo-Indian Society is satisfied with things as they are, and enjoys life in its own fashion with vigour and zest. And in truth, if the generosity and good feeling evinced towards our native fellow-subjects in its upper ranks were displayed in the lower ones, the Englishman or woman out from home would find very little that is unworthy of our jealously maintained British traditions.

CHAPTER XIV.

NOTES ON TRAVELLING AND OUTFIT.

"Beware of sudden change in any great point of diet, and if necessity enforce it, fit the rest to it; for it is a secret both in nature and state that it is safer to change many things than one. . . . As for the passions and studies of the mind, avoid envy, anxious fears, anger, fretting inwards, subtle and knotty inquisitions, joys and exhilarations in excess, sadness not communicated. Entertain hopes, mirth rather than joy, variety of delights rather than surfeit of them, wonder and admiration, and therefore novelties; studies that fill the mind with splendid and illustrious objects as histories, fables, and contemplations of nature."—LORD BACON.

WHEN I left England, I was under editorial instructions to take the journeys from Madras to Calcutta, and Bombay to Colombo turning homewards, by coasting steamers, in order that I might see as much as possible of the average woman's life in the working and mercantile classes in the comparatively rarely visited commercial cities of the Coromandel and Malabar shores. It was therefore deemed advisable by my editor and myself that I should do the whole of my sea travelling by one company's fleet, and of course there was little choice then left in the matter, as it is only by the British India Steam Navigation Company that such a programme could be carried out. The advantages of such a course to a rapidly moving tourist are obvious. One has reliable addresses for home letters to be sent to; one can dispense with or pick up baggage at convenience with security; and by no means least in importance is the knowledge that through a company to whom one is well known, an English bank-note or cheque is readily cashed by them. The majority of travellers take circular notes; I took, however, a sufficiency of gold for immediate uses, and had notes sent out later. This not very orthodox plan served me, nevertheless, very well.

As to the comfort and delight of travelling by the "B. I.," as one soon learns to call it, I have no words too good. It may be unsociable, but I think it is possible to have too many passengers on board a ship. Now, with the "B. I." none of its vessels afford first-class accommodation for more than seventy-five to ninety voyagers. The tonnage of their London-Calcutta boats ranges from 4800 to 6200, so that with no more than this number the deck and saloon are never overcrowded. I went out on the *Golconda,* which has the reputation of being the absolutely steadiest ship on the whole Eastern carrying service, and I would say at the outset that she bore out her good character; but she only is the wise woman at sea who has set her cabin in order while the vessel is still in the river. When all one's small arrangements are made, then is the time both to look round at fellow-passengers and to examine what will be one's floating home for between three and four weeks to come.

I travelled direct to Trincomalie, which would be one of the "show places" of the world were it only a little more easy of access, and to enter its harbour by sunrise is one of the sights to remember in one's life. Save naval men, so few know it, that I can never forbear speaking of its beauties; and though so little is heard about it in our times of calm and quiet, it is really one of the places on which, to paraphrase a sentence from the Articles of War, "under the good Providence of God, our Wealth, Prosperity, and Peace depend." For it is the great naval store and depot of the whole of the East Indies Station, and to it come for refitting, repairing, and recommissioning those ships of the command which range the seas from Rangoon to Rodriguez, from the Mauritius to Zanzibar.

The glinting rays from Foul Point Lighthouse were still shooting out in the grey haze of dawn when I came up on deck, and there stretched out a long promontory of low, sandy waste. Presently Fort Ostenburg could be discerned, but so far the entrance to the harbour seemed invisible, or else barred by several rugged-looking islets upon which the surf was beating. Then, after a few minutes' delay, while the native pilot came on board, and under a glorious morning glow of amber and rose, the narrow passage had opened out, and we were swinging into what Tennent, the historian of Ceylon, has called "the magnificent basin of Trincomalie, which, in extent, security, and beauty, is unsurpassed by any haven in the world." Standing boldly up in the steep height of brown laterite rock upon which Fort Ostenburg is situated, the lavish profusion of tropical vegetation, which grows down to the very water's edge, conceals not only its stony formation, but one of the most powerful fortifications belonging to the British crown. Under these gorgeous flowering trees and feathery palms are hidden masked batteries, with all their grim armament, while mines under water protect every yard of possible approach. Each revolution of the screw reveals, however, a fresh beauty, whether it be the beautifully kept grounds of the naval yard, the white outlines of Admiralty House, surrounded as it is with a perfect park of exotic greenery, the trim barracks with their red-tiled roofs, or the shore itself with its gaily turbaned and draped crowds of Tamils and Cinhalese grouped around their native boats.

Here I stayed a few weeks, making pleasant excursions in Eastern Ceylon, and I left it for Madras in the *Nuddea,* under Captain Cave. We enjoyed a pleasant interval at Negapatam, which is a growing port of commerce at the present time, and it is said, indeed, that as much passes across its wharves as at Madras itself. It has little, however, to show of sight-seeing, or in educational or mission work, save by the Roman

THE LOCAL HANSOM, NEGAPATAM.

Catholics, who all along the coast of the Presidency are very active. Curiously impressive was it to see the funeral procession of a little baptized infant, with its banners and emblems of the Roman Church, and chanting to strident Tamil words the old air "Adeste Fideles," while an attendant crowd of scantily clad natives followed behind. It is a place of long sunny streets and picturesque groups, though its modes of locomotion are limited, as may be judged from a snapshot of a jutka, which has to fill the position of the local hansom cab.

Quiet steaming during the dark but peaceful night brought the *Nuddea* next morning to Cuddalore, a place of real interest to all students of history from its association with Clive's earlier fighting, but it involved all the energy for sight-seeing that one possessed to face going through the heavy surf to be seen rolling in over the bar that lay between the ship and the shore. Captain Cave had promised me the use of his gig for the trip, but the sea-going wiseacres of

A CARGO LIGHTER, CUDDALORE.

the port assured him that a cargo lighter would be safer, which I realized was probably the case when a bigger roll than usual sent me and my camera down into the bottom of the boat. It is a strange old-world little place, with a church that reminds one of some of those of East Anglia, and round it are memorials to many who acted under "John Company," whose services are commemorated in quaintly old-fashioned terms upon fast perishing slabs of soft stone. Cuddalore was an important centre in the old Company's work, and up to very lately several of the aged pensioners who were in receipt of its always generous bounty continued to live there.

My passage onwards from Madras was taken on the *Khandalla*, commanded by Captain Kendall, after which port of call Coconada is the first, in itself almost like a Dutch city in the busy bustle at the juncture of the canal which has been brought down from the Godavari river. Then comes Vizagapatam, offering the first really pretty bit of scenery on the East coast. It lies under a bold rock, known as the

MADRAS FROM THE SEA.

Jarada Hill, 1174 feet high, which slopes gradually towards the sea, and terminates abruptly to the northward in the Dolphin's Nose, a bluff headland with a masonry tower and flagstaff on its summit, and several houses on its north side. Certainly, under the cloud-flecked sky of a delightfully crisp, fresh November morning, the place is one of the most charming one could wish to see, with the quaint old Dutch House now converted into offices, the old military cantonment that dates from East India

Company's days, and the white buildings of the fine schools and convent maintained here by the Roman Catholics for mission purposes, while away under the Jarada Hill can be distinguished the mouth of the Maonderu, a small river which drains the high land district. The exigencies of commerce did not detain us here for more than three hours, and so I did not land; but at Bimlipatam, the next port, which we reached at noon, I did, going, as at Cuddalore, in one of the big flat-bottomed cargo-boats.

A RUSH FOR CARGO AT VIZAGAPATAM—A VIEW TAKEN DOWNWARDS FROM THE BRIDGE.

A curious feature of all these craft on the Coromandel coast is that they have not got a nail about them. They are all built of some soft and elastic jungle wood which is stitched together with a vast amount of strong twine, and the result is that they can go through the heavy surf which sets into almost all this shore far more safely than a less yielding structure could do. I found very little of interest at Bimlipatam, save a small native toddy or drink-shop, which was evidently built chiefly from the timbers of some British wreck, for it had two pairs of cabin-doors as its entrance, over which still stood, with delightful ignorance as to its meaning, "Certified to accommodate three seamen." The day I was there happened to be the closing one of the Hindu "Feast of Lights," and

THE DUTCH HOUSE, BIMLIPATAM.

during the afternoon, processions accompanied by bands of monotonous tom-toms had paraded the little town, but as we steamed away between eight and nine this festival gave to us one of the most beautiful effects of illumination it has ever been my lot to see. For upon a steep hill-side of about six hundred feet high, which forms an impressive background to the town, there is a large temple and pagoda, and this was entirely outlined after dark with tiny lamps. The ground plan of the buildings formed almost a perfect imperial crown, and this flashing tracery of fire upon the sombre hill-side, with its foreground of deep dark blue sea, as it has probably shone out on this particular night for hundreds of years, was one of the most striking and weird recollections of the East that I carried home.

This part of the coast is bounded by a chain of low hills covered with short grass, and often curiously conical and detached in form. The further ones, seen under the soft violet haze of late afternoon, sometimes recall bits of our English shores, though we can seldom see at home anything to approach the intense vividness of the sunset glow. At Callingapatam, however, we had come back to low stretches of sand bounded by long sweeps of palm trees, and the place with its few commercial offices and closely packed rows of native huts was not sufficiently enticing to induce me to take a journey ashore in a cargo lighter, and I reserved my energies for next day at Gopalpore, at which a busy amount of trade is done. In days gone by, however, it was such an unimposing place in appearance that it was often passed by the skippers who had to call at it, and to arrest seafaring attention, an enormous board bearing the word "Gopalpore" in huge white letters upon a black ground was placed high above the offices of the British India Company's office.

Then there is the rather tedious run up the Hooghly, for it is so wide that there is little to be distinguished on either shore, and Calcutta, but for its strange craft and the great Sailers lying at Budge Budge, might almost be Blackwall or Poplar under a Turneresque effect of grey and rose-shot haze.

To cruise down the Malabar coast, I had fixed to travel

in the *Booldana*, one of the trimmest and most comfortable of all the British India fleet. I had to go on board late at night, for which my consolation was the loveliness of the harbour under the young moon, where one caught shadowy reflections of the lights on the shore, the mysteriously indefinite forms of the great ships, cruisers of the Royal Indian marine, merchantmen of all tonnage and from all ports, "Clippers wing and wing that race the Southern wool," truly side by side "with crawling cargo tanks from

ON THE HOOGHLY—THE FASTEST STEAM TUG IN THE WORLD.

Bremen, Leith, and Hull," with the sombre heights of the Western ghats towering darkly against the star-strewn heaven.

In the morning, Bombay, with pleasant recollections, claimed an *au revoir* of parting glimpse, and never, surely, does Malabar Hill, with its fine bungalows and well-wooded steeps, look prettier than under the rosy flush of sunrise. Goa has long ceased to have merchandise enough to induce any of the great shipping lines to call there, and to reach by rail it is a tedious journey. As my interests in India were human and feminine, rather than ecclesiastical and mediæval, I abandoned the idea of visiting it, and had to be satisfied during the day, after leaving Bombay, to have its direction pointed out to me by Captain Hugill, R.N.R., the *Booldana's* commander, than whom I could have wished no more cultured and sympathetic guide, alike to people and places on this western coast.

With daybreak, after forty-eight hours run, came "slowing down," and the noisy rush of the anchor cables being paid out, and we were lying off Mangalore, which was our first port of call. The few houses and business-offices which lie along its shore give very little idea of its extent or population, which numbers close upon thirty-five thousand, and, indeed, from no point of view does one see anything to suggest that its inhabitants are one hundredth part of this total. Thanks to a kindly invitation "to come ashore with the ship's paper," I found, on landing, a handsome pair of bulls and well-equipped jhatka—for it is one of the peculiarities of the place that horses do not thrive well in its climate—in waiting, and the first point of vantage to which the traveller is taken is the hill on which stands the lighthouse. Close beside this is the fine pile of buildings of St. Aloysius' Jesuit College, an institution which has done notably good educational work, and is affiliated to the University of Madras, while below stretches a vast expanse of cocoanut and other palms. It is under these that the natives live, for the most part in detached and substantially built huts, but so thick and close are the trees that it is almost impossible to realize that they overshadow a populous city. Roman Catholicism has made many converts here, and it is curious to see the native women going to and returning from mass habited in long white robes girt in at the waist with a thick black cord, and wearing over their heads an immense Capuchin hood.

THE LIGHTHOUSE AND ST ALOYSIUS' COLLEGE, MANGALORE.

Another evangelizing body which is especially active at this and several more of the West-coast ports is the Basel Mission, the only Protestant effort, I believe, of its class on the Malabar shores, which I find maintains some very efficient schools for girls. In the earlier days of this agency's exertions, it was found that conversion imposed great labour disabilities upon those who accepted it, and to assist such, a very modest effort in the direction of weaving was started. The enterprise succeeded, and from a strictly commercial point of view alone gave great promise for future development. The factories were extended, and at the present time at Mangalore, and the next port of Cannanore—whose rajah enjoys the sovereignty of the Laccadive Islands, including Minicoy, which is virtually under a Home Rule of women,—it possesses flourishing establishments for the manufacture of cotton goods, which are turned out in good quality and finish. Another branch of industry which the mission has taken up is the making of the semicircular tiles for roofing which are now so much used on even poor huts and cottages throughout India. A very large amount of raw coffee passes across the wharves of Mangalore, and constitutes one of its chief exports.

Thus it was possible to spend a day very profitably at Mangalore, and although we were detained for some hours while a fierce thunderstorm raged—with wonderful flashes, or rather sheets, of pale amber and amethyst and sapphire lightning, which showed instantaneous pictures, sharp and clear as daylight, of the native craft lying near the harbour bar—a night of steady steaming brought us to Cannanore. Here time was very short, and though it possesses features of historical interest, I did not go ashore, as I did not wish to overtire myself. Tellicherry, which we should reach about three the same afternoon, promised to be even more interesting. This is still a great centre of the trade in pepper, cardamoms, beloved of every true Oriental, and spices, and, indeed, it was to secure to themselves the mastery over these important articles of commerce that the old East India Company made this its first regular settlement on the Malabar coast. Ships anchor about two miles out, and the place with its back waters affords a really charming drive. The population here and on to Calicut include a large percentage of the Nayars.

At Calicut, which is the next port reached after Tellicherry, there are a few horses available for hire, and the day that the ship is lying there at anchor may be interestingly spent in driving about the town and the surrounding country. To the ordinary mind, the name of the place conveys few associations, unless it be that from its early exports of cotton cloth our own word calico is derived; but besides the fact that it was here that Vasco de Gama, nigh upon four hundred years ago—in May, 1498, to be exact—first landed in India, it was the place from which the notorious Captain Kydd began his career of piracy. As 1895 will see the bicentenary of this fierce old sea-robber's embarkation from England, when his ship, the *Adventure,* a galley of thirty guns and two hundred men, was equipped by the subscriptions of several noblemen, the story is worth telling again. On the Madagascar coast was the central stronghold of a great body of daring buccaneers, who preyed so relentlessly upon the native trading craft of the Malabar coast that the Honourable Company felt in duty bound to take some protective measures, and Captain Kydd undertook the mission with this strength. His intentions in this task may or may not have been conscientious, but he failed over it, and then, almost in the Calicut roadstead, seized a Dutch barque, adding insult to injury by himself carrying it off to Madagascar. His next great prize was the *Queddah*

Merchant, with a cargo estimated at four hundred thousand rupees in value, and he then placed himself at the head of a piratical fleet which ranged the seas from Mangalore down to Cape Comorin. In due course the treasure was divided, and the commander saw fit to try his knavish fortune in the West Indies. He was arrested in America through Lord Bellamont, one of those who had assisted in starting him, and was hanged at Tilbury in 1701, Queen Anne presenting his forfeited property to Greenwich Hospital. For a long time, however, piracy remained strong along these shores.

In writing of marriage I have already spoken of the immense importance in the family of the Nayar women, and as a result of this the women of the coast and backwaters possess an independence and frankness that many of those of other parts, whose hereditary instincts are of greater humility and servility, are wanting in. At the same time, they have preserved their womanly modesty, and, indeed, among the Nambutiri or Brahmins, the word used to express the sex means "indoor folk," as the caste women are very rarely seen outside their own houses. I have alluded before to the scanty clothing worn in the Malabar district, and this I found did not increase as one went southwards. They are, however, very clean in their personal habits, and keep their heavy jewellery, sometimes of silver gilt, and sometimes of plain silver, beautifully bright. No less fastidious are they with regard to their houses, and if the list of furniture sounds scanty, and comprises, so far as I could see, little more than a brass or earthen *chattie*, or water vessel, a cooking-pot or two, some round plates and trays of brass or bell metal, and a wooden chest in which to keep the rice or grain, all were polished and clean as ashes and tamarinds could make them. The houses of those of any caste were guarded by high fences, and one is rather struck by the amount of space kept clear between each dwelling; but among those whom one might define as the respectable or well-to-do there is a great dread of pollution from the too near approach of those whose very atmosphere, shadow, or touch might convey uncleanness. Another point that one observes is the exceeding neatness with which these outer compounds are kept. The dirt and the untidy litter which disfigures the surroundings of even the wealthiest houses of, say, Madras, Calcutta, or Bombay do not exist here, where repeated watering and sweeping keeps all fresh and tidy. Many even of the poorest houses are now tile-roofed, instead of, as formerly, palm thatched. For many centuries only palaces and temples were tiled, but gradually this restriction became slackened, and now, thanks largely to the enterprise of the Basel Mission, which has developed very largely the industry of tile-making down the coast, this form of roofing has come into general use.

Hospital accommodation and medical aid I find is still backward in most parts of this district, though for the poorer and working women some special wards are usually available in the civil hospitals. Some of the Roman Catholic nursing Sisters who are settled at the larger industrial centres also lend useful assistance in this direction, but there is room for considerable development of the work by the Dufferin Fund or private enterprise. Nor is educational progress making any marked advances. Government schools of course there are, for all these ports belong to the great seaboard of the Presidency of Madras, whose wide system of public instruction and encouragement of girls' learning extends in limited degree to its northernmost fishing or agricultural village. But trade is of somewhat local character, views do not expand rapidly in the absence of emulative influences or outside incentives, traditional prejudices remain strong, and at present little has been done by refined women to raise the condition of the enormous female population of this great district. The Basel Mission deserves all honour with the Roman Catholics for whatever voluntary effort has been made.

The small ports of Beypore and Narakal, this latter often the only place along the coast which affords a safe anchorage during the south-west monsoon, when the sea, then so oily and smooth in its deep turquoise blue, is lashed into one fierce turmoil of steaming, boiling surf, are passed by the *Booldana* in the clear moonlight of a breezy February night, and at daybreak again we are anchored about three miles off Cochin.

"And in all this space of two months' journey, there is not a span free from cultivation. For everybody has here a garden, and his house is placed in the middle of it, and there is a fence of wood up to which the ground of each inhabitant comes. No one travels in these parts upon beasts of burden; nor is there any horse found except with the king, who is therefore the only person who rides." So said the Sheikh Ibu Batuta, of Tangiers, writing in 1342–47 of the Malabar coast, and the description is still so entirely true that one is quite justified in quoting it, though the district collector now may ride where a king formerly did; and at Cochin the sightseer goes to gaze on its features of interest in an exaggerated perambulator known as a "push-push," which is propelled by two coolies and guided by one who pulls in front.

Historically, Cochin offers interest enough to have a book of its own, for even to-day one looks with some wonder upon the place in India which first possessed European fortifications, at which Vasco da Gama breathed his last in 1524, at which St. Francis Xavier preached in 1530, and which saw the printing by the Jesuits of the first book published in India in 1577. But besides its associations, there is plenty for the modern traveller to see in the miles of canal and backwater upon which the town stands, the latter of which runs many miles inland, with shores fringed with the richest vegetation, and dotted by prosperous village communities. Very bright, bustling, and picturesque is the scene along the canal which runs through the town, with its bank filled with an animated, moving crowd, and upon its waters a busy fleet of the curious flat-bottomed barges, with their thatched awnings, by which a great amount of the trade of the place is carried on. This comprises a variety of merchandise, including coir yarn, rope and fibre, cocoanut and other oils, as well as of late years an enormous amount of dried fish. Both the sea and the back waters abound with fish, and a very large proportion of it finds its way to Ceylon, where it is consumed chiefly by the coolies upon the tea and coffee estates. Whole fleets of strangely rigged fishing-craft, the men wearing a huge piece of headgear, combining in itself the attributes both of hat and umbrella, are to be seen all down the coast, but most particularly round Calicut and Cochin, while at the latter place primitive supports carrying great nets are erected at close intervals along the shore. These are generally in charge of two or three men, who continually lower them into the water, where they are borne down by heavy stones, and when hauled up contain, it may be, the delicious pomfret (this, however, is eaten at its best at Bombay), the tasty mullet, the seer, the barmin, or more probably the sardine of the East, a small and extremely plentiful fish, which approximates closely to its brethren of the Mediterranean.

Some years ago an effort to develop trade in packing these in oil, as is done in Europe, was made, but the Merchandise Marks Act compelled their correct descriptive registration, and buyers would not be convinced that genuine sardines could be found in places other than those

Fishing nets Cochin

they were accustomed to regard as their sources. In the business of curing the fish for export, the women do most of the work. Salt is not employed, and the fish are merely spread out in air and sun until they are sufficiently dried to pack in palm matting. It is, perhaps, unnecessary to explain that they are powerfully malodorous after this simple treatment, and in damp weather do not constitute a pleasant cargo to travel with.

As a home of curious religions Cochin is one of the most interesting of Indian cities, and with its colony of the Nestorian and Syrian Christians is, perhaps, the last place in the world that retains any after-glows of the fierce blaze of religious controversies over which the Fathers and the schoolmen quarrelled with such vehement warmth. For Cochin is the centre of the Catholics of the Syrian rite in India, a body who are estimated to number 221,550, and who hold themselves curiously aloof from the Roman Catholics converted direct from heathenism. Among themselves, however, they have been divided for more than two hundred years, the followers of the older form retaining the Syrian language in their services, and admitting the supremacy of the pope, while the adherents of the new Church, who call themselves Jacobites, are opposed to the teachings alike of Arius and Nestorius, and deny any allegiance to Rome. Very mixed indeed are their tenets, as they hold that the bread and wine of the Sacrament become the Real Presence, yet they give it in both kinds; they honour the Virgin and Saints as holy persons and friends of God, pray for the dead, deny purgatory, practise confession, and use the sign of the cross. Among themselves controversy runs high and keen, but in their civil relations of life they are pronounced peaceable and law abiding, while they are industrious and their women quiet and modest.

Besides these Christians, however, there is a colony of Jews, black as well as white. How they came there is a lost tradition, though a belief obtains that Malabar, with its gold (from the Western ghats), its ivory, apes, and peacocks, its myrrh, aloes, cassia, and cinnamon, was the Ophir of King Solomon, and that the Jews came with the fleets of Hiram of Tarshish to seek its treasure. If this be mythical, however, there is no question but that they have many reasons for believing that Jews were settled on the coast after the time of the captivity under Cyrus in the sixth century B.C.

To reach the Jewish town, one is taken through the long, narrow street of the native bazaar, a place of strange smells and unwonted commodities of food, but where also one is surprised to recognize familiar British biscuits, baking powder, soap, and matches. Close, narrow, and dirty are the streets of Jews' town, with little to distinguish them from any ordinary native quarter, though the characteristics of Jewish racial features are strongly marked upon those who come out to gaze upon the rather unwonted sight of a stranger in their midst.

The old synagogue is the chief point of interest, and the connoisseur of old china knows the pangs of envy over the delightful early blue Delft tiles with which it is paved. One is shown two strange old mitres in silver and precious stones, and other things used in ceremonial observance, and curiously graven sheets of copper, which one takes on trust that they are deeds conferring rights and property upon the community, and of great antiquity, and one gazes upon beautifully inscribed rolls of the law in silken wrappings, one of which was seized by the Portuguese during the siege of Cochin in 1668, but which was subsequently recovered uninjured. Then I was taken up to the women's gallery, whence the female worshippers can see and follow the service, after ideas perhaps not wholly uninfluenced by native *purdah* customs, and where a fragment of lovely old Persian carpet won all one's admiration; going afterwards to the Jewish school attached to the synagogue, where the bright, intelligent looks of the little girls impressed me very much. Among the girls education is by no means neglected, for with their usual foresight the Jews here have been quick to see its possible advantages.

Lastly, there is a lingering visit to be paid to the old Dutch church, too, with its crumbling monuments of two to three centuries old to long-forgotten Mynheers and Mevrouws, and the stone bearing the one word "Vasco" is pointed out as the spot under which, for a time, the remains of the great explorer laid, though there is little doubt that prior to their removal to Portugal they rested rather in the Franciscan chapel at Cochin. Then, in the sunset again, the *Booldana* weighs anchor, and our next port is Alleppey. But one must be an insatiable sightseer to land here, even to buy the dainty lace which the women have learnt to make with admirable skill from European monitresses; while Tuticorin, though rising into importance commercially, has no calls whatever to induce one to face a tedious six miles' pull or sail over the murky, shallow water, and would, moreover, be an unpleasant spot to bear in mind as one's last reminiscence of Indian soil.

As to the accommodation offered for so extensive a "round tour," I may say that the boats are all large, Glasgow-built, and almost unexceptionally splendid sea-goers. Their passenger accommodation is excellent, their sanitation and cleanliness are everything to be desired; and if they are not swift as a rule, it is on account of the exigencies of cargo, and a day or so is no very great matter surely when one is travelling for pleasure and health.

With the annually increasing number of ladies in India having independent work of their own to carry out—whether as missionaries, doctors, teachers, or artists, or in the official positions they are beginning to take up in appreciable numbers as inspectresses of schools or directresses of public institutions—the company finds it well worth while to pay attention to the wants of its feminine passengers. It is true that these, at present, are hardly sufficient to warrant the placing of a stewardess on all the boats, but as a rule the woman who is independent enough to be travelling alone either has her own ayah with her, or can dispense altogether with such services as the stewardess is supposed to perform. As far as possible the cabins of either the port or starboard side are reserved for lady passengers, and a bath-room, on whichever side it is, is kept exclusively for them. The cabins are all constructed with three berths, are commodious and roomy, and are supplied with all requisites. It is, however, seldom that so many ladies are travelling that one cannot feel sure of that greatest of all ship's luxuries—a cabin to one's self. Tea and toast, generally accompanied with fruit, is brought to your cabin door any time you order it between 6 and 7.30 by your special "table boy," a native functionary who never dreams of entering without permission, and—well, wise lady travellers always have a nice dressing-gown, and keep it handy. After *chota hazri* has thus been taken in, the most embarrassed spinster has nothing to dread from the absence of a stewardess, and the bath, hot or cold, is ready whenever one chooses to go for it.

An institution famous in Eastern seas is the "B.I. chop," provided from the daily diminishing live stock carried in some obscure part of the deck, and certainly as it is served for breakfast, brought up on the frizzling gridiron, and "cooked to a turn," it is a rival that some of our best-reputed London restaurants might fear. Tiffin is a simple meal of cold meats, but I have known nice little dainties of sweets and cakes made specially for afternoon tea when lady passengers have been on board. Dinner is never less than five or six courses, and, when the weather is warm and the ship not full, is often served, like the other meals, on deck. Of course, after the dances, the theatricals, and the sports organized by the passengers on the great out or home liners, there is not much of gaiety or excitement over the voyage, and the usual rule of steaming hard at night and spending the days in port, with the noise and bustle of taking on and discharging freight, may grow monotonous. But given a certain amount of work to be done, say in reading or writing, a temperament that is interested rather than bored over busy and unfamiliar sights, the intention to go ashore wherever practicable, and a hand camera, and any woman can derive a vast amount of pleasure from the journey.

Then one may profitably spend a couple of nights at the "Clapham Junction of the Shipping World," as Colombo, always bright, bustling, cosmopolitan, and hospitable, loves to hear itself called. There is a pleasant run up to Kandy over some of the most beautiful and sensationally engineered railway in the world, and there is plenty to fill the time even should one's homeward boat be a little late. But the *Dilwara*, in which my passage home was taken, was punctual to an hour, and in the rose and violet haze of twilight glow Colombo faded out of sight, a gracious vision to the last. Happy is the voyage that is uneventful as ours was until we met really bad weather in the Bay of Biscay, but the same hints will serve for the home as for the outward journey. The ship is the latest addition to the B.I. fleet, and with her genial and popular commander, bade fair to be a great favourite with travellers. For in her fitting, an innovation most commendable in the eyes of lone voyagers, was the inclusion of a number of snug and cosy single-berth cabins. Even the nicest woman develops unexpectedly disagreeable attributes when a cabin is shared with her and perhaps a third one for three weeks or a month. She either rises at unholy hours, or wants to dress when you do, or takes your *Eau de Cologne* to the bath-room, where it disappears altogether, even if she cannot exercise a terror by hinting that she might reveal to a possible rival that she has noticed how your hair is eked out by tresses from the barber, or that your teeth are false, as such might be harmless secrets that some ladies might wish to keep. But the Admiralty, in the recent changes that have been made in the trooping and transport service, were aware of the recommendations of the ship, and had known Captain Mann honourably of old. So she has been chartered on a long period, and it is doubtful how far she may ever be again available for ordinary passenger carrying.

One word as to hotels may fittingly be spared here, though I may admit that, thanks to my many and weighty introductions, my experiences of them were limited. They are the least enjoyable items, as a rule, in a traveller's experience, and with rare and notable exceptions are very bad. As a matter of fact, they are too cheap, and the average tourist, to whom a few pounds more or less are of no great matter, would gladly pay a couple of rupees or so more a day to have better accommodation. Five to seven rupees a day for a bedroom, with its accompanying bath-room, and including breakfast, tiffin, afternoon tea, and dinner, is the usual charge, and even taking into consideration the lower prices for ordinary provisions and service, this sum cannot be expected to ensure very high-class accommodation. In the Government rest-houses, which are maintained in the smaller

THE MUTINY MEMORIAL WELL AT CAWNPORE.

towns and at intervals upon main roads, it will be found that a fixed and reasonable tariff has been drawn up, and that generally speaking, though very simple and primitive, the shelter they afford is at least clean. Few, however, who are merely tourists find occasion to visit them, but if necessity arises, it is well to have in reserve some simple tinned provisions and a small quantity of brandy, whisky, or wine, as their resources in provisions are not usually extensive, and indeed generally dwindle down to eggs and fowls.

Then, again, the conditions of railway travelling are completely different to those with us, and the mere amount of it alone is a point that few grasp when they leave home, even if one intends to do no more than visit the "show cities," as Cawnpore and Benares, of the dependency, which lie along the great main lines between Bombay and Calcutta. Even if this journey be taken direct it occupies three and a half days, which is a novel experience to her who has regarded the run from London to Brighton as a long journey, and a trip to Scarborough as a great undertaking. Out in India it is considered quite a small detour if one spends twenty-four hours in the train to reach some interesting spot, and two nights and a day in the railway carriage are occupied over many expeditions. Europeans scarcely ever, unless of the very humblest order, go anything but first or second class, and one's first lesson is to become used to the different patterns upon which the carriages are built. The compartments of these classes are about double the size of those at home, and the seats are set the opposite way to our own, that is, instead of sitting with one's face or back to the engine, the places are set sideways, and are long enough to lie down upon in comfort. The first-class carriages are nominally constructed for six, though more than four are never put into

THE MONKEY TEMPLE AT BENARES.

them save under the greatest pressure of traffic. In the second-class the seats are somewhat narrower, not quite so well cushioned, and nine is the regulation number, another bench being placed down the middle.

For night accommodation two extra bunks, which are hinged and can be folded back during the day, are provided above the lower ones, which latter the experienced *voyageuse* always endeavours to secure. Each compartment has its lavatory, with marble basin and a supply of cold water, which is contained in a cistern under the carriage roof, and is replenished at intervals along the line by the scantily clad *bheesti*, or water-carrier, with his dripping *mussick* made from a whole goat-hide. Though one makes the best of the sleeping arrangements at night, during the day time one is inclined to think regretfully of the cushioned ease of the first-class compartment or, better still, the Pullman car at home, for the seats are too high from the ground and are too wide, as well as lacking in well-placed arms or support for comfort in sitting. Unless, therefore, one is well provided with cushions, among which an air one is desirable, a really restful position is somewhat hard to obtain.

The ladies' compartment is, as a rule, well patronized, and woe betide the unfortunate male who inadvertently opens its door. Though socially he might be possessed of every attraction, he is scowled at as an iniquitous intruder, and does not receive even a gracious glance for his hasty apology and lifted hat. Every one travels as a rule by night rather than by day, and prudent people at the great railway termini, like the Presidency towns or Delhi, either book places in advance or come in good time before the train starts to make sure of the coveted lower berths. In Indian railway travelling, it must be conceded, the virtues of the sex are not exhibited in their most pleasing light, while the amount of belongings and their characteristics that the average woman manages to bring into the carriage with her would exasperate the equanimity of the suavest of British guards. With such long journeys, bedding becomes a necessity, this being a baggage adjunct that the unfortunate uninitiated ones never possess. A proper bedding kit should include two *razias*, or quilts, made of gaily printed cotton, and wadded like eider downs with cotton wool, a blanket or two, and two pillows. These are rolled up, and when strapped form a bundle about as big as an ordinary portmanteau; but with such materials a native servant, or even one's self, after a little practice, can convert either the seat or upper bunk into a tolerably comfortable couch.

To enjoy the situation by the mail thoroughly and philosophically, starting say north-westwards from Calcutta, one absolutely must either book a place in advance or arrive very early to secure one's own berth, and "turn in" at once. The windows, it should be explained, have wooden shutters like Venetian blinds, so that even in the most bustling station there is no fear of prying eyes. The hat is put on the rack above, dress and petticoat are hung up, smaller articles, with your camera, dressing-bag, and such things, are disposed under the seat, and, instead of the usual *robe de nuit,* one puts on the lace-trimmed flannel dressing-gown, which is all-essential in one's travelling outfit. The door opens, and two more ladies, apparently friends, one quite middle-aged, the other younger but decidedly stout, enter. They have no shyness whatever as to letting you know that they think you a nuisance there, and generally begin by shrieking to the guard to know if there is not a vacant carriage. He says, in the usual high-pitched Eurasian voice, "This ladies' carriage," and repeats it, and they return, having dragged in, from the coolies by the door, their own two bundles of bedding and a miscellaneous variety of packages, which probably include a portly handbag, a wooden box or two, several toys awkward of shape but fragile of construction, a carpet bag—a form of receptacle which flourishes abundantly in the native bazaar—and an assortment of solar topies in different degrees of size and ugliness, umbrellas and shawls, while one asks the other ominously, "Where is the tiffin basket?" This is forthcoming at last, and then they proceed to dispose of their chattels, an undertaking which generally consists in their placing temporarily a heavy package or so upon your feet, and ultimately piling them up against the door that you will want to open to get out. As they undress one gains sundry evidences of the scantiness of underwear in India, and one watches furtively the gymnastic efforts of the stouter lady to climb into the upper berth, she the while scowling at the privilege that coming early obtained for yourself.

The train moves off, and she draws the green flannel cap over the carriage lamp with an angry snap. We pass through roadside stations, and hear the noise and clamour of native voices, and the vendors of parched grain and sweetmeats call their wares in strident tones. An impressionist painter could find many worse subjects than an Indian railway station at night, with its spluttering oil lamps, the softly moving, ghostly native figures coated up in all the clothing they can find, and the glare upon brass chatties and dishes. But a junction is reached, and, horror! the door opens. Then we all scowl and say in chorus, "We're very full here." A voice plaintively says, "I can't find any other place," and she comes in, adding her full share to the incumbrances already there, which, in her well-meant efforts to undress without removing the shade from the light, she generally manages to displace and upset, while her attempts to lower the unused bunk involve assistance from the one lying below it.

It is usually at a station reached between six and seven

TIME, TWO A.M.—VACANT PLACES AT A PREMIUM.

in the morning that the door opens, and one may obtain the *chota hazri*, or early (literally, "little") breakfast, the acceptance of which is one of the first Anglo-Indian habits one acquires. A cup of tea, generally tolerable, but occasionally very bad, and bread, with the white and tasteless buffalo butter, is what is offered, and for it one pays from fourpence to eightpence. For breakfast the train generally makes a stop of about half an hour at the largest station it reaches between nine and eleven, and, with the exception of Burdwhan, where I once got an excellent meal, this is seldom a satisfactory repast. It is wont to consist of tough mutton chops, eggs, and very salt bacon, and the bones of aged fowls disguised under the name of curry. Dinners as a rule are better, but two rupees are charged for them, for which, taking into consideration the cheapness of provisions in India, an excellent meal ought to be given. Anglo-Indian domestic economy, however, views meals at refreshment rooms as an extravagance, as well as leaving much to be desired on the score of quality. Hence the important part that the tiffin-basket always plays in the travelling equipment, and careful individuals appear to enjoy even the delights of a picnic long drawn out, though a breakfast of sandwiches, oranges and cake, with claret or whisky and soda, can scarcely be regarded as, in a favourite word of one of our most graceful of minor poets, "conducive." Of course there are degrees of tiffin-baskets, and I entertain pleasant recollections of the daintily served roast chicken and tongue, the delicate pastry and fruit, and the glass of '80 champagne that a maharajah's hospitality provided for me, but as a rule eating is not to be classed among the joys of Eastern railway travelling.

In the matter of ladies' travelling accommodation, however, there are one or two points upon which some of our English companies might well come to India for instruction. On the Bombay, Baroda, and Central India line, for instance, the arrangements are notably satisfactory; and in the ladies' waiting-rooms baths may be obtained in privacy and comfort, while a civilly spoken ayah will perform any little attentions required—such as hair-dressing or sewing on a loose button. This line, however, with its courteous *personnel*, from Mr. O'Callaghan, its traffic manager, and Mr. Kennedy, the station-master at its terminus at Delhi, deserves the best of feminine thanks for the attention it bestows in many ways upon the well-being of its lady travellers, even to providing at several of its larger junctions and stations retiring-rooms furnished with couches and long chairs, in which a few hours' rest and quiet may be secured. It often happens that one is obliged to leave the train at some unusual hour like four in the morning, it may be to go sight-seeing or visiting, or to wait till another train comes up, and in such instances these retiring-rooms prove a true boon. No fee whatever is asked in them, even for the use of the bath, and a "tip" of a quarter to half a rupee, according to the amount of trouble that has been given, is quite enough for the ayah.

Thus the traveller must be equipped for things to which she is totally unaccustomed, yet which, to the woman who has experienced them, seem such ordinary matters of fact that she seldom troubles herself to mention them to any who seeks her advice. For one's wear on the voyage, the first point to be borne in mind is, that unless one is in the rare position of wealth or personal favour to command an unshared cabin, nothing larger than the company's "regulation size" trunk will be admitted. This varies a little on the different lines, but information as to what it is, is always given on taking a ticket, and averages three feet six inches long, fifteen inches deep, and eighteen inches wide. Truly, not a liberal allowance for the many "things" a woman wants. In this, however, should be taken three or four complete changes of underwear, and it is a good plan, if one is nervous as to sea-going physique, to have these just tied together in sets, containing everything from stockings to camisole, so as to lessen as far as possible the *malaise* of hunting for the different items. Another advisable step is to collect up one's oldest *lingerie*, get it repaired, buttoned and taped, to last "one wear more," and throw it overboard when soiled. This obviates keeping a quantity of unwashed linen to the end of the journey, and having this never very pleasant encumbrance to take ashore.

For wear on board ship, blue serge is always useful and appropriate, and nothing is nattier or more practical than a well-made skirt and coat of this. As large a number as possible of shirts or blouses should be taken, and a striped flannel one is advisable for the first few days of the voyage. Any sensible and tailor-made gown is useful, however; but after Port Said is passed lighter things become a necessity. Smart cottons or washing silks are wanted then, but loose lace or flying ribbon ends do not add to comfort, and should be avoided. One wants a couple of evening gowns for the voyage, and a dainty tea-gown is useful, but a black silk, with bodice not markedly *décolleté*, is never amiss, and with a couple of pretty silk blouses can be made to furnish desirable variations. White petticoats should be worn with discretion, as tar and pitch are not unknown if one moves off the holystoned snowiness of the upper deck. Light-coloured cottons, and made rather short, are less extravagant wear. A comfortable cape, a waterproof and a close-fitting cap are all useful if the weather is not perfectly calm.

Of course, however, it is impossible to condense all these necessaries into the limited cabin trunk, and therefore one packs all not wanted during the first week and all the rest of one's belongings in the stronger larger boxes or trunks which go into the ship's hold, marking each legibly, "Wanted on voyage." Once a week all these are brought up, but to the uninitiated traveller "baggage day" is a terror rather than a joy, and is apt to confirm the average woman in a view that in the matter of packing and

"BAGGAGE DAY,"—A SCENE ON THE LOWER DECK.

raiment, at least, the other sex holds the superior position. As the weather grows warmer the necessity for lighter clothing becomes pressing; still, it requires some courage to disturb the well-placed orderliness of the big trunk down below. The occasion is preceded by a notice placed in the saloon to the effect that "baggage will be upon the lower deck at eleven to-morrow," and prudent persons then overhaul the contents of their cabin portmanteaux, roll soiled linen into clean bags, and generally prepare to substitute what is not required for what is. Meantime, the luggage has been brought up, an awning has been spread, and the scene of piled-up boxes and bags, tins, trunks, and traps would do credit to the busiest London terminus in the height of the holiday season. The fourth officer is on duty to superintend, and she who has found her particular belongings can command the services of one of the swarthy lascars of the crew to uncord it for her. This is the juncture at which the true genius of packing becomes apparent, for it is annoying to have to work through a stratum or two of smart "going ashore" gowns, and lightest "Red Sea" cotton skirts, not to speak of solar topies, to discover that the intermediate things for wear in the Mediterranean, before Port Said is reached, are packed at the very bottom. After the first "baggage day" dress on board is apt to become rather more elaborate, for at starting the view obtains that "anything will do for the ship," but presently true feminine rivalry comes up, and nice frocks that had been meant for future wear in India often make their first appearances at sea.

Among the most important items of an outfit are to be placed dressing-gowns. They cannot be too elaborate for success, for whatever purpose they may be required. One runs the gauntlet of male passengers, to say nothing of table boys, to reach the bath-room in the morning, and in the ante-chamber of this one waits one's turn in company with perhaps half one's female fellow-travellers on board. It is recognized at "Scandal Point," as this trysting-place is usually called, that neither age nor rank confers any precedence in the "order of the bath," and the rule of first come first served is unswervingly carried out, even though the much harassed stewardess looks pathetically regretful when she has to call little Miss Missionary Spinster before Lady Major-General or Mrs. High Court Judge. There is no rule, however, that is not set at defiance; and I have seen a lady, who did not disdain to wait her turn, clad in an antiquated waterproof with a crotchet wrap over her head, amid crepons and laces around her. Then, in the event of illness, and the

FIRST IMPRESSIONS OF MADRAS—SOME PUBLIC BUILDINGS.

necessity for summoning the usually young and often good-looking surgeon of the ship, one is also able to be becomingly ill, even in face of the limp draggle of sea-sickness. Moreover, on arrival in India, where one rests and writes much in one's own room, it is often a welcome relief to change even the easiest of dresses and corsets for an easy *robe de chambre.* Bath-room slippers should not be forgotten.

To keep the hair in curl at sea is among one's minor troubles, and many women when they start are unaware of the extremely stringent rule on all the lines against the use of the usual spirit lamp and tongs. The stewardess is generally under orders to remove these and any spirit or matches found in a cabin. The Orient Company, I believe, allows the use of these appliances in the bath-room under certain conditions, but it is better if possible to use Hindes' pins or some similar device, and an Anglo-Indian "dodge" worth knowing is to sprinkle a little violet powder over the hair before twisting it up to curl. This is of great assistance in averting the effect of the moisture around, and I have found it quite equal to any of the advertised and costly preparations sold for this purpose. Many women regard a false fringe as quite allowable at sea, even though they would not dream of wearing it ashore. But its aggressive neatness and frizziness generally reveal its secret.

A very useful adjunct to the cabin equipment is one of the Holland bags that are made by the Irish Ladies' Work Society. These are hung above the berth, and with their numerous pockets can contain an infinity of small necessities of everyday use.

There is only one other essential not to be forgotten for the voyage, and that is a strong, comfortable chair. The average Anglo-Indian takes a *chaise longue*, which allows of a recumbent attitude, and this I believe is a great comfort to sea-sick subjects. The tourist is, however, generally satisfied with a "hammock" or folding chair, but an addition of much value is a good air cushion. This also is useful later for railway travelling.

But the most earnestly asked, I find, of all questions is, "What is the best thing for sea-sickness?" To those making a big voyage for the first time, as I was, I recommend my own mental attitude, which was that numbers of persons crossed the ocean without suffering from it, and why should not I prove to be one of them? It is a great mistake to make up one's mind beforehand that one has got to be ill. Happily for myself, I discovered that I could "stand anything," and in the pride of my heart I thought I could not be made ill at all. Leaving Madras, however, we came into a fearfully regular monsoon pitch, and that I must admit humbled me. Some find their panacea in champagne, others in bottled stout. The steward of the *Khandalla*, however, undertook my cure, and I commend it to others, as two tiny slices cut from the breast of a well-roasted fowl, served very hot, without any gravy or sauce, a slice of thin, crisp dry toast, a daintily peeled and quartered orange, and a claret glassful—no more—of iced brandy and soda, was a little meal that had no disconcerting horror whatever, after a day of decided *malaise*. The point of it is to have the chicken as hot as possible.

Now as to what must be taken for Indian winter wear. Combinations of the finest but purest wool, or else mixed silk and wool, are *absolutely essential*, and upon that point it is impossible to insist too strongly. Not only is cotton next the skin the most fruitful source of chill and rheumatism, but with the unavoidable saturation of perspiration is extremely objectionable in all ways. A dozen of either, or half-a-dozen of each (keeping the silk for the hottest wear), ought to suffice for the usual seven or eight months' tour.

Belts made of thick but soft flannel should also be worn night and day round the lower abdomen, as it is of the first importance to women to avoid anything like cold in the organs peculiar to the sex. These belts should be made five or six inches deep, of the finest and best quality of material doubled, and fastened with three sets of tapes. A little shaping over the hips on each side is a great improvement.

I personally prefer very fine flannel for my night dresses in the East, and though this is by no means universally adopted or urged, I think it is a great safeguard against night chills. They are, however, somewhat extravagant wear, as the bad washing that they often meet causes them to shrink alarmingly and soon makes them anything but fascinating in colour.

White petticoats are of course required, as there is no substitute for them under light gowns, but it is advisable to avoid choosing them with handsome or delicate lace trimmings, as they will be assuredly spoiled after a washing or two. Good Swiss embroidery is more satisfactory and stands rough treatment remarkably well. A pretty silk petticoat or two, one flannel lined, is a desirable addition to the wardrobe, and it must be borne in mind that an ample allowance of every separate article of wear must be taken, as complete change is more frequently essential than it is here, while one often cannot stay long enough in a place to get everything washed.

Sanitary towels should be taken rather than the old-fashioned description, as in many parts caste prejudices forbid the washing of these latter. The want of knowledge of this fact often causes lady travellers extreme unpleasantness and inconvenience.

It is a mistake to suppose that nothing but light cotton can be worn in India, and for a winter trip a couple of really warm dresses at least ought to be in the outfit. Delhi, for example, in December or January is really chilly, and I well remember how amused I was at a party of tourists I saw there on a day that I was wearing a thick serge gown and my sealskin with comfort. These misguided folk were shivering in their cottons, and had on solar topies, green veils, and blue spectacles, as well as carrying large double umbrellas. They were truly the *rcductio ad absurdum* of the average English tourist's preconceived notions of India. Of course, if one is going further north still, there will be still greater occasion for warm clothes. Kharkie, with its very hard, dust-resisting surface, made me one of my most useful travelling dresses, and if this be bought at a genuine army outfitters like Firmin's in the Strand, and in its best qualities, wears really well and is not at all objectionable in colour. It does not crease and look tumbled as readily as

PACK CAMELS AT DELHI.

the more feminine brown Holland. White drill or duck is also good and durable for dress wear. Quite the coolest dress that I took with me was a grey alpaca, lined with a decisive yellow silk and made with a yellow silk blouse. This was in accordance with a suggestion by Sir George Birdwood, who had a sound scientific theory for his recommendation. No one, he argues, ever got sunstroke or heat fever from exposure to a dark source of warmth, or even to the most powerful furnace. It is the chemical rays of the sun that work the mischief, and it is the photographer who gives us the hint for their exclusion. He glazes his windows, and uses lamps shaded with red or yellow, and thus manipulates his plates with safety. It is quite immaterial for wear whether the yellow is inside or out, and as fashion does not usually favour our appearance in such brilliant colouring, I allied, or rather, Messrs. Howell and James did for me, mine with light grey alpaca, and brought, for once, artistic effect and hygiene into excellent accord. The natives, it may be mentioned, have used yellow linings for their tents for countless generations. It would, of course, be quite practicable to wear petticoats and camisoles of yellow surah or washing silk.

Besides the demi-toilettes for board ship and *table d'hôte* wear, it is necessary to take three or four good evening gowns at least, if one intends going into Anglo-Indian society even to a moderate extent, while if one expects any official recognition from the Government Houses, they are also essential, as a dinner or dance is usually the first hospitality shown to a new arrival. These must be of the very latest fashion and really well made, for dress in Calcutta especially is no whit behind that of London or Paris, and the lady traveller who thought her last season's gowns would "do" would find she cut a sorry figure beside her Indian hostesses, whether these belonged to the administrative, military, or leading commercial sets. Soft *broché* satins pack as well as any material, and come out fresh even after some crushing.

Gloves are worn for state dinners, and invariably for balls, but for less formal entertainments society allows latitude, and they are often dispensed with entirely. To keep them in good condition they should be left in the tissue-paper wrapping in which they are bought, and folded up in flannel. They should then be placed in an air-tight tin box, or better still, in a large bottle tightly corked.

As to hats, I find that Anglo-Indians stand aghast when

I tell them that I never wore one of the very unbecoming sun helmets or solar topies the whole time I was absent from England. Perhaps during the hot season, and if one intended to ride much during the day, it would not be a very wise course to pursue, nor would I recommend it to any one subject to heat headache, but I found no inconvenience whatever by dispensing with it. It is true that I have a quantity of hair, which I wear at the back of my head, and it is at the base of the skull that protection is most important, and that I had a white and yellow sunshade that I always carried. Round straw boating hats lined with flannel and yellow silk are very useful wear, and Heath's, in Oxford Street, carried me out a very good idea in providing each one with three or four ribbon bands and bows of different colours. These had a tiny buckle concealed behind the bow, and could be changed at a minimum of trouble to match every dress. A smarter bonnet, toque, or hat or two ought to be taken for visiting, lunching, or tennis-party wear.

Cotton coats over shirts are favoured for riding, and the habit skirt should be well cut, but made of very light tweed or serge. Kharkie is often used for the latter, but if it is found that this is required, a native tailor can always be found to copy one's English pattern in it with absolute accuracy. Up country, however, riding gear need not have the smart perfection of the Row, and numbers of women turn out in the simplest of serge skirts and loose blouses.

A couple of evening wraps, one slightly thicker than the other, are advisable, as people generally drive in their open carriages to dinners and dances, and the night air, however delightful it seems, is wont to be treacherous.

Every woman has her individual fads and fancies about

her dress, and will modify these fragmentary hints accordingly. But two things I would repeat. One is, under no circumstances to disdain the wearing of flannel belts, and silk and wool, or unmixed wool combinations. The other is, not to be led away by stories that warm clothing is never wanted on an Indian tour. In the winter months the Punjab and the North-West Provinces can give one really cold days, and one finds fireplaces in the houses. The natives are to be seen muffled up in quilted coats, and besides putting on a thick serge dress, one can follow their example in wearing with comfort a thick, or even fur-lined jacket or cloak. A fur-lined cloak, I may say, is a particularly cosy addition to one's wardrobe on the first few and last few days of an average voyage during the popular seasons for going out or returning.

As to medicine, a few simple remedies may be taken in case of emergency, but few parts of the dependency are now so benighted that medical assistance is not soon attainable. The most useful things to take are a box of Dixon's or Cockle's pills, a little castor oil in capsules, a small quantity of the old-fashioned but efficacious Gregory powder, some ipecacuanha in powder, sulphate of quinine, soda, chlorodyne (for cholera or dysentery), and a small bottle, say half an ounce, of essential oil of cinnamon.

The reason for this latter I may explain. Most Indian doctors are agreed that there is a sound hygienic reason for the quantity of curry that enters into the native diet, and that the amount of spice-oil that through it is taken into the system is a powerful safeguard against malarial or choleraic maladies. It is a good plan, therefore, to carry a little of this in its most potent form, and if it is feared that one is in a malarial or unhealthy district, to wet the tip of a finger with the oil and touch the back of the tongue once or twice a day.

Other hints, which were privately given to me by one of the most noted authorities on health and sanitation in the East, and by the carrying into practice of which I never suffered a single day's incapacitation, included advice always to sleep as high as possible off the ground or floor, and to protect one's self from any land wind or breeze. The daily bath must not be omitted, and even twice a day is often not too much. Animal food should be reduced as far as practicable, and vegetables and fruits substituted for it. Malt liquors should be used with caution, and wine is advisable only in extreme moderation. Aërated waters are exceedingly cheap, and can be obtained everywhere, and the drink that is most generally favoured is very mild whisky and soda with abundant ice. Tea and coffee, the former generally good, are widely drunk. Neither milk nor water should be drunk till it has been boiled, and the latter ought to be filtered in addition. Fresh lime-juice and soda, with a small quantity of sugar, may be commended as the most thoroughly refreshing and thirst-quenching beverage.

Sunstroke is the greatest horror of most travellers, who seem to be terrified by the mere strength and clearness of the light around them, and it is well for the timid to avoid the direct rays of the sun. A light and nutritious but sufficient diet proves a considerable preventive against attack; and, besides protecting the head, many Anglo-Indians have much faith in a small square of flannel placed inside the shirt or dress body and covering the nape of the neck and spinal column. For the consolation of the fearful, I may say that the first symptom of a stroke is the cessation of perspiration. So long as this is felt freely there is no danger whatever, even in the greatest heat, but the instant that the skin becomes dry there is cause for alarm, and it is well at once to go into a cool place and sip a little water.

The slightest diarrhœa should never be neglected, and on the least sign of this a dose of chlorodyne should be taken, and medical advice called. In the same way, any straining should be regarded as a possible indication of dysentery, and for this a few grains of ipecacuanha may be swallowed in the interval before a doctor can arrive. Constipation must not be permitted for a single day, and if it is experienced, either a capsule of castor oil or a pill should be immediately taken. Indigestion, too, is not to be ignored, as it is a symptom of disordered liver, and a doctor should be consulted; while for the feeling of bilious nausea, which I believe overcomes many and deprives them of appetite, ten to fiften grains of quinine often affords prompt relief. Like the other troubles I have mentioned, if it recurs it should not be regarded as of no moment.

With such simple precautions any woman of average health—and one not possessing this should not venture upon the journey—need not fear illness or even temporary *malaise.* The sanitation of European houses, if primitive, is at least sound, and even in the crowded native quarters of the town vast improvements are being made. The odours encountered are wont to be startling, and besides the "spicy, garlic smell" which is all-pervading towards sundown, as the simple evening meals are being cooked, there is the sickly and altogether indescribable pungency of the rank *ghi,* or oiled butter, that constitutes such a delight in the indigenous *cuisine.* Decaying vegetable matter contributes an offensive addition to the other disagreeables, but the loathsomeness of putrid animal refuse is, fortunately, rare. I think, however, for penetrative horror it would be hard to find anything much worse than the stench with which one is met rowing round Bombay harbour on a close and steamy night, if one happens to pass under the bows of one of the top-heavy Arabian buggaloes, which have come up from the Persian Gulf to carry back a malodorous cargo of partially dried fish.

Mosquitoes and other disagreeables of insect life will certainly be encountered, and it is difficult to suggest any efficacious prophylactic against or remedy for their bites and stings. Eucalyptus oil is said to fulfil the former condition, but, unfortunately, any lavish employment of it renders one hardly a desirable addition to society. A favourite native prescription for relief is the repeated application of fresh lime-juice round the part stung, and this certainly reduces swelling and allays irritation. In spite of all unpleasant predictions, I never found snakes in my shoes, though it is well to acquire the habit of shaking these before putting them on. Nor were my possessions eaten by white ants or ruined by damp, both of which calamities are emphatically promised, and in making this statement I fully foresee all sorts of criticisms, that I only saw India at its best, and only one side of it.

But to me it is hard to write of India without enthusiasm. Its warmth, its colour, its art, and, above all, its people, are so real and so intensely interesting that our Western attitude of critical aloofness seems chilling and inadequate towards it. I have, indeed, every reason to remember my time in the East with gratitude, for it was one long succession of kindness from the great administrators, native importancies, and hosts of friends, old and new, European and Parsee, Hindu and Muslim; but beyond that it has its own subtle attraction, its own beautiful fascination of age with vigour, of art the oldest, yet in fullest vitality, of ideas, customs, prejudices, which go back to the dimmest mists of antiquity, and still continue in the face of the most pronounced modernity, and how this all may influence one is best summed up in the words of India's own laureate, who says—

> "An' I'm learnin' 'ere in London what the ten-year soldier tells;
> 'If you've 'eard the East a-callin', you won't never 'eed aught else.'"

THE END.

INDEX OF AUTHORS.

NEW AND FORTHCOMING BOOKS.

GENERAL SIR C. P. BEAUCHAMP WALKER, K.C.B.

Days of a Soldier's Life. Written during active service in the Crimean, Chinese, Austro-Prussian ('66), and Franco-German ('70–'71) Wars, by General Sir C. P. BEAUCHAMP WALKER. Demy 8vo., with Portrait.

COLONEL G. B. MALLESON, C.S.I.

Life of Warren Hastings: First Governor-General of India. By Colonel G. B. MALLESON, C.S.I. With Portrait. Demy 8vo.

LIEUT.-COLONEL COOPER-KING.

Life of George Washington. By Lieut.-Colonel COOPER-KING. With Maps and Plans. Large Crown 8vo. *6s.*

FITZHUGH LEE.

General Lee, of the Confederate Army. By FITZHUGH LEE, his Nephew. With Portrait and Maps. Crown 8vo. *6s.*

AUGUSTUS GRIMBLE.

Highland Sport. By AUGUSTUS GRIMBLE. With Illustrations by A. THORBURN. Large Paper Edition, uniform with "Deer Stalking," "Shooting and Salmon Fishing." *£2 2s. net.*

COLONEL POLLOK.

Incidents of Foreign Sport and Travel. By Colonel POLLOK, Author of "Sport in British Burma." With Illustrations by A. T. ELWES. Demy 8vo. *16s.*

"SNAFFLE."

Gun, Rifle, and Hound, in East and West. By "SNAFFLE." With Illustrations by H. DIXON. Demy 8vo.

OSWALD CRAWFURD.

A Year of Sport and Natural History. Shooting, Hunting, Coursing, Falconry, and Fishing. Edited by OSWALD CRAWFURD. With Chapters on Birds of Prey, Nidifications of Birds, and Tricks of Poachers. With numerous Illustrations by FRANK FELLER, BRYAN HOOD, CECIL ALDIN, A. T. ELWES, E. NEALE, JOHN BEER, P. VIENZENY, STANLEY BERKELEY, and G. E. LODGE. Large Paper Edition.

CHARLES DIXON.

The Migration of British Birds: including their Post-Glacial Emigration as Traced by the Application of a New Law of Dispersal. By CHARLES DIXON. With Maps. Crown 8vo.

The Nests and Eggs of Non-Indigenous British Birds; or, such Species that do not Breed within the British Archipelago. By CHARLES DIXON. With Coloured Frontispiece of Eggs. Crown 8vo. *6s.*

MARY FRANCES BILLINGTON.

Woman in India. By MARY FRANCES BILLINGTON. With an Introduction by the Marchioness of DUFFERIN AND AVA, C.I., and numerous Illustrations by HERBERT JOHNSON, and others. Dedicated by permission to H.R.H. the DUCHESS of CONNAUGHT. Demy 8vo.

CHARLES G. HARPER.

The Marches of Wales: Notes and Impressions on the Welsh Borders, from the Severn Sea to the Sands o' Dee. By CHARLES G. HARPER. With 114 Illustrations. Demy 8vo.

V. MARMERY.

The Progress of Science: its Origin, Course, Promoters and Results. By V. MARMERY. Demy 8vo.

PERROT AND CHIPIEZ.

The History of Art in Primitive Greece. (Mycenian Art.) By GEORGES PERROT and CHARLES CHIPIEZ. With 553 Illustrations. Two vols. Imperial 8vo.

MRS. R. HENRY.

Queen of Beauty: or, The Adventures of Prince Elfrestan. By Mrs. R. HENRY. Illustrated by JOHN JELLICOE. One vol.

CHARLES DICKENS AND GEORGE CRUIKSHANK.

The Adventures of Oliver Twist: or, the Parish Boy's Progress. By CHARLES DICKENS. An Edition de Luxe. With Twenty-six Water-colour Drawings by GEORGE CRUIKSHANK. Imperial 8vo., 42*s*. net.

GEORGE V. C. HOLMES.

Naval Architecture and Shipbuilding. By GEORGE V. C. HOLMES, Author of "Marine Engines and Boilers." With Illustrations. Crown 8vo.

HENRY ADAMS, M.I.C.E.

Machine Construction and Drawing. (Elementary.) A Key to the Examinations of the Science and Art Department. By HENRY ADAMS, M.I.C.E., Author of "Building Construction." Crown 8vo.

W. J. LINEHAM.

A Text-book of Mechanical Engineering. By WILFRID J. LINEHAM, Head of the Engineering Department at the Goldsmiths' Institute. With numerous Illustrations. Crown 8vo., 10*s*. 6*d*. *net*.

JOHN HARRISON.

The Decoration of Metals: Chasing, Repoussé, and Saw Piercing. By JOHN HARRISON. With 180 Illustrations. Crown 8vo., 3*s*. 6*d*.

H. FOSTER NEWEY.

Elementary Drawing: a Few Suggestions for Students and Teachers. By H. FOSTER NEWEY, Birmingham School of Art. Illustrated. Crown 8vo., 2*s*. 6*d*.

H. H. STATHAM.

Architecture for General Readers: to which is added an Historical Sketch of Architecture. By H. HEATHCOTE STATHAM. With hundreds of Illustrations by the Author.

PROFESSOR A. HUMBOLDT SEXTON.

Home Work in Inorganic Chemistry: a Series of Exercises with Explanations and Worked Examples. By A. HUMBOLDT SEXTON, F.I.C., &c. Third Edition. Crown 8vo., 1*s*.

HENRY ANGEL.

Practical Plane and Solid Geometry. By HENRY ANGEL, Lecturer at the Birkbeck Institute. Crown 8vo.

R. G. HATTON.

Figure Drawing and Composition. By R. G. HATTON, Author of "Text-book of Elementary Design." Illustrated. Crown 8vo.

New Novels.

Grandborough. By the EARL OF DESART. Two vols.

A Black Squire. By Mrs. ALFRED HUNT. One vol.

The Pilgrims. By W. CARLTON DAWE. Two vols.

Queen of the Hamlet. By H. F. LESTER. Two vols.

Through a Field Glass. By G. F. UNDERHILL and H. S. SWEETLAND. With Illustrations by L. THACKERAY, Crown 8vo.

The Mystery of the Patrician Club. By ALBERT D. VANDAM. A New Edition in One Volume. Crown 8vo.

The Star of Fortune: A Story of the Indian Mutiny. By J. E. MUDDOCK. A New Edition in one Volume. Crown 8vo.

Clove Pink: a Study from Memory. By ANNA C. STEELE, Author of "Gardenhurst," &c. Second Edition. Crown 8vo., 3*s*. 6*d*.

'Midst the Wild Carpathians. By MAURUS JOKAI. Translated by R. NISBET BAIN. A New Edition. Crown 8vo., 3*s*. 6*d*.

CATALOGUE OF BOOKS

PUBLISHED BY

CHAPMAN & HALL, LIMITED.

Agriculture, Farming, Horticulture, &c.

Agricultural Science (Lectures on), AND OTHER PROCEEDINGS OF THE INSTITUTE OF AGRICULTURE, SOUTH KENSINGTON, 1883–84. Crown 8vo., sewed, 2*s*.

Agricultural Zoology. By Dr. J. RITZEMA BOS. Translated by Professor J. R. AINSWORTH DAVIS, B.A., F.C.P. With an Introduction by MISS E. A. ORMEROD, F.R.Met.S., F.R.M.S., etc. With 149 Illustrations. Crown 8vo., 6*s*.

About Orchids: A Chat. By FREDERICK BOYLE. With Coloured Illustrations. Large crown 8vo., 8*s*.

Food Grains of India. By Professor A. H. CHURCH, M.A. Oxon. With numerous Woodcuts. Small 4to., 6*s*.

Animal Plagues: THEIR HISTORY, NATURE, AND PREVENTION. By GEORGE FLEMING, F.R.C.S. 8vo., cloth, 15*s*.

Practical Lessons in Botany. Adapted for Beginners in all Classes. By the Rev. Professor HENSLOW. Illustrated. Crown 8vo., sewn, 6*d*.

The Pleasures and Profits of our Little POULTRY FARM. By Miss G. HILL. Small 8vo., 3*s*.

Dairy Farming. To which is added a Description of the Chief Continental Systems. By JAMES LONG. With numerous Illustrations. Crown 8vo., 9*s*.

Illustrations of the Principal Natural ORDERS OF THE VEGETABLE KINGDOM, PREPARED FOR THE SCIENCE AND ART DEPARTMENT, SOUTH KENSINGTON. By D. OLIVER, LL.D., F.L.S., F.R.S., &c. New Edition, revised by Author. With 109 Coloured Plates. Royal 8vo., 16*s*.

British Bee Farming: Its Profits and Pleasures. By JAMES F. ROBINSON. Large crown 8vo., 5*s*.

Farming for Pleasure and Profit. By ARTHUR ROLAND. Edited by WILLIAM ABLETT. 8 vols. Crown 8vo., 5*s*. each.

- DAIRY-FARMING, MANAGEMENT OF COWS, etc.
- POULTRY-KEEPING.
- TREE-PLANTING, FOR ORNAMENTATION OR PROFIT.
- STOCK-KEEPING AND CATTLE-REARING.
- DRAINAGE OF LAND, IRRIGATION, MANURES, etc.
- ROOT-GROWING, HOPS, etc.
- MANAGEMENT OF GRASS LANDS, LAYING DOWN GRASS, ARTIFICIAL GRASSES, etc.
- MARKET GARDENING, HUSBANDRY FOR FARMERS AND GENERAL CULTIVATORS.

Prairie Experiences in Handling CATTLE AND SHEEP. By Major SHEPHERD, R.E. With Illustrations and Map. Demy 8vo., 10*s*. 6*d*.

Holt Castle; or, Threefold Interest in Land. By Professor TANNER, F.C.S. Crown 8vo.

Jack's Education; or, How He Learnt Farming. By Professor TANNER, F.C.S. Second Edition. Crown 8vo.

Principles of Agricultural Practice AS AN INSTRUCTIONAL SUBJECT. By Prof. JOHN WRIGHTSON, M.R.A.C., F.C.S., &c., President of the College of Agriculture, Downton. With Geological Map. Second Edition. Crown 8vo., 5*s*.

Fallow and Fodder Crops. By Prof. JOHN WRIGHTSON, M.R.A.C., F.C.S., &c., President of the College of Agriculture, Downton. Crown 8vo., 5*s*.

Art.

Written Design. By T. R. ABLETT. Oblong, sewed, *6d.*

Practical Plane and Solid Geometry. By HENRY ANGEL, Lecturer at the Birkbeck Institute. Crown 8vo.

Alfred Stevens (Sculptor). A Biographical Sketch. By W. ARMSTRONG. Fully illustrated. Imp. 4to., handsomely bound, *10s. 6d.*

Charts for Model Drawing. By T. C. BARFIELD. *8s.*

Principles of the Science of Colour. By W. BENSON. 4to., *15s.*

The Industrial Arts of India. By Sir GEORGE C. M. BIRDWOOD, C.S.I. With Map and 174 Illustrations. New Edition. Demy 8vo., *14s.*

Elements of Geometrical Drawing. By THOMAS BRADLEY, Royal Military Academy, Woolwich. In Two Parts, with Sixty Plates. Oblong folio, half bound, each Part *16s.*

Linear Perspective, for the Use of Schools of Art. By R. BURCHETT. New Edition. With Illustrations. Post 8vo., cloth, *7s.*

Practical Geometry: The Course of Construction of Plane Geometrical Figures. By R. BURCHETT. With 137 Diagrams. Eighteenth Edition. Post 8vo., cloth, *5s.*

Definition of Geometry. By R. BURCHETT. 18mo., sewed, *5d.*

English Porcelain: A Handbook to the China made in England during the 18th Century. By Prof. A. H. CHURCH, M.A. Oxon. With numerous Woodcuts. Large crown 8vo., *3s.*

English Earthenware: A Handbook to the Wares made in England during the 17th and 18th Centuries. By Prof. A. H. CHURCH, M.A. Oxon. With numerous Woodcuts. Large crown 8vo., *3s.*

Precious Stones: Considered in their Scientific and Artistic relations. By Prof. A. H. CHURCH, M.A. Oxon. With a Coloured Plate and Woodcuts. Second Edition. Large crown 8vo., *2s. 6d.*

College and Corporation Plate. A Handbook for the Reproduction of Silver Plate. By WILFRED JOSEPH CRIPPS, M.A., F.S.A. With numerous Illustrations. Large crown 8vo., cloth, *2s. 6d.*

Interior Architecture. Doors, Vestibules, Staircases, Anterooms, Drawing, Dining, and Bed Rooms, Libraries, Bank and Newspaper Offices, Shop Fronts and Interiors. By E. DAUBOURG. Half-imperial, cloth, *£2 12s. 6d.*

Tapestry. By ALFRED DE CHAMPEAUX. With numerous Woodcuts. Cloth, *2s. 6d.*

Art in the Modern State. By Lady DILKE. With facsimile. Demy 8vo., *9s.*

Drawing Book of the Government SCHOOL OF DESIGN. By WILLIAM DYCE, R.A. Fifty selected Plates. Folio, sewed, *5s.*; mounted, *18s.*

Elementary Outlines of Ornament. By WILLIAM DYCE, R.A. Plates I. to XXII., containing 97 Examples, adapted for Practice of Standards I. to IV. Small folio, sewed, *2s. 6d.*

Selection from Dyce's Drawing Book. Fifteen Plates. Sewed, *1s. 6d.*; mounted on cardboard, *6s. 6d.*

Text to Dyce's Drawing Book. By WILLIAM DYCE, R.A. Crown 8vo., sewed, *6d.*

Musical Instruments. By CARL ENGEL. With numerous Woodcuts. Large crown 8vo., cloth, *2s. 6d.*

Maiolica. By C. D. E. FORTNUM, F.S.A. With numerous Woodcuts. Large crown 8vo., cloth, *2s. 6d.*

Bronzes. By C. D. E. FORTNUM, F.S.A. With numerous Woodcuts. Large crown 8vo., cloth, *2s. 6d.*

Japanese Pottery. Being a Native Report, with an Introduction and Catalogue. By A. W. FRANKS. With numerous Illustrations and Marks. Large crown 8vo., cloth, *2s. 6d.*

Ironwork: From the Earliest Time to the End of the Mediæval Period. By J. STARKIE GARDNER. With 57 Illustrations. Large crown 8vo., *3s.*

French Pottery. By PAUL GASNAULT and ED. GARNIER. With Illustrations and Marks. Large crown 8vo., *3s.*

A Practical Handbook of Drawing FOR MODERN METHODS OF REPRODUCTION. By CHARLES G. HARPER. With many Illustrations showing comparative results. Crown 8vo., *7s. 6d.*

ART—*CONTINUED.*

The Decoration of Metals: Chasing, REPOUSSÉ AND SAW PIERCING. By JOHN HARRISON. With 180 Illustrations. Crown 8vo., 3*s.* 6*d.*

Elementary Design: Being a Theoretical and Practical Introduction in the Art of Decoration. By RICHARD G. HATTON, Durham College of Science, Newcastle-on-Tyne. With 110 Illustrations. Crown 8vo., 2*s.* 6*d.*

Figure Drawing and Composition. By R. G. HATTON, author of "Text-book of Elementary Design." Illustrated. Crown 8vo.

Industrial Arts of Scandinavia in the PAGAN TIME. By HANS HILDEBRAND. With numerous Woodcuts. Large crown 8vo., 2*s.* 6*d.*

Twelve Heads After Holbein. Selected from Drawings in Her Majesty's Collection at Windsor. Reproduced in Autotype in portfolio. £1 16*s.*

Industrial Arts: Historical Sketches. With numerous Illustrations. Large crown 8vo., 3*s.*

Theory and Practice of Design: An Advanced Text Book on Decorative Art. By FRANK G. JACKSON, Master in the Birmingham Municipal School of Art. With 700 Illustrations. Large crown 8vo., 9*s.*

Decorative Design. An Elementary Text Book of Principles and Practice. By FRANK G. JACKSON. With numerous Illustrations. Second Edition. Crown 8vo., 7*s.* 6*d.*

Handbook to Perspective. By HENRY A. JAMES, M.A. Crown 8vo., 2*s.* 6*d.*

Perspective Charts, for use in Class Teaching. By HENRY A. JAMES, M.A. 2*s.*

Hints to Amateurs. A Handbook on Art. By LOUISE JOPLING. With Diagrams. Crown 8vo., 1*s.* 6*d.*

The Street of Human Habitations. By Mrs. RAY S. LINEHAM. Fully Illustrated. Crown 8vo., 6*s.*

Russian Art and Art Objects in Russia. A Handbook to the Reproduction of Goldsmiths' Work and other Art Treasures. By ALFRED MASKELL. With Illustrations. Large crown 8vo., 4*s.* 6*d.*

Ivories: Ancient and Mediæval. By WILLIAM MASKELL. With numerous Woodcuts. Large crown 8vo., cloth, 2*s.* 6*d.*

Handbook to the Dyce and Forster COLLECTIONS. By WILLIAM MASKELL. With Illustrations. Large crown 8vo., cloth, 2*s.* 6*d.*

Life in Ancient Egypt and Assyria. By G. MASPÉRO, late Director of Archæology in Egypt, and Member of the Institute of France. Translated by A. P. MORTON. With 188 Illustrations. Third Thousand. Crown 8vo., 5*s.*

Raphael: His Life, Works, and Times. By EUGENE MUNTZ. Illustrated with about 200 Engravings. A New Edition, revised from the Second French Edition by W. ARMSTRONG, B.A. Oxon. Imperial 8vo., 25*s.*

Glass. By ALEXANDER NESBITT. With numerous Woodcuts. Large crown 8vo., cloth, 2*s.* 6*d.*

Elementary Drawing: A Few Suggestions for Students and Teachers. By H. FOSTER NEWEY, Birmingham School of Art. Illustrated. Crown 8vo., 2*s.* 6*d.*

A History of Ancient Art in Primitive GREECE. By GEORGES PERROT and CHARLES CHIPIEZ. With about 500 Illustrations. 2 vols. Imperial 8vo.

A History of Ancient Art in Persia. By GEORGES PERROT and CHARLES CHIPIEZ. With 254 Illustrations, and 12 Steel and Coloured Plates. Imperial 8vo., 21*s.*

A History of Ancient Art in Phrygia — LYDIA, AND CARIA — LYCIA. By GEORGES PERROT and CHARLES CHIPIEZ. With 280 Illustrations. Imperial 8vo., 15*s.*

A History of Ancient Art in Sardinia, JUDÆA, SYRIA, AND ASIA MINOR. By GEORGES PERROT and CHARLES CHIPIEZ. With 395 Illustrations. 2 vols. Imperial 8vo., 36*s.*

A History of Ancient Art in Phœnicia AND ITS DEPENDENCIES. By GEORGES PERROT and CHARLES CHIPIEZ. With 654 Illustrations. 2 vols. Imperial 8vo., 42*s.*

A History of Art in Chaldæa and ASSYRIA. By GEORGES PERROT and CHARLES CHIPIEZ. With 452 Illustrations. 2 vols. Imperial 8vo., 42*s.*

ART—*CONTINUED.*

A History of Art in Ancient Egypt. By GEORGES PERROT and CHARLES CHIPIEZ. With 600 Illustrations. 2 vols. Imperial 8vo., 42*s.*

Gold and Silver Smith's Work. By J. H. POLLEN. With numerous Woodcuts. Large crown 8vo., cloth, 2*s.* 6*d.*

Ancient and Modern Furniture and Woodwork. By J. H. POLLEN. With numerous Woodcuts. Large crown 8vo., cloth, 2*s.* 6*d.*

The Art of the Saracens in Egypt. By STANLEY LANE POOLE, B.A., M.R.A.S. With 108 Woodcuts. Large crown 8vo., 4*s.*

Ten Lectures on Art. By E. J. POYNTER, R.A. Third Edition. Large crown 8vo., 9*s.*

Sciography, or Parallel and Radial PROJECTION OF SHADOWS. Being a Course of Exercises for the use of Students in Architectural and Engineering Drawing, and for Candidates preparing for the Examinations in this subject and in Third Grade Perspective conducted by the Science and Art Department. By ROBERT PRATT, Headmaster School of Science and Art, Barrow-in-Furness. Oblong quarto, 7*s.* 6*d.*

Outlines of Historic Ornament. Translated from the German. Edited by GILBERT REDGRAVE. With numerous Illustrations. Crown 8vo., 4*s.*

Manual of Design. By RICHARD REDGRAVE, R.A. With Woodcuts. Large crown 8vo., cloth, 2*s.* 6*d.*

Elementary Manual of Colour, with a Catechism on Colour. By RICHARD REDGRAVE, R.A. 24mo., cloth, 9*d.*

A Descriptive Catalogue of the HisTORICAL COLLECTION OF WATER-COLOUR PAINTINGS IN THE SOUTH KENSINGTON MUSEUM. By SAMUEL REDGRAVE. With numerous Chromo-lithographs and other Illustrations. Royal 8vo., £1 1*s.*

The Industrial Arts in Spain. By JUAN F. RIANO. With numerous Woodcuts. Large crown 8vo., cloth, 4*s.*

Italian Sculpture of the Middle Ages AND PERIOD OF THE REVIVAL OF ART. By J. C. ROBINSON. With 20 Engravings. Royal 8vo., cloth, 7*s.* 6*d.*

Textile Fabrics. By the Very Rev. Canon ROCK, D.D. With numerous Woodcuts. Large crown 8vo., cloth 2*s.* 6*d.*

Egyptian Art. An Elementary Handbook for the use of Students. By CHARLES RYAN, late Head Master of the Ventnor School of Art. With 56 Illustrations. Crown 8vo., 2*s.* 6*d.*

The Sculptor and Art Student's Guide to the Proportions of the Human Form, with Measurements in feet and inches of Full-grown Figures of Both Sexes and of Various Ages. By Dr. G. SCHADOW. Plates reproduced by J. SUTCLIFFE. Oblong folio, 31*s.* 6*d.*

Wood-Carving in Practice and THEORY, AS APPLIED TO HOME ARTS. With Notes on Designs having special application to Carved Wood in different Styles. By F. L. SCHAUERMANN. Containing 124 Illustrations. Second Edition. Large crown 8vo., 5*s.*

The Mythology of Greece and Rome, with Special Reference to its Use in Art. From the German. By O. SEEMAN. Edited by G. H. BIANCHI. 64 Illustrations. New Edition. Crown 8vo., 5*s.*

Persian Art. By Major R. MURDOCK SMITH, R.E. With Map and Woodcuts. Second Edition. Large crown 8vo., 2*s.*

Architecture for General Readers, to which is added an Historical Sketch of Architecture. By H. HEATHCOTE STATHAM With hundreds of Illustrations by the author. Large crown 8vo.

Early Christian Art in Ireland. By MARGARET STOKES. With 106 Woodcuts. Crown 8vo., 4*s.*

Elementary Art Teaching: An Educational and Technical Guide for Teachers and Learners, including Infant School-work; The Work of the Standards; Freehand; Geometry; Model Drawing, Nature Drawing; Colours; Light and Shade; Modelling and Design. By EDWARD R. TAYLOR, Head Master of the Birmingham Municipal School of Art. With over 600 Diagrams and Illustrations. 8vo., 10*s.* 6*d.*

The Barbizon School of Painters: Corot, Rousseau, Diaz, Millet, and Daubigny. By D. C. THOMSON. With 130 Illustrations, including 36 Full-page Plates, of which 18 are Etchings. 4to., cloth, 42*s.*

Drawing-Book. By G. WALLIS. Sewed, 3*s.* 6*d.*; mounted, 8*s.*

ART—*CONTINUED.*

The Principles of Ornament. By JAMES WARD. Edited by GEORGE AITCHINSON, A.R.A. Large crown 8vo., *7s. 6d.*

Elementary Principles of Ornament. By JAMES WARD. With 122 Illustrations in the Text. Large crown 8vo., *5s.*

Church Embroidery—Designs for. By A. R. Letterpress by the Hon. Mrs. WIEL. With numerous Illustrations. 4to., *12s.* net.

Analysis of Ornament: The Characteristics of Styles. An Introduction to the History of Ornamental Art. By R. N. WORNUM. With many Illustrations. Ninth Edition. Royal 8vo., cloth, *8s.*

Industrial Arts of Denmark, from THE EARLIEST TIMES TO THE DANISH CONQUEST OF ENGLAND. By J. J. A. WORSAAE. With Maps and Woodcuts. Large crown 8vo., *3s. 6d.*

Biography and Reminiscences.

Alfred Stevens (SCULPTOR). A Biographical Sketch. By W. ARMSTRONG. Fully illustrated. Imp. 4to., handsomely bound, *10s. 6d.*

From Sinner to Saint; or, Character Transformations. By JOHN BURN BAILEY. Crown 8vo., *6s.*

Modern Methuselahs; or, Short Biographical Sketches of a few advanced Nonagenarians or actual Centenarians. By JOHN BURN BAILEY. Demy 8vo., *10s. 6d.*

A Journalist's Jottings. By W. BEATTY-KINGSTON. 2 vols. Demy 8vo., *24s.*

A Wanderer's Notes. By W. BEATTY-KINGSTON. 2 vols. Demy 8vo., *24s.*

Music and Manners: Personal Reminiscences and Sketches of Character. By W. BEATTY-KINGSTON. 2 vols. Demy 8vo., *30s.*

Memoir of Benjamin Lord Bloomfield, G.C.B., &c. By GEORGIANA LADY BLOOMFIELD. With Portraits. 2 vols. Demy 8vo., *28s.*

A Girl's Life Eighty Years Ago. Selections from the Letters of Eliza Southgate Bowne, with an Introduction by CLARENCE COOK. Illustrated with Portraits and Views. Crown 4to., *12s.*

Frederick the Great. By Col. C. B. BRACKENBURY. With Maps and Portrait. Large crown 8vo., *4s.*

Musical Celebrities: Portraits and Biographies. By F. F. BUFFEN. Second Series. Crown 4to., *21s.*

The Life of Sir Richard Francis BURTON. By Lady ISABEL BURTON. With Portraits, numerous Coloured and other Illustrations, and Maps. 2 vols. Demy 8vo., *42s.*

Life of Frederick Schiller and Exami-NATION OF HIS WORKS. By THOMAS CARLYLE. With Supplement of 1872. Portrait and Plates. Demy 8vo., *9s.* and *8s.*; crown 8vo., *2s. 6d.*, *2s.*, and *1s.*

Oliver Cromwell's Letters and SPEECHES. By THOMAS CARLYLE. With Portraits. 5 vols., demy 8vo., *9s.* each; 3 vols., demy 8vo., *8s.* each; 3 vols., crown 8vo., *2s. 6d.* each; 5 vols., crown 8vo., *1s.* each; 1 vol., crown 8vo., *2s. 6d.*

Life of John Sterling. By THOMAS CARLYLE. With Portrait. Demy 8vo., *9s.* and *8s.*; crown 8vo., *2s. 6d.* and *1s.*

History of Frederick the Second. By THOMAS CARLYLE. 10 vols., demy 8vo., *9s.* each; 6 vols., demy 8vo., *8s.* each; 5 vols., crown 8vo., *2s. 6d.* each; 10 vols., crown 8vo., *1s.* each.

Early Kings of Norway. By THOMAS CARLYLE. With Portrait Illustrations. Demy 8vo., *9s.* and *8s.*; crown 8vo., *2s. 6d.* and *1s.*

Life and Letters of Charlotte Elizabeth, Princess Palatine and mother of Philippe d'Orléans, Regent of France, 1652–1722. With Portraits. Demy 8vo., *10s. 6d.*

George Washington. By Lieut.-Colonel COOPER-KING. With Portrait and Maps. Large crown 8vo., *6s.*

BIOGRAPHY AND REMINISCENCES—*CONTINUED.*

Memoirs of a Royalist. By the Count DE FALLOUX. Edited by C. B. PITMAN. 2 vols. With Portraits. Demy 8vo., 32*s.*

The Salon of Madame Necker. By VICOMTE D'HAUSSONVILLE. 2 vols. Crown 8vo., 18*s.*

Recollections of Forty Years. By FERDINAND DE LESSEPS. 2 vols. Demy 8vo., 24*s.*

Experiences of a Woolwich Professor DURING FIFTEEN YEARS AT THE ROYAL MILITARY ACADEMY. By Major-General A. W. DRAYSON. Demy 8vo., 8*s.*

Englishman in Paris: Notes and Recollections during the Reign of Louis Philippe and the Empire. Eighth Thousand. Crown 8vo., 7*s.* 6*d.*

Life and Letters of Edward Livingstone Youmans. By JOHN FISKE. Comprising Correspondence with Spencer, Huxley, Tyndall, and others. Crown 8vo., 8*s.*

Henry Irving: A Record of Twenty Years at the Lyceum. By PERCY FITZGERALD, M.A., F.S.A. With Portrait. Demy 8vo., 14*s.*

The Life of Charles Dickens. By JOHN FORSTER. Original Edition. Vol. I., 8vo., cloth, 12*s.* Vol. II., 8vo., cloth, 14*s.* Vol. III., 8vo., cloth, 16*s.*

Uniform with the Illustrated Library Edition of Dickens's Works. 2 vols. Demy 8vo., 20*s.*

Uniform with the "C. D." Edition. With numerous Illustrations. 2 vols. 7*s.*

Uniform with the Crown Edition. Crown 8vo., 5*s.*

Uniform with the Household Edition. With Illustrations by F. BARNARD. Crown 4to., cloth, 5*s.*

Uniform with the Pictorial Edition. With 40 Illustrations by F. BARNARD and others. Royal 8vo., 3*s.* 6*d.*

Letters from the Crimea, the Danube, AND ARMENIA. By General GORDON. Edited by DEMETRIUS C. BOULGER. Second Edition. Crown 8vo., 5*s.*

Secrets of the Prison House. By Major ARTHUR GRIFFITHS, H.M. Inspector of Prisons. With numerous Illustrations by GEORGE D. ROWLANDSON. 2 vols. Demy 8vo., 30*s.*

French Revolutionary Generals. By Major ARTHUR GRIFFITHS, H.M. Inspector of Prisons. Large crown 8vo., 6*s.*

Swift: THE MYSTERY OF HIS LIFE AND LOVE. By the Rev. JAMES HAY. Crown 8vo., 6*s.*

Behind the Scenes of the Comédie FRANCAISE, AND OTHER RECOLLECTIONS. By ARSÉNE HOUSSAYE. Translated from the French. Demy 8vo., 14*s.*

Turenne. By H. M. HOZIER. With Portrait and two Maps. Large crown 8vo., 4*s.*

Creators of the Age of Steel. Memoirs of Sir W. Siemens, Sir H. Bessemer, Sir J. Whitworth, Sir J. Brown, and other Inventors. By W. T. JEANS. Second Edition. Crown 8vo., 7*s.* 6*d.*

The Life of Miguel de Cervantes SAAVEDRA: a Biographical, Literary, and Historical Study, with a Tentative Bibliography from 1585 to 1892, and an Annotated Appendix on the "Canto de Calíope." By JAMES FITZMAURICE KELLY. Demy 8vo., 16*s.*

Convivial Caledonia: Inns and Taverns of Scotland, and some Famous People who have Frequented Them. By ROBERT KEMPT. Crown 8vo., 2*s.* 6*d.*

General Lee of the Confederate Army. By FITZHUGH LEE, his Nephew. With Portrait and Maps. Crown 8vo., 6*s.*

A Waterbiography. By R. C. LESLIE. With Illustrations by the Author. Crown 8vo.

A Sea Painter's Log. By R. C. LESLIE. With 12 Full-page Illustrations by the Author. Large crown 8vo., 12*s.*

H. M. Stanley: HIS LIFE, WORKS, AND EXPLORATIONS. By the Rev. H. W. LITTLE. Demy 8vo., 10*s.* 6*d.*

The Life of Warren Hastings, First Governor of India. By Col. G. B. MALLESON, C.S.I. With Portrait. Demy 8vo.

Loudon: A Sketch of the Military Life of Gideon Ernest, Freicherr von Loudon. By Col. G. B. MALLESON, C.S.I. With Portrait and Maps. Large crown 8vo., 4*s.*

Reminiscences of a Regicide. Edited from the Original MSS. of SERGENT MARCEAU, Member of the Convention, and Administrator of Police in the French Revolution of 1789. By M. C. M. SIMPSON. Demy 8vo., with Illustrations and Portraits, 14*s.*

BIOGRAPHY AND REMINISCENCES—*CONTINUED.*

Raphael: his Life, Works, and Times. By EUGENE MUNTZ. Illustrated with about 200 Engravings. A New Edition, revised from the Second French Edition. By W. ARMSTRONG, B.A. Imperial 8vo., 25*s.*

Life of Richard Cobden. By the Right Hon. JOHN MORLEY, M.P. With Portrait. New Edition. Crown 8vo., 7*s.* 6*d.*
Popular Edition, with Portrait, 4to., sewed, 1*s.*; cloth, 2*s.*

Memoir of Lieutenant Rudolph de LISLE, R.N., of the Naval Brigade. By the Rev. H. N. OXENHAM, M.A. Third Edition. Crown 8vo., 7*s.* 6*d.*

The Earl of Peterborough and Mon-MOUTH (Charles Mordaunt): A Memoir. By Colonel FRANK RUSSELL, Royal Dragoons. With Illustrations. 2 vols. Demy 8vo., 32*s.*

The Life of the Right Hon. W. E. For-STER. By Sir T. WEMYSS REID. With Portraits. Fourth Edition. 2 vols. Demy 8vo., 32*s.*
Fifth Edition, in one volume, with new Portrait. Demy 8vo., 10*s.* 6*d.*

Recollections of My Youth. By ERNEST RENAN. Translated from the French, and Revised by MADAME RENAN. Second Edition. Crown 8vo., 3*s.* 6*d.*

Elisabeth of Roumania: A Study. With Two Tales from the German of Carmen Sylva, Her Majesty Queen of Roumania. By BLANCHE ROOSEVELT. With Two Portraits and Illustrations. Demy 8vo., 12*s.*

Early Days Recalled. By Mrs. JANET ROSS. With Illustrations and Portrait. Crown 8vo., 5*s.*

Friedrich Frobel: A Short Sketch of his Life, including Fröbel's Letters from Dresden and Leipzig to his Wife, now first Translated into English. By EMILY SHIRREFF. Crown 8vo., 2*s.*

Life of Suvóroff. By Lieut.-Col. SPALDING. Crown 8vo., 6*s.*

Parliamentary Generals of the Great CIVIL WAR. By Major WALFORD, R.A. With Maps. Large crown 8vo., 4*s.*

Days of a Soldier's Life. Written during active service in the Crimean, Chinese, Austro-Prussian ('66), and Franco-German ('70-'71) Wars. By General Sir C. P. BEAUCHAMP WALKER. Demy 8vo., with Portrait.

Parallel Lives of Ancient and Modern HEROES. By C. D. YOUNGE. New Edition. 12mo, cloth, 4*s.* 6*d.*

Cookery, &c.

Hilda's "Where is it?" of Recipes. Containing many old CAPE, INDIAN, and MALAY DISHES and PRESERVES; also Directions for Polishing Furniture, Cleaning Silk, &c.; and a Collection of Home Remedies in Case of Sickness. By HILDAGONDA J. DUCKITT. Fifth Thousand. Crown 8vo., 4*s.* 6*d.*

Dinners in Miniature. By Mrs. EARL. Crown 8vo., 2*s.* 6*d.*

The Royal Confectioner: English and Foreign. By C. E. FRANCATELLI. With Illustrations. Sixth Thousand. Crown 8vo., 5*s.*

The Pytchley Book of Refined Cook-ERY AND BILLS OF FARE. By Major L——. Fifth Edition. Large crown 8vo., 8*s.*

Breakfasts, Luncheons, and Ball SUPPERS. By Major L——. Crown 8vo., 4*s.*

Table Decoration. By WILLIAM LOW. With 19 Full Illustrations. Demy 8vo., 6*s.*

Official Handbook of the National TRAINING SCHOOL FOR COOKERY. Containing Lessons on Cookery, forming the Course of Instruction in the School. Compiled by "R. O. C." Twenty-fourth Thousand. Large crown 8vo., 6*s.*

Breakfast and Savoury Dishes. By "R. O. C." Ninth Thousand. Crown 8vo., 1*s.*

Sick-Room Cookery. Compiled by "R. O. C." Crown 8vo., sewed, 6*d.*

How to Cook Fish. Compiled by "R. O. C." Crown 8vo., sewed, 3*d.*

St. James's Cookery Book. By LOUISA ROCHFORT. Crown 8vo., 3*s.* 6*d.*

The Kingswood Cookery Book. By H. F. WICKEN. Crown 8vo., 2*s.*

Fiction.

A Romance of N'Shabe: Being a Record of Startling Adventures in South Central Africa. By ANDREW A. ANDERSON. With Illustrations. Crown 8vo., *5s.*

The Story of Allan Gordon. By Captain LINDSAY ANDERSON. With Illustrations. Crown 8vo., *5s.*

Among Typhoons and Pirate Craft. By Captain LINDSAY ANDERSON. With Illustrations by STANLEY WOOD. Crown 8vo., *5s.*

A Cruise in an Opium Clipper. By Captain LINDSAY ANDERSON. With Illustrations. Crown 8vo., *6s.*

Altavona: Fact and Fiction from my Life in the Highlands. By JOHN STUART BLACKIE, F.R.S.E. Third Edition. Crown 8vo., *6s.*

Babylon Electrified: The History of an Expedition undertaken to restore Ancient Babylon by the Power of Electricity, and how it Resulted. Translated from the French. By A. BLEUNARD. Illustrated. Royal 8vo., *12s.*

From the Frontier: Sketches and Stories of Savage Life. By FREDERICK BOYLE. Crown 8vo., *3s. 6d.*

The Prophet John: A Romance. By FREDERICK BOYLE. Crown 8vo., *5s.*

The Orchid Seekers: A Story of Adventure in Borneo. By FREDERICK BOYLE and ASHMORE RUSSAN. Illustrated by ALFRED HARTLEY. Crown 8vo., *7s. 6d.*

Rachel and Maurice, and other Tales. By the Hon. MARGARET COLLIER, Madame Galletti di Cadilliac. Crown 8vo., *3s. 6d.*

The Lazy Tour of Two Idle Apprentices. By WILKIE COLLINS and CHARLES DICKENS. With 8 Illustrations. Crown 8vo., *5s.*

CHARLES DICKENS'S WORKS.

Pickwick Papers.
Martin Chuzzlewit.
Dombey and Son.
Nicholas Nickleby.
David Copperfield.
Bleak House.
Little Dorrit.
Our Mutual Friend.
Barnaby Rudge.
Old Curiosity Shop.
Edwin Drood and Other Stories.
Christmas Stories, from "Household Words."
Sketches by "Boz."
Christmas Books.
Oliver Twist.
Great Expectations.
Tale of Two Cities.
Hard Times.
Uncommercial Traveller.

*** *For detailed List of the different editions of Charles Dickens's Works see pages 27–31.*

Innocencia: A Story of the Prairie Regions of Brazil. By SYLVIO DINARTE. Translated from the Portuguese and Illustrated by JAMES W. WELLS, F.R.G.S. Crown 8vo., *6s.*

The Secret of the Princess: A Tale of Country, Camp, Convict, and Cloister Life in Russia. By MRS. SUTHERLAND EDWARDS. Crown 8vo., *3s. 6d.*

South African Sketches. By Colonel A. B. ELLIS. Crown 8vo., *6s.*

Undine: a Romance translated from the German. By DE LA MOTTE FOUQUÉ. With an Introduction by JULIA CARTWRIGHT. Illustrated by HEYWOOD SUMNER. Crown 4to., *5s.*

The New Academe: An Educational Romance. By EDWARD HARTINGTON. Crown 8vo., *5s.*

Queen of Beauty: or, The Adventures of Prince Elfreston. By Mrs. RE HENRY. Illustrated by JOHN JELLICOE.

The Vyvyans: or, the Murder in the Rue Bellechasse. By ANDRÉE HOPE. Crown 8vo., *3s. 6d.*

A Black Squire. By Mrs. ALFRED HUNT. Crown 8vo.

'Midst the Wild Carpathians. By MAURUS JOKAI. Translated by R. NISBET BAIN. Crown 8vo., *3s. 6d.*

A Human Document. By W. H. MALLOCK. Sixth Thousand. Crown 8vo., *3s. 6d.*

FICTION—*CONTINUED.*

GEORGE MEREDITH'S WORKS.

Lord Ormont and his Aminta. 3 vols. 31*s.* 6*d.*

A Uniform Edition. Crown 8vo., 3s. 6d. each.

One of our Conquerors.

Diana of the Crossways.

Evan Harrington.

The Ordeal of Richard Feverel.

The Adventures of Harry Richmond.

Sandra Belloni.

Vittoria.

Rhoda Fleming.

Beauchamp's Career.

The Egoist.

The Shaving of Shagpat; and Farina.

The 6s. Edition is also to be had.

Wanneta, the Sioux. By WARREN K. MOOREHEAD. With Illustrations from Life. Large crown 8vo., 6*s.*

A Partner from the West. By ARTHUR PATERSON. Crown 8vo., 5*s.*

The Goldsmith's Ward: A Tale of London City in the Fifteenth Century. By Mrs. R. H. READE. With 27 Illustrations by W. BOWCHER. Crown 8vo., 6*s.*

Miss Parson's Adventure, and other STORIES. By W. CLARK RUSSELL, W. E. NORRIS, JULIAN HAWTHORNE, Mrs. L. B. WALFORD, J. M. BARRIE, F. C. PHILIPS, Mrs. ALEXANDER, and WILLIAM WESTALL. With 16 Illustrations. 1 vol. Crown 8vo., 5*s.*

Karma. A Novel. By A. P. SINNETT. New Edition. Crown 8vo., 3*s.*

Clove Pink: a Study from Memory. By ANNA C. STEELE. Second Edition. Crown 8vo., 3*s.* 6*d.*

The Chronicles of Barsetshire. By ANTHONY TROLLOPE. A Uniform Edition, in 8 vols., large crown 8vo., handsomely printed, each vol. containing Frontispiece. 6*s.* each:—

THE WARDEN AND BARCHESTER TOWERS. 2 vols.

DR. THORNE.

FRAMLEY PARSONAGE.

THE SMALL HOUSE AT ALLINGTON. 2 vols.

LAST CHRONICLE OF BARSET. 2 vols.

A Princess of Chalco. By A. WALL. With Illustrations. Crown 8vo., 6*s.*

Supplejack: a Romance of Maoriland. By R. WARD. With 8 Illustrations. Crown 8vo., 6*s.*

Stories from "Black and White." By GRANT ALLEN, Mrs. LYNN LINTON, J. M. BARRIE, Mrs. OLIPHANT, W. CLARK RUSSELL, THOMAS HARDY, W. E. NORRIS, and JAMES PAYN. With numerous Illustrations. Crown 8vo., 3*s.* 6*d.*

TWO SHILLINGS EACH.

Eline Vere. By LOUIS COUPERUS. Translated from the Dutch by J. T. GREIN. Crown 8vo.

Cross Currents: A Novel. By MARY A. DICKENS. Third Thousand.

The Story of Helen Davenant. By VIOLET FANE. Crown 8vo.

Pretty Michal. By MAURUS JOKAI. Translated by R. NISBET BAIN. Cr. 8vo.

A Deputy Providence. By HENRY MURRAY. Crown 8vo.

The Queen of Spades and other STORIES. By A. S. PUSHKIN. With a Biography. Translated from the Russian by Mrs. SUTHERLAND EDWARDS. Illustrated. Crown 8vo.

In Low Relief: A Bohemian Transcript. By MORLEY ROBERTS. Crown 8vo.

Through a Field Glass. By G. F. UNDERHILL and H. S. SWEETLAND. With Illustrations by L. THACKERAY. Crown 8vo.

ONE SHILLING EACH.

In the Shade of Schiehallion. By C. BLATHERWICK. With 8 Illustrations. Crown 8vo.

Cynthia. By C. BLATHERWICK. With 4 Illustrations. Crown 8vo.

The Chumplebunnys and some other ODDITIES. Sketched from Life. By W. BEATTY-KINGSTON. Illustrated. Crown 8vo.

Arcadian Life. By S. S. BUCKMAN, F.G.S. With Illustrations. Crown 8vo.

A Poppy's Tears. By MANNINGTON CAFFYN. Crown 8vo.

FICTION—*CONTINUED.*

ONE SHILLING EACH—*continued.*

Notches on the Rough Edge of Life. By LYNN CYRIL D'OYLE. Crown 8vo.

The Waif from the Waves: A Story of Three Lives, touching this World and Another. By the Rev. Canon KNOX LITTLE. Fifth Thousand. Crown 8vo.

The Child of Stafferton: A Chapter from a Family Chronicle. By the Rev. Canon KNOX-LITTLE. Twelfth Thousand. Crown 8vo.

The Broken Vow: A Story of Here and Hereafter. By the Rev. Canon KNOX LITTLE. Eighteenth Thousand. Crown 8vo.

Who is the Man? A Tale of the Scottish Border. By J. S. TAIT. Crown 8vo.

The Helterskelter Hounds: or Mr. Flopkin's Sporting Memoirs. By G. F. UNDERHILL. With Illustrations by L. THACKERAY. 4th Thousand. Crown 8vo.

In and Out of the Pigskin. By G. F. UNDERHILL. With Illustrations by WALLIS MACKAY. Second Edition. Crown 8vo.

History and Politics.

The Scottish Highlanders and the LAND LAWS. By JOHN STUART BLACKIE, F.R.S.E. Demy 8vo., 9*s.*

Frederick the Great. By Colonel C. B. BRACKENBURY. With Maps and Portrait. Large crown 8vo., 4*s.*

The British Army. By the Author of "Greater Britain." Demy 8vo., 12*s.*

Court Life in Egypt. By A. J. BUTLER. Second Edition. Illustrated. Large crown 8vo., 12*s.*

History of Frederick the Second. By THOMAS CARLYLE. 10 vols. Demy 8vo., 9*s.* each; 6 vols., demy 8vo., 8*s.* each; 5 vols., crown 8vo., 2*s.* 6*d.* each; 10 vols., Crown 8vo., 1*s.* each.

Oliver Cromwell's Letters and SPEECHES. By THOMAS CARLYLE. With Portraits. 5 vols., demy 8vo., 9*s.* each; 3 vols., demy 8vo., 8*s.* each; 3 vols., crown 8vo., 2*s.* 6*d.* each; 5 vols., crown 8vo., 1*s.* each; 1 vol., crown 8vo., 2*s.* 6*d.*

On Heroes, Hero Worship, and the HEROIC IN HISTORY. By THOMAS CARLYLE. Demy 8vo., 7*s.* 6*d.*, 8*s.*; crown 8vo., 2*s.* 6*d.*, 2*s.*, 1*s.*

The French Revolution. A History. By THOMAS CARLYLE. 3 vols., demy 8vo., 9*s.* each; 2 vols., demy 8vo., 8*s.* each; 2 vols., crown 8vo., 2*s.* 6*d.* each; 3 vols., crown 8vo., 1*s.* each; 1 vol., crown 8vo., 2*s.*

Early Kings of Norway; Essay on the Portraits of John Knox. By THOMAS CARLYLE. With Portrait Illustrations. Demy 8vo., cloth, 9*s.* and 8*s.*; crown 8vo., 2*s.* 6*d.*, and 1*s.*

Ireland in the Days of Dean Swift. By J. B. DALY, LL.D. Crown 8vo., 5*s.*

Germany and the Germans: Social Life, Culture, Religious Life, etc., etc. By WILLIAM HARBUTT DAWSON. In 2 vols. Demy 8vo., 26*s.*

Paddy at Home; OR, IRELAND AND THE IRISH AT THE PRESENT TIME, AS SEEN BY A FRENCHMAN. By Baron E. DE MANDAT-GRANCEY. Fifth Edition. Crown 8vo., 1*s.*; in cloth, 1*s.* 6*d.*

Siberia as it is. By H. DE WINDT. With numerous Illustrations. Demy 8vo., 18*s.*

A Child's History of England. By CHARLES DICKENS. Illustrated. Demy 8vo., 10*s.*; post 8vo., 8*s.*; crown 8vo., 5*s.*; 4to., 3*s.*; royal 8vo., 3*s.* 6*d.*; crown 8vo., 3*s.* 6*d.*; crown 8vo., 2*s.* 6*d.*; small fcap. 8vo., 1*s.* 6*d.*

The History of Ancient Civilisation. A Handbook based upon M. Gustave Ducoudray's "Histoire Sommaire de la Civilisation." Edited by Rev. J. VERSCHOYLE, M.A. With Illustrations. Large crown 8vo., 6*s.*

HISTORY AND POLITICS—*CONTINUED.*

The History of Modern Civilisation. By GUSTAVE DUCOUDRAY. With Illustrations. Large crown 8vo., 9*s*.

Old Court Life in Spain. By FRANCES MINTO ELLIOT. 2 vols. Demy 8vo., 24*s*.

History of the Gold Coast of West AFRICA. By A. B. ELLIS, Colonel 1st West India Regiment. Demy 8vo., 10*s*. 6*d*.

The Yoruba-Speaking Peoples of the SLAVE COAST OF WEST AFRICA: their Religion, Manners, Customs, Laws, Language, &c. By A. B. ELLIS. With an Appendix and Map. Demy 8vo., 10*s*. 6*d*.

The Ewe-Speaking People of the SLAVE COAST OF WEST AFRICA. By A. B. ELLIS. With Map. Demy 8vo., 10*s*. 6*d*.

The Tshi-Speaking Peoples of the Gold COAST: their Religion, Manners, Customs, Laws, Language, &c. By A. B. ELLIS. With Map. Demy 8vo., 10*s*. 6*d*.

Politics and Letters. By T. H. S. ESCOTT. Demy 8vo., 9*s*.

England; Its People, Polity, and Pursuits. By T. H. S. ESCOTT. New and Revised Edition. Eighth Thousand. Demy 8vo., 3*s*. 6*d*.

The Present Position of European POLITICS. By the Author of "Greater Britain." Demy 8vo., 12*s*.

Chronicles of Bow Street Police Office. By PERCY FITZGERALD, F.S.A. New and Cheaper Edition.

The History of Pickwick. An Account of its Characters, Localities, Allusions, and Illustrations. By PERCY FITZGERALD, F.S.A. With a Bibliography. Demy 8vo., 8*s*.

Italy: Present and Future. By ANTONIO GALLENGA. 2 vols. Demy 8vo., 21*s*.

An Election Manual. Containing the Parliamentary Elections (Corrupt and Illegal Practices) Act, 1883, with Notes. By Sir J. E. GORST, Q.C., M.P. Third Edition. Crown 8vo., 1*s*. 6*d*.

Our South African Empire. By WILLIAM GRESWELL, M.A., F.R.C.I. With Map. 2 vols. Crown 8vo., 21*s*.

The Great Republic. By Sir LEPEL HENRY GRIFFIN, K.C.S.I. Second Edition Crown 8vo., 4*s*. 6*d*.

China and Her Neighbours. France in Indo-China, Russia and China, India and Thibet, &c. By R. S. GUNDRY. With Maps. Demy 8vo., 9*s*.

Chronicles of an Old Inn: or, a Few Words about Gray's Inn. By ANDRÉE HOPE. Crown 8vo., 5*s*.

Middlesex County Records. Indictments, Recognizances, Coroners' Inquisitions, Post Mortem, Orders, Memoranda, and Certificates of Convictors of Conventiclers, *temp.* 19 Charles II. to 4 James II. By J. CORDY JEAFFRESON, B.A. 4 vols. With Portraits, Illustrations, and Facsimiles. Demy 8vo., 25*s*. each.

Russian Characteristics. By E. B. LANIN. Reprinted, with Revisions, from *The Fortnightly Review.* Demy 8vo., 14*s*.

Egypt under Ismail: A Romance of History. By J. C. MCCOAN. With Portrait and Appendix of Official Documents. Crown 8vo., 7*s*. 6*d*.

British East Africa. A History of the Formation and Work of the Imperial British East Africa Company. Compiled with the Authority of the Directors from Official Documents and the Records of the Company. By P. L. M'DERMOTT. With Maps and Illustrations. Crown 8vo., 6*s*.

Our Ocean Railways; or, The Rise, Progress, and Development of Ocean Steam Navigation, etc., etc. By A. F. MACDONALD. With Maps and Illustrations. Large crown 8vo., 6*s*.

The Emancipation of South America. By General DON BARTOLOME MITRE. Being a Condensed Translation, by WILLIAM PILLING, of "The History of San Martin." Demy 8vo., with Maps, 12*s*.

History of England from the Year 1830 TO THE RESIGNATION OF THE GLADSTONE MINISTRY, 1874. By W. NASSAU MOLESWORTH. Twelfth Thousand. 3 vols. Crown 8vo., 18*s*.

Poland: AN HISTORICAL SKETCH. By Field-Marshal Count VON MOLTKE. With Biographical Notice by E. S. BUCHHEIM. Crown 8vo., 4*s*. 6*d*. and 1*s*.

Tonkin; or, France in the Far East. By C. B. NORMAN. With Maps. Demy 8vo., 14*s*.

HISTORY AND POLITICS—*CONTINUED.*

The Victories of the British Army in THE PENINSULA AND THE SOUTH OF FRANCE from 1808 to 1814. An Epitome of Napier's History of the Peninsular War, and Gurwood's Collection of the Duke of Wellington's Despatches. By ROBERT O'BYRNE, F.R.G.S. Crown 8vo., 5*s*.

Toryism and the Tory Democracy. By STANDISH O'GRADY. Crown 8vo., 5*s*.

The Radical Programme. From the *Fortnightly Review*, with Additions. With a Preface by the Right Hon. J. CHAMBERLAIN, M.P. Thirteenth Thousand. Crown 8vo. Paper Covers, 1*s*.

History of the People of Israel. By ERNEST RENAN.

FIRST DIVISION. Till the Time of King David. Demy 8vo., 14*s*.

SECOND DIVISION. From the Reign of David up to the Capture of Samaria. Demy 8vo., 14*s*.

THIRD DIVISION. From the Time of Hezekiah till the Return from Babylon. Demy 8vo., 14*s*.

The Future of Science: Ideas of 1848. By ERNEST RENAN. Demy 8vo., 18*s*.

A History of Vagrants and Vagrancy AND BEGGARS AND BEGGING. By C. J. RIBTON-TURNER. With Illustrations. Demy 8vo., 21*s*.

The Republic as a Form of Government; or, The Evolution of Democracy in America. By JOHN SCOTT. Crown 8vo., 7*s*. 6*d*.

The First Technical College: a Sketch of the History of "The Andersonian" and the Institutions descended from it, 1796–1894. By A. HUMBOLDT SEXTON. With Portraits and Illustrations. Cr. 8vo. 3*s*. 6*d*.

Castle St. Angelo. By W. W. STORY. With Illustrations. Crown 8vo., 10*s*. 6*d*.

Galileo and His Judges. By F. R. WEGG-PROSSER. Demy 8vo., 5*s*.

Literature, Belles Lettres, and Poetry.

Songs and Verses. By H. CUMBERLAND BENTLEY. Illustrated by FINCH MASON, and dedicated to J. G. WHYTE MELVILLE. Crown 8vo., 4*s*.

Sartor Resartus. By THOMAS CARLYLE. With a Portrait. Demy, 7*s*. 6*d*. and 8*s*.; crown 8vo., 2*s*. 6*d*., 2*s*. and 1*s*.; 4to., sewed, 6*d*.

Life of Frederick Schiller and Examination of his Works. By THOMAS CARLYLE. With Supplement of 1872. Portrait and Plates. Demy, 9*s*. and 8*s*.; crown, 2*s*. 6*d*., 2*s*. and 1*s*.

Critical and Miscellaneous Essays. By THOMAS CARLYLE. With Portrait. 6 vols. Demy, 9*s*. each; 3 vols., demy 8vo., 8*s*. each; 4 vols., crown 8vo., 2*s*. 6*d*. each; 2 vols., crown, 2*s*. each; 7 vols., crown 8vo., 1*s*. each; 4to., sewed, 6*d*.

On Heroes, Hero Worship, and the HEROIC IN HISTORY. By THOMAS CARLYLE. Demy 8vo., 7*s*. 6*d*. and 8*s*.; crown 8vo., 2*s*. 6*d*., 2*s*. and 1*s*; 4to., sewed.

Past and Present. By THOMAS CARLYLE. Demy 9*s*. and 8*s*.; crown 8vo., 2*s*. 6*d*., 2*s*. and 1*s*.

Latter-day Pamphlets. By THOMAS CARLYLE. Demy 8vo., 9*s*. and 8*s*.; crown 8vo., 2*s*. 6*d*., 2*s*. and 1*s*.

Translations from the German. By THOMAS CARLYLE. 3 vols., demy, 9*s*. each; 3 vols., demy 8vo., 8*s*. each; 3 vols., 2*s*. 6*d*. each; 5 vols., 1*s*. each.

Essay on the Portraits of John Knox. By THOMAS CARLYLE. With Portrait Illustrations. Demy 8vo., 9*s*. and 8*s*.; crown 8vo., 2*s*. 6*d*. and 1*s*.

The Canterbury Tales. Selections from the Tales of Geoffrey Chaucer rendered into Modern English. By FRANK PITT TAYLOR. Crown 8vo., 6*s*.

English of Shakespeare. Illustrated in a Philological Commentary on "Julius Cæsar." By GEORGE LILLIE CRAIK. Eighth Edition. Post 8vo., cloth, 5*s*.

LITERATURE, &c.—*CONTINUED.*

Outlines of the History of the English LANGUAGE. By GEORGE LILLIE CRAIK. Eleventh Edition. Post 8vo., cloth, 2*s*. 6*d*.

Studies at Leisure. By W. L. COURTNEY, M.A., LL.D., of New College, Oxford. Crown 8vo., 6*s*.

Studies New and Old. By W. L. COURTNEY, M.A., LL.D., of New College, Oxford. Crown 8vo., 6*s*.

Some French Writers. By EDWARD DELILLE. Contents: Bourget, Pierre Loti, Baudelaire, Guy de Maupassant, Verlaine, Maurice Barres, &c. Crown 8vo., 5*s*.

Handbook to the Dyce and Forster COLLECTIONS IN THE SOUTH KENSINGTON MUSEUM. With Portraits and Facsimiles. 2*s*. 6*d*.

Autumn Songs. By VIOLET FANE. Crown 8vo., 6*s*.

Life and Works. By W. S. LANDOR. 8 vols.:

Vol. I. Out of Print.

Vol. II. Out of Print.

Vol. III. CONVERSATIONS OF SOVEREIGNS AND STATESMEN, AND FIVE DIALOGUES OF BOCCACCIO AND PETRARCA. Demy 8vo., 14*s*.

Life and Works. By W. S. LANDOR—*Continued.*

Vol. IV. DIALOGUES OF LITERARY MEN. Demy 8vo., 14*s*.

Vol. V. DIALOGUES OF LITERARY MEN (*continued*). FAMOUS WOMEN. LETTERS OF PERICLES AND ASPASIA. And Minor Prose Pieces. Demy 8vo., 14*s*.

Vol. VI. MISCELLANEOUS CONVERSATIONS. Demy 8vo., 14*s*.

Vol. VII. GEBIR, ACTS AND SCENES AND HELLENICS. Poems. Demy 8vo., 14*s*.

Vol. VIII. MISCELLANEOUS POEMS AND CRITICISMS ON THEOCRITUS, CATULLUS, AND PETRARCH. Demy 8vo., 14*s*.

Dante for Beginners: a Sketch of the "Divina Commedia." By ARABELLA SHORE. With Translations, Biographical and Critical Notices, and Illustrations. With Portrait. Crown 8vo., 6*s*.

Essays, Speculative and Suggestive. By JOHN ADDINGTON SYMONDS. New Edition. Demy 8vo., 9*s*.

Cosmopolitan Essays. By Sir RICHARD TEMPLE, Bart., M.P., G.C.S.I. With Maps. Demy 8vo., 16*s*.

Military.

Frederick the Great. By Col. C. B. BRACKENBURY. With Maps and Portrait. Large crown 8vo., 4*s*.

The British Army. By the Author of "Greater Britain." Demy 8vo., 12*s*.

Historical Record of the First or Royal REGIMENT OF DRAGOONS. By General DE AINSLIE. Illustrated. Royal 8vo., 21*s*.

History of Frederick the Second. By THOMAS CARLYLE. 10 vols., demy 8vo., 9*s*. each; 6 vols., demy 8vo., 8*s*. each; 5 vols., 2*s*. 6*d*. each; 10 vols., 1*s*. each.

George Washington. By Lieut.-Colonel COOPER-KING. Large crown 8vo. With Portrait and Maps.

Practical Military Surveying and SKETCHING. By Major-General A. W. DRAYSON. Fifth Edition. Post 8vo., 4*s*. 6*d*.

History of the 1st West India Regi-MENT. By Colonel A. B. ELLIS. With Coloured Illustrations. Demy 8vo., 14*s*.

With the Camel Corps up the Nile. By Count GLEICHEN. With numerous Sketches by the Author. Third Edition. Large crown 8vo., 9*s*.

Letters from the Crimea, the Danube, AND ARMENIA. By General GORDON. Edited by DEMETRIUS C. BOULGER. Second Edition. Crown 8vo., 5*s*.

French Revolutionary Generals. By Major ARTHUR GRIFFITHS. Large crown 8vo., 6*s*.

Turenne. By H. M. HOZIER. With Portrait and Two Maps. Large crown 8vo., 4*s*.

General Lee of the Confederate Army. By FITZHUGH LEE, his Nephew. With Portrait and Maps. Crown 8vo., 6*s*.

On Active Service. By W. W. LLOYD, late 24th Regiment. Printed in Colours. Oblong 4to., 5*s*.

Sketches of Indian Life. By W. W. LLOYD, late 24th Regiment. Printed in Colours. 4to., 6*s*.

MILITARY—*CONTINUED.*

The Life of Warren Hastings, First Governor-General of India. By Colonel G. B. MALLESON, C.S.I. With Portrait. Demy 8vo.

Prince Eugene of Savoy. By Colonel G. B. MALLESON. C.S.I. With Portrait and Maps. Large crown 8vo., 6*s*.

Loudon: A Sketch of the Military Life of Gideon Ernest, Freicherr von Loudon. By Colonel G. B. MALLESON, C.S.I. With Portrait and Maps. Large crown 8vo., 4*s*.

The Victories of the British Army in THE PENINSULA AND THE SOUTH OF FRANCE from 1808 to 1814. An Epitome of Napier's History of the Peninsular War, and Gurwood's Collection of the Duke of Wellington's Despatches. By ROBERT O'BYRNE, F.R.G.S. Crown 8vo., 5*s*.

The Earl of Peterborough and Mon-MOUTH (Charles Mordaunt): A Memoir. By Colonel FRANK RUSSELL, Royal Dragoons. With Illustrations. 2 vols. Demy 8vo., 32*s*.

Life in the Army: Every-day Incidents in Camp, Field, and Quarters. By R. SIMKIN. Printed in Colours. Oblong 4to., 5*s*.

Life of Suvoroff. By Lieut.-Col. SPALDING. Crown 8vo., 6*s*.

Martial Law and Custom of War; or, Military Law and Jurisdiction in Troublous Times. By Lieut.-Col. TOVEY, R.E. Crown 8vo., 6*s*.

Parliamentary Generals of the Great CIVIL WAR. By Major WALFORD, R.A. With Maps. Large crown 8vo., 4*s*.

Days of a Soldier's Life. Written during active service in the Crimean, Chinese, Austro-Prussian ('66), and Franco-German ('70–'71) Wars. By General Sir C. P. BEAUCHAMP WALKER. With Portrait. Demy 8vo.

The Young Officer's "Don't." Crown 8vo., 1*s*.

Miscellaneous.

The Carlyle Birthday Book. By THOMAS CARLYLE. Second Edition. Small fcap. 8vo., 3*s*.

Character in the Face. Physiognomical Sketches. Our Looks and what they Mean. Crown 8vo., 5*s*.

The Charles Dickens Birthday Book. With Five Illustrations. In a handsome fcap. 4to. volume, 12*s*.

The Humour and Pathos of Charles DICKENS. By CHARLES KENT. With Portrait. Crown 8vo., 6*s*.

Animal Plagues: THEIR HISTORY, NATURE, AND PREVENTION. By GEORGE FLEMING, F.R.C.S. 8vo., cloth, 15*s*.

Practical Horse-Shoeing. By GEORGE FLEMING, F.R.C.S. With 37 Illustrations. Fifth Edition, enlarged. 8vo., sewed, 2*s*.

Rabies and Hydrophobia: THEIR HISTORY, NATURE, CAUSES, SYMPTOMS, AND PREVENTION. By GEORGE FLEMING, F.R.C.S. With 8 Illustrations. 8vo., cloth, 15*s*.

A Travelling Atlas of the English COUNTIES. By SIDNEY HALL. Fifty Maps, coloured. New Edition, including the Railways, corrected up to the present date. Demy 8vo., in roan tuck, 10*s*. 6*d*.

English Composition Exercises. By J. M. LAINÉ, M.A. Crown 8vo., 2*s*. 6*d*.

The Tarot of the Bohemians. The most Ancient Book in the World. For the exclusive use of the Initiates. An Absolute Key to Occult Science. By PAPUS. With numerous Illustrations. Large crown 8vo., 7*s*. 6*d*.

The Dickens' Dictionary. A Key to the Characters and Principal Incidents in the Tales of Charles Dickens. By GILBERT PIERCE and W. A. WHEELER. New Edition. Large crown 8vo., 5*s*.

Austrian Health Resorts Through-OUT THE YEAR. By W. FRASER RAE. A New and Enlarged Edition. Crown 8vo., 5*s*.

A Birthday Book. By Lady GWENDOLEN RAMSDEN. Containing 46 Illustrations from Original Drawings. Royal 8vo., 21*s*.

Home Education in Relation to the KINDERGARTEN. By EMILY SHIRREFF. Two Lectures. Crown 8vo., 1*s*. 6*d*.

Coach Trimming. By GEORGE A. THRUPP and WILLIAM FARR. With 60 Illustrations. Crown 8vo., 2*s*. 6*d*.

Music, Drama, &c.

Music and Manners: Personal Reminiscences and Sketches of Character. By W. BEATTY-KINGSTON. 2 vols. Demy 8vo., 30*s.*

Musical Celebrities: Portraits and Biographies. By F. F. BUFFEN. Second Series. Crown 4to., 21*s.*

English of Shakespeare. Illustrated in a Philological Commentary on "Julius Cæsar." By GEORGE LILLIE CRAIK. Eighth Edition. Post 8vo., cloth, 5*s.*

Musical Instruments. By CARL ENGEL. With numerous Woodcuts. Large crown 8vo., cloth, 2*s.* 6*d.*

Henry Irving. A Record of Twenty Years at the Lyceum. By PERCY FITZGERALD, M.A., F.S.A. With Portrait. Demy 8vo., 14*s.*

The French Stage in the Eighteenth CENTURY. By FREDERICK HAWKINS. With Portraits. 2 vols. Demy 8vo., 30*s.*

Annals of the French Stage: FROM ITS ORIGIN TO THE DEATH OF RACINE. By FREDERICK HAWKINS. Four Portraits. 2 vols. Demy 8vo., 28*s.*

Behind the Scenes of the Comédie FRANCAISE, AND OTHER RECOLLECTIONS. By ARSÉNE HOUSSAYE. Translated from the French. Demy 8vo., 14*s.*

Half a Century of Music in England, 1837—1887. By F. HUEFFER. Demy 8vo., 8*s.*

Acrobats and Mountebanks. By H. LE ROUX. With over 200 Illustrations by J. GARNIER. Royal 8vo., 16*s.*

Form and Design in Music: A Brief Outline of the Æsthetic Conditions of the Art, addressed to General Readers. By H. H. STATHAM. With Musical Examples. Demy 8vo., 2*s.* 6*d.*

My Thoughts on Music and Musicians. By H. H. STATHAM. Illustrated with Frontispiece of the Entrance-front of Handel's Opera House and Musical Examples. Demy 8vo., 18*s.*

Natural History.

Agricultural Zoology. By Dr. J. RITZEMA BOS. Translated by Professor J. R. AINSWORTH DAVIS, B.A., F.C.P. With an Introduction by Miss E. A. ORMEROD, F.R.Met.S., F.R.M.S., etc. With 149 Illustrations. Crown 8vo., 6*s.*

Log-Book of a Fisherman and ZooloGIST. By FRANK BUCKLAND. With Illustrations. Sixth Thousand. Cr. 8vo., 3*s.* 6*d.*

A Year of Sport and Natural History: Shooting, Hunting, Coursing, Falconry, and Fishing. Edited by OSWALD CRAWFURD. With Chapters on Birds of Prey, Nidifications of Birds, and Tricks of Poachers. With numerous Illustrations by FRANK FELLER, BRYAN HOOD, CECIL ALDIN, A. T. ELWES, E. NEALE, JOHN BEER, P. VIENZENY, STANLEY BERKELEY, and G. E. LODGE. Large Paper Edition.

The Migration of British Birds, including their Post Glacial Emigration as traced by the Application of a New Law of Dispersal. By CHARLES DIXON. With Maps. Crown 8vo.

The Nests and Eggs of Non-IndigenOUS BRITISH BIRDS; or, such species that do not Breed within the British Archipelago. By CHARLES DIXON. With Coloured Frontispiece. Crown 8vo., 6*s.*

Jottings about Birds. By CHARLES DIXON. With Coloured Frontispiece by J. SMIT. Crown 8vo., 6*s.*

The Nests and Eggs of British Birds: When and Where to Find Them. Being a Handbook to the Oölogy of the British Islands. By CHAS. DIXON. Cr. 8vo., 6*s.*

*** *A Large Paper Edition, containing 157 Coloured Illustrations, Demy 8vo., 15s. net.*

The Game Birds and Wild Fowl of THE BRITISH ISLANDS. By CHARLES DIXON. Illustrated by A. T. ELWES. Demy 8vo., 18*s.*

The Migration of Birds: An Attempt to Reduce the Avian Season-flight to Law. By CHARLES DIXON. Crown 8vo., 6*s.*

The Birds of Our Rambles: A Companion for the Country. By CHARLES DIXON. With Illustrations by A. T. ELWES. Large crown 8vo., 7*s.* 6*d.*

Idle Hours with Nature. By CHARLES DIXON. With Frontispiece. Cr. 8vo., 6*s.*

Annals of Bird Life: A Year-Book of British Ornithology. By CHARLES DIXON. With Illustrations. Crown 8vo., 7*s.* 6*d.*

Birds in a Village. By W. H. HUDSON, C.M.Z.S. Joint Author of "Argentine Ornithology." Square crown 8vo., 7*s.* 6*d.*

NATURAL HISTORY—*CONTINUED.*

Idle Days in Patagonia. By W. H. HUDSON, C.M.Z.S. Joint Author of "Argentine Ornithology." With numerous Illustrations by J. SMIT and A. HARTLEY. Demy 8vo., 14*s.*

The Naturalist in La Plata. By W. H. HUDSON, C.M.Z.S. With numerous Illustrations by J. SMIT. Second Edition. Demy 8vo.

Creatures of Other Days. By the Rev. H. N. HUTCHINSON, F.G.S. With a Preface by Sir W. H. FLOWER, K.C.B., F.R.S., and numerous Illustrations by J. SMIT and others. Large Demy 8vo., 14*s.*

Extinct Monsters. A Popular Account of some of the larger forms of Ancient Animal Life. By the Rev. H. N. HUTCHINSON, F.G.S. With numerous Illustrations by J. SMIT and others. Third Thousand, Revised and Enlarged. Demy 8vo., 12*s.*

Economic Entomology. APTERA. By ANDREW MURRAY, F.L.S. With numerous Illustrations. Large crown 8vo., 3*s.* 6*d.*

The Typical Parts in the Skeletons of A CAT, DUCK, AND CODFISH. With comparative descriptions arranged in a Tabular Form. By E. TULLEY NEWTON, F.G.S. Demy 8vo., 3*s.*

The Habits of the Salmon. By Major TRAHERNE. Crown 8vo., 3*s.* 6*d.*

Science and Technology.

Building Construction. Key to Examinations of Science and Art Department. By HENRY ADAMS, M.Inst.C.E., M.I. Mech.E., F.S.I., etc. Professor of Engineering at the City of London College. Crown 8vo., 4*s.*

Machine Construction: A Key to the Examinations of the Science and Art Department. By HENRY ADAMS, M.Inst.C.E. Crown 8vo.

Mechanics and Experimental Science. As required for the Matriculation Examination of the University of London. By EDWARD AVELING, D.Sc., Fellow of University College, London.

MECHANICS. With numerous Woodcuts. Crown 8vo., 6*s.* Key to Problems in ditto. Crown 8vo., 3*s.* 6*d.*

CHEMISTRY. With numerous Woodcuts. Crown 8vo., 6*s.* Key to Problems in ditto. Crown 8vo., 2*s.* 6*d.*

MAGNETISM AND ELECTRICITY. With numerous Woodcuts. Crown 8vo., 6*s.*

LIGHT AND HEAT. With numerous Woodcuts. Crown 8vo., 6*s.* Key to the last two volumes in one vol. Crown 8vo., 5*s.*

The Beam: or, Technical Elements of Girder Construction. By W. L. BAKER, A.M.I.C.E. Crown 8vo., 4*s.*

The Chemistry of Foods. By JAMES BELL, Ph.D., &c., Principal of the Somerset House Laboratory. With Microscopic Illustrations. PART I. TEA, COFFEE, COCOA, SUGAR, ETC. Large crown 8vo., 2*s.* 6*d.* PART II. MILK, BUTTER, CHEESE, CEREALS, PREPARED STARCHES, ETC. Large crown 8vo., 3*s.*

Elements of Human Physiology for THE HYGIENE EXAMINATIONS OF THE SCIENCE AND ART DEPARTMENT. By Dr. J. H. E. BROCK, Assistant Examiner in Hygiene, Science and Art Department. Crown 8vo., 1*s.* 6*d.*

Plain Words About Water. By Professor A. H. CHURCH, M.A. Oxon. Illustrated. Crown 8vo., sewed, 6*d.*

Food: Some Account of its Sources, Constituents, and Uses. By Professor A. H. CHURCH, M.A. Oxon. A New and Revised Edition. Large crown 8vo., cloth, 3*s.*

Sketch of the First Principles of PHYSIOGRAPHY. By JOHN DOUGLAS. With Maps and numerous Illustrations. Crown 8vo., 6*s.*

Thirty Thousand Years of the Earth's PAST HISTORY. By Major-General A. W. DRAYSON. Large crown 8vo., 5*s.*

Practical Metallurgy: An Elementary Text-Book. By A. R. GOWER, Royal School of Mines. With Illustrations. Crown 8vo., 3*s.*

Naval Architecture and Shipbuilding. By GEORGE C. V. HOLMES, Secretary of the Institution of Naval Architects. [*In the Press.*

Marine Engines and Boilers. By GEORGE C. V. HOLMES. With 69 Woodcuts. Large crown 8vo., 3*s.*

The Sea Boat: How to Build, Rig, and Sail Her. By R. C. LESLIE. With numerous Illustrations by the Author. Crown 8vo., 4*s.* 6*d.*

SCIENCE AND TECHNOLOGY—*CONTINUED.*

A Text-Book of Mechanical Engineering. By WILFRED J. LINEHAM, late Professor of Engineering at the Science and Art Department. Fully Illustrated with Cuts and Diagrams. Cr. 8vo. 10*s.* 6*d.* *net.*

Practical Manual of Chemical Assaying, as applied to the Manufacture of Iron. By L. L. DE KONINCK and E. DIETZ. Edited, with notes, by ROBERT MALLET. Post 8vo., cloth, 6*s.*

Advanced Physiography (Physiographic Astronomy). Designed to meet the Requirements of Students preparing for the Elementary and Advanced Stages of Physiography in the Science and Art Department Examinations, and as an Introduction to Physical Astronomy. By JOHN MILLS. Crown 8vo., 4*s.* 6*d.*

Elementary Physiographic Astronomy. By JOHN MILLS, formerly Assistant to the Solar Physics Committee. Crown 8vo., 1*s.* 6*d.*

Alternative Elementary Physics. By JOHN MILLS. Second Edition. Crown 8vo., 2*s.* 6*d.*

Quantitative Analysis (INTRODUCTORY LESSONS ON). By JOHN MILLS and BARKER NORTH. With numerous Woodcuts. Crown 8vo., 1*s.* 6*d.*

Handbook of Quantitative Analysis. By JOHN MILLS and BARKER NORTH. Crown 8vo., 3*s.* 6*d.*

Wood-Working Positions. By W. NELSON, Organiser, Manual Instruction, Manchester School Board. Twelve Illustrations by HERBERT COLE. Royal 4to., 2*s.* 6*d.* Large size, 6*s.*

Handbook to the Special Loan Collection of Scientific Apparatus. 3*s.*

A Catalogue of Modern Works on Science and Technology. Classified under Authors and Subjects. Twenty-second Edition. With Index. Cr. 8vo., 1s.

Solutions to the Questions in Pure Mathematics—Stages 1 and 2—Set at the Science and Art Examinations from 1881 to 1886. By THOMAS T. RANKIN, C.E., Rector of the Gartsherrie Science School, and West of Scotland Mining College. Crown 8vo., 2*s.*

Elementary Building Construction. By GEORGE ROBSON. Illustrated by a Design for an Entrance Lodge and Gate. Fifteen Plates. Oblong folio, sewed, 8*s.*

Home Work in Chemistry (Inorganic): a Series of Exercises with Explanations and Worked Examples. By A. HUMBOLDT SEXTON, F.I.C., F.C.S. Third Edition. Crown 8vo., 1*s.*

Animal Products: Their Preparation, Commercial Uses, and Value. By T. L. SIMMONDS. With numerous Illustrations. Large crown 8vo., 3*s.* 6*d.*

Sport.

The Sea and the Rod. By F. G. AFLALO and Surgeon-General C. T. PASKE. With Illustrations. Crown 8vo., 4*s.* 6*d.*

Congo Free State and its Big Game Shooting, Travel and Adventures. By Captain H. BAILEY (BULA N'ZAU). Illustrated from the Author's sketches. Demy 8vo., 14*s.*

Sport: Fox Hunting, Salmon Fishing, Covert Shooting, Deer Stalking. By the late W. BROMLEY-DAVENPORT, M.P. With numerous Illustrations by General CREALOCK, C.B. New Cheap Edition. Post 8vo., 3*s.* 6*d.*

Log-Book of a Fisherman and Zoologist, By FRANK BUCKLAND. With Illustrations. Sixth Thousand. Crown 8vo., 3*s.* 6*d.*

English and American Yachts. By EDWARD BURGESS. Illustrated with 50 beautiful Photogravure Engravings. Oblong folio, 42*s.*

A Year of Sport and Natural History: Shooting, Hunting, Coursing, Falconry, and Fishing. Edited by OSWALD CRAWFURD. With Chapters on Birds of Prey, Nidifications of Birds, and Tricks of Poachers. With numerous Illustrations by FRANK FELLER, BRYAN HOOD, CECIL ALDIN, A. T. ELWES, E. NEALE, JOHN BEER, F. VIENZENY, STANLEY BERKELEY, and G. E. LODGE. Large Paper Edition.

A Mirror of the Turf; or, The Machinery of Horse-racing Revealed, showing the Sport of Kings as it is to-day. By LOUIS HENRY CURZON. Crown 8vo., 8*s.*

The Racehorse in Training, with Hints on Racing and Racing Reform. By WILLIAM DAY. Fifth Thousand. Demy 8vo., 9*s.*

The Highlands of Central India: Notes on their Forests and Wild Tribes, Natural History and Sports. By Captain FORSYTH. With Map and Coloured Illustrations. A New Edition. Demy 8vo., 12*s.*

SPORT—*CONTINUED.*

The Hunter's Arcadia. By PARKER GILLMORE. With numerous Illustrations. Demy 8vo., 10*s.* 6*d.*

Shooting and Salmon Fishing: HINTS AND RECOLLECTIONS. By A. GRIMBLE. Second Edition. With Illustrations. Demy 8vo., 16*s.*

Highland Sport. By AUGUSTUS GRIMBLE. With Twelve Illustrations by A. Thornburn. Large Paper Edition, 42*s.* net.

Gun, Rifle, and Hound in the East AND WEST. By "SNAFFLE." With Illustrations. Demy 8vo.

Travels, Sports, and Politics in the EAST OF EUROPE. By the Marquis of HUNTLY. With Illustrations. Large crown 8vo., 12*s.*

Norwegian Sketches: Fishing in Strange Waters. By EDWARD KENNARD. Illustrated with 30 beautiful Sketches. Second Edition. 14*s.*

How to Buy a Horse. With Hints on Shoeing and Stable Management. By PELAGIUS. Third Thousand. Crown 8vo., 1*s.*

Incidents of Foreign Sport and TRAVEL. By Colonel POLLOK, Author of "Sport in British Burma." With Illustrations. Demy 8vo., 16*s.*

Bear Hunting in the White Moun- TAINS; or, Alaska and British Columbia Revisited. By H. W. SETON-KARR, F.R.G.S., etc. Illustrated. Large crown, 4*s.* 6*d.*

Ten Years' Travel and Sport in FOREIGN LANDS; or, Travels in the Eighties. By H. W. SETON-KARR, F.R.G.S., etc. Large crown 8vo., 5*s.*

The Habits of the Salmon. By Major TRAHERNE. Crown 8vo., 3*s.* 6*d.*

Poachers and Poaching. By JOHN WATSON. With Frontispiece. Crown 8vo., 7*s.* 6*d.*

Sketches of British Sporting Fishes. By JOHN WATSON. With Frontispiece. Crown 8vo., 3*s.* 6*d.*

Five Months' Sport in Somali Land. By Lord WOLVERTON. With Illustrations. Demy 8vo., 7*s.* 6*d.*

Theology, Philosophy, Sociology, etc.

Handbook of Social Economy; or, The Worker's A B C. From the French. By EDMOND ABOUT. With a Biographical and Critical Introduction by W. FRASER RAE. Second Edition, revised. Crown 8vo., 4*s.*

Constructive Ethics: A Review of Modern Philosophy in its Three Stages of Interpretation, Criticism, and Reconstruction. By W. L. COURTNEY, M.A., LL.D., Demy 8vo., 12*s.*

The Yoruba-Speaking Peoples of the SLAVE COAST OF WEST AFRICA: their Religion, Manners, Customs, Laws, Language, &c. By A. B. ELLIS, Colonel 1st West India Regiment. With an Appendix and Map. Demy 8vo., 10*s.* 6*d.*

The Ewe-Speaking People of the SLAVE COAST OF WEST AFRICA. By A. B. ELLIS. With Map. Demy 8vo., 10*s.* 6*d.*

The Tshi-Speaking Peoples of the GOLD COAST; their Religion, Manners, Customs, Laws, Language, &c. By A. B. ELLIS. With Map. Demy 8vo., 10*s.* 6*d.*

The Science of Language: LINGUISTICS PHILOLOGY, AND ETYMOLOGY. By ABEL HOVELACQUE. With Maps. Large crown 8vo., cloth, 3*s.* 6*d.*

Philistines and Israelites: A New Light on the World's History. By H. MARTYN KENNARD. Demy 4to., 6*s.*

Jesus Christ; God; and God and Man. Conferences delivered at Notre Dame in Paris. By PERE LACORDAIRE. Seventh Thousand. Crown 8vo., 3*s.* 6*d.*

Human Origins: Evidence from History and Science. By S. LAING. With Illustrations. Twelfth Thousand. Demy 8vo., 3*s.* 6*d.*

Problems of the Future and Essays. By S. LAING. Thirteenth Thousand. Demy 8vo., 3*s.* 6*d.*

Modern Science and Modern Thought. By S. LAING. Nineteenth Thousand. Demy 8vo., 3*s.* 6*d.*

A Modern Zoroastrian. By S. LAING. Ninth Thousand. Demy 8vo., 3*s.* 6*d.*

THEOLOGY, &c.—*CONTINUED.*

Words of a Believer, and the Past AND FUTURE OF THE PEOPLE. By F. LAMENNAIS. Translated from the French by L. E. MARTINEAU. With a Memoir of Lamennais. Crown 8vo., 4*s.*

The Elements of Political Economy. By EMILE DE LAVELEYE. Translated by W. POLLARD, B.A., St. John's College, Oxford. Crown 8vo., 6*s.*

Evolution: Its Nature, Its Evidences, and Its Relations to Religious Thought. By JOSEPH LE CONTE, Professor of Geology and Natural History in the University of California. A New and Revised Edition. Crown 8vo. 6*s.*

Philosophy, Historical and Critical. By ANDRÉ LEFEVRE. Translated, with an Introduction, by A. W. KEANE, B.A. Large crown 8vo., 3*s.* 6*d.*

Papacy, Socialism, and Democracy. By ANATOLE LEROY-BEAULIEU, Member of the Institute of France. Translated by Professor B. L. O'DONNELL. Crown 8vo., 7*s.* 6*d.*

Sociology. Based upon Ethnology. By Dr. CHARLES LETOURNEAU. Large crown 8vo., 3*s.* 6*d.*

Biology. By Dr. CHARLES LETOURNEAU. With 83 Illustrations. A New Edition. Demy 8vo., 3*s.* 6*d.*

The Claims of Christianity. By W. S. LILLY. Demy 8vo., 12*s.*

On Shibboleths. By W. S. LILLY. Demy 8vo., 12*s.*

On Right and Wrong. By W. S. LILLY. Second Edition. Demy 8vo., 12*s.*

Chapters on European History. By W. S. LILLY. With an Introductory Dialogue on the Philosophy of History. 2 vols. Demy 8vo., 21*s.*

A Century of Revolution. By W. S. LILLY. Second Edition. Demy 8vo., 12*s.*

Ancient Religion and Modern THOUGHT. By W. S. LILLY. Second Edition. Demy 8vo., 12*s.*

The Progress of Science: Its Origin, Course, Promoters and Results. By V. MARMERY. Demy 8vo.

The Future of Science: Ideas of 1848. By ERNEST RENAN. Demy 8vo., 18*s.*

History of the People of Israel. By ERNEST RENAN.

FIRST DIVISION. Till the Time of King David. Demy 8vo., 14*s.*

SECOND DIVISION. From the Reign of David up to the Capture of Samaria. Demy 8vo., 14*s.*

THIRD DIVISION. From the time of Hezekiah till the return from Babylon. Demy 8vo., 14*s.*

Esoteric Buddhism. By A. P. SINNETT. Annotated and enlarged by the Author. Seventh Edition. Crown 8vo., 3*s.* 6*d.*

Aphorisms from the Writings of HERBERT SPENCER. Selected by JULIA RAYMOND GINGELL. With a Photogravure Portrait. Second Thousand. Crown 8vo., 3*s.*

Anthropology. By Dr. PAUL TOPINARD. With a Preface by Professor PAUL BROCA. With 49 Illustrations. Demy 8vo., 3*s.* 6*d.*

Æsthetics. By EUGENE VERON. Translated by W. H. ARMSTRONG. Large crown 8vo., 3*s.* 6*d.*

A Modern Layman's Faith Concern-ING THE CREED AND THE BREED OF THE "THOROUGHBRED MAN." By W. B. WOODGATE. Demy 8vo., 14*s.*

Travel.

Woman in India. By MARY FRANCES BILLINGTON. With a preface by the Marchioness of DUFFERIN and AVA, C.I., and numerous Illustrations by HERBERT JOHNSON and others. Demy 8vo.

Through the Heart of Asia over the PAMIR TO INDIA. By GABRIEL BONVALOT. Translated from the French by C. B. PITMAN. With 250 Illustrations by ALBERT PÉPIN. Royal 8vo., 32*s.*

Winters in Algeria. By F. A. BRIDGMAN. With 62 Illustrations. Royal 8vo., 10*s.* 6*d.*

Two Summers in Greenland: An Artist's Adventures among Ice and Islands in Fjords and Mountains. By A. RIIS CARSTENSEN. With numerous Illustrations by the Author. Demy 8vo., 14*s.*

The Ancient Cities of the New World. Being Travels and Explorations in Mexico and Central America, 1857–1882. By DÉSIRÉ CHARNAY. With upwards of 200 Illustrations. Super royal 8vo., 31*s.* 6*d.*

Round the Calendar in Portugal. By OSWALD CRAWFURD. With numerous Illustrations. Royal 8vo., 18*s.*

TRAVEL—*CONTINUED.*

Sketches of Hindoo Life. By DEVENDRA N. DAS. Crown 8vo., 5*s*.

Three Months' Tour in Ireland. By MADAME DE BOVET. Translated and Condensed by Mrs. ARTHUR WALTER. With Illustrations. Crown 8vo., 6*s*.

Around Tonkin and Siam. By Prince HENRY D'ORLEANS. Translated by C. B. PITMAN. With 28 Illustrations. Demy 8vo., 14*s*.

From Pekin to Calais by Land. By H. DE WINDT. With numerous Illustrations by C. E. FRIPP from Sketches by the Author. New and Cheaper Edition. 7*s*. 6*d*.

A Ride to India Across Persia and BELUCHISTAN. By H. DE WINDT. With numerous Illustrations. Demy 8vo., 16*s*.

American Notes and **Pictures from** ITALY. By CHARLES DICKENS. With 8 Illustrations. Demy 8vo., 10*s*.; post 8vo., 8*s*.; crown 8vo., 5*s*., 3*s*. 6*d*., 2*s*. 6*d*. and 2*s*.; 4to., 3*s*.; royal 8vo., 3*s*. 6*d*.; fcap. 8vo., 1*s*. 6*d*.

Gibraltar. By HENRY M. FIELD. With numerous Illustrations. Demy 8vo., 7*s*. 6*d*.

The Highlands of Central India: Notes on their Forests and Wild Tribes, Natural History and Sports. By Captain FORSYTH. With Map and Coloured Illustrations. A new Edition. Demy 8vo., 12*s*.

Round About the Crooked Spire. By ALBERT J. FOSTER, M.A. With Illustrations. Crown 8vo., 5*s*.

With the Camel Corps up the Nile. By Count GLEICHEN. With numerous Sketches by the Author. Third Edition. Large crown 8vo., 9*s*.

A Land of Mosques and Marabouts. By the Hon. Mrs. GREVILLE-NUGENT. Illustrated. Demy 8vo., 14*s*.

The Marches of Wales: Notes and Impressions on the Welsh Borders, from the Severn Sea to the Sands o' Dee. By CHARLES G. HARPER. With 114 Illustrations. Demy 8vo.

A Week's Tramp in Dickens-Land. By W. R. HUGHES, F.L.S. With upwards of 100 Illustrations by F. G. KITTON, HERBERT RAILTON, and others. Second Edition. Demy 8vo., 7*s*. 6*d*.

Travels, Sports, and Politics in the EAST OF EUROPE. By the Marquis of HUNTLY. With Illustrations. Large crown 8vo., 12*s*.

Life Aboard a British Privateer in the Time of Queen Anne. Being the Journals of Captain Woodes Rogers, Master Mariner. With Notes and Illustrations by R. C. LESLIE. A New and Cheaper Edition. Large crown 8vo., 3*s*. 6*d*.

Travels in Africa. By Dr. WM. JUNKER. Translated from the German by Professor KEANE.

Vol. I. DURING THE YEARS 1875 TO 1878. Containing 38 Full-page Plates and 125 Illustrations in the Text and Map. Demy 8vo., 21*s*.

Vol. II. DURING THE YEARS 1879 TO 1883. Containing numerous Full-page Plates and Illustrations in the Text and Map. Demy 8vo., 21*s*.

Vol. III. DURING THE YEARS 1882 TO 1886. Containing numerous Full-page Plates and Illustrations in the Text and Maps. Demy 8vo., 21*s*.

Across the Border; or, Pathan and Biloch. By E. E. OLIVER, Under-Secretary to the Public Works Department, Punjaub. With numerous Illustrations by J. L. KIPLING, C.I.E. Demy 8vo., 14*s*.

Round about New Zealand. Being Notes from a Journal of Three Years' Wandering in the Antipodes. By E. W. PAYTON. With Twenty Original Illustrations by the Author. Large crown 8vo., 12*s*.

Incidents of Foreign Sport and Travel. By Colonel POLLOK, Author of "Sport in British Burma." With Illustrations by A. T. ELWES. Demy 8vo., 16*s*.

A Suburb of Yedo. By the late THEOBALD A. PURCELL. Illustrated. Crown 8vo., 2*s*. 6*d*.

Spanish Cities: with Glimpses of Gibraltar and Tangiers. By C. A. STODDARD. With 18 Illustrations. Large crown 8vo., 7*s*. 6*d*.

Across Russia from the Baltic to the DANUBE. By C. A. STODDARD. With numerous Illustrations. Large crown 8vo., 7*s*. 6*d*.

With Stanley's Rear Column. By J. ROSE TROUP. With Portraits and Illustrations. Second Edition. Demy 8vo., 16*s*.

Untrodden Paths in Roumania. By Mrs. WALKER. With 77 Illustrations. Demy 8vo., 10*s*. 6*d*.

Eastern Life and Scenery, with Excursions to Asia Minor, Mitylene, Crete, and Roumania. By Mrs. WALKER. 2 vols., with Frontispiece to each vol. Crown 8vo., 21*s*.

A Month in Yorkshire. By WALTER WHITE. With a Map. Fifth Edition. Post 8vo., 4*s*.

A Londoner's Walk to the Land's END, AND A TRIP TO THE SCILLY ISLES. By WALTER WHITE. With 4 Maps. Third Edition. Post 8vo., 4*s*.

THOMAS CARLYLE'S WORKS.

THE ASHBURTON EDITION.

Handsomely printed, containing all the Portraits and Illustrations, in Twenty Volumes, demy 8vo., 8s. each.

THE FRENCH REVOLUTION AND PAST AND PRESENT. 2 vols.
SARTOR RESARTUS; HEROES AND HERO WORSHIP. 1 vol.
LIFE OF JOHN STERLING—LIFE OF SCHILLER. 1 vol.
LATTER-DAY PAMPHLETS—EARLY KINGS OF NORWAY—ESSAY ON THE PORTRAIT OF JOHN KNOX. 1 vol.
LETTERS AND SPEECHES OF OLIVER CROMWELL. 3 vols.
HISTORY OF FREDERICK THE GREAT. 6 vols.
CRITICAL AND MISCELLANEOUS ESSAYS. 3 vols.
TRANSLATIONS FROM THE GERMAN. 3 vols.

LIBRARY EDITION.

Handsomely printed in 34 Vols., demy 8vo., £15 3s.

SARTOR RESARTUS. With a Portrait, 7*s.* 6*d.*

THE FRENCH REVOLUTION. A History. 3 vols., each 9*s.*

LIFE OF FREDERICK SCHILLER AND EXAMINATION OF HIS WORKS. With Supplement of 1872. Portrait and Plates, 9*s.*

CRITICAL AND MISCELLANEOUS ESSAYS. With Portrait. 6 vols., each 9*s.*

ON HEROES, HERO WORSHIP, AND THE HEROIC IN HISTORY. 7*s.* 6*d.*

PAST AND PRESENT. 9*s.*

OLIVER CROMWELL'S LETTERS AND SPEECHES. With Portraits. 5 vols., each 9*s.*

LATTER-DAY PAMPHLETS. 9*s.*

LIFE OF JOHN STERLING. With Portrait, 9*s.*

HISTORY OF FREDERICK THE SECOND. 10 vols., each 9*s.*

TRANSLATIONS FROM THE GERMAN. 3 vols., each 9*s.*

EARLY KINGS OF NORWAY; ESSAY ON THE PORTRAITS OF JOHN KNOX; AND GENERAL INDEX. With Portrait Illustrations. 8vo., cloth, 9*s.*

PEOPLE'S EDITION.

37 *vols., small crown 8vo.,* 37*s.; separate vols.,* 1*s. each.*

SARTOR RESARTUS. With Portrait of Thomas Carlyle.

FRENCH REVOLUTION. A History. 3 vols.

OLIVER CROMWELL'S LETTERS AND SPEECHES. 5 vols. With Portrait of Oliver Cromwell.

ON HEROES AND HERO WORSHIP AND THE HEROIC IN HISTORY.

PAST AND PRESENT.

CRITICAL AND MISCELLANEOUS ESSAYS. 7 vols.

THE LIFE OF SCHILLER AND EXAMINATION OF HIS WORKS. With Portrait.

LATTER-DAY PAMPHLETS.

WILHELM MEISTER. 3 vols.

LIFE OF JOHN STERLING. With Portrait.

HISTORY OF FREDERICK THE GREAT. 10 vols.

TRANSLATIONS FROM MUSÆUS, TIECK, AND RICHTER. 2 vols.

THE EARLY KINGS OF NORWAY; Essay on the Portraits of Knox.

Or in sets, 37 *vols. in* 18, 37*s.*

THOMAS CARLYLE'S WORKS—*Continued.*

THE HALF-CROWN EDITION.

This Edition includes the whole of Carlyle's Writings and Translations, together with the Portraits and Maps, and is complete in twenty volumes. Crown 8vo. Price 2*s.* 6*d.* each.

SARTOR RESARTUS AND LATTER-DAY PAMPHLETS. With a Portrait of Thomas Carlyle.

PAST AND PRESENT AND ON HEROES AND HERO WORSHIP.

LIFE OF JOHN STERLING AND LIFE OF SCHILLER.

CRITICAL AND MISCELLANEOUS ESSAYS, EARLY KINGS OF NORWAY, AND ESSAY ON THE PORTRAITS OF KNOX. *In four volumes.*

FRENCH REVOLUTION: A HISTORY. *In two volumes.*

OLIVER CROMWELL'S LETTERS AND SPEECHES, with Portrait of Oliver Cromwell. *In three volumes.*

HISTORY OF FREDERICK THE GREAT. *In five volumes.*

WILHELM MEISTER. *In two volumes.*

TRANSLATIONS FROM MUSÆUS, TIECK AND RICHTER. *In one volume.*

CHEAP ISSUE.

Bound in Blue Cloth.

THE FRENCH REVOLUTION. One volume. With Portrait. Crown 8vo., 2*s.*

SARTOR RESARTUS, HEROES AND HERO WORSHIP, PAST AND PRESENT, AND CHARTISM. One volume. Crown 8vo., 2*s.*

OLIVER CROMWELL'S LETTERS AND SPEECHES. Crown 8vo., 2*s.* 6*d.*

CRITICAL AND MISCELLANEOUS ESSAYS. 2 vols. 4*s.*

WILHELM MEISTER. One volume, 2*s.*

LIVES OF SCHILLER AND STERLING. With Portraits. One volume, 2*s.*

SIXPENNY EDITION. *4to., sewed.*

SARTOR RESARTUS. Eightieth Thousand.

HEROES AND HERO WORSHIP.

ESSAYS: BURNS, JOHNSON, SCOTT, THE DIAMOND NECKLACE.

The above in 1 vol., cloth, 2s. 6d.

CHARLES DICKENS'S WORKS.

ORIGINAL EDITIONS.

In demy 8vo.

THE MYSTERY OF EDWIN DROOD. With Illustrations by S. L. FILDES, and a Portrait engraved by BAKER. Cloth, 7*s.* 6*d.*

OUR MUTUAL FRIEND. With Forty Illustrations by MARCUS STONE. Cloth, £1 1*s.*

THE PICKWICK PAPERS. With Forty-three Illustrations by SEYMOUR and PHIZ. Cloth, £1 1*s.*

NICHOLAS NICKLEBY. With Forty Illustrations by PHIZ. Cloth, £1 1*s.*

SKETCHES BY "BOZ." With Forty Illustrations by GEORGE CRUIKSHANK. Cloth, £1 1*s.*

MARTIN CHUZZLEWIT. With Forty Illustrations by PHIZ. Cloth, £1 1*s.*

DOMBEY AND SON. With Forty Illustrations by PHIZ. Cloth, £1 1*s.*

DAVID COPPERFIELD. With Forty Illustrations by PHIZ. Cloth, £1 1*s.*

BLEAK HOUSE. With Forty Illustrations by PHIZ. Cloth, £1 1*s.*

LITTLE DORRIT. With Forty Illustrations by PHIZ. Cloth, £1 1*s.*

THE OLD CURIOSITY SHOP. With Seventy-five Illustrations by GEORGE CATTERMOLE and H. K. BROWNE. A New Edition. Uniform with the other volumes, £1 1*s.*

BARNABY RUDGE: A Tale of the Riots of 'Eighty. With Seventy-eight Illustrations by GEORGE CATTERMOLE and H. K. BROWNE. Uniform with the other volumes, £1 1*s.*

CHRISTMAS BOOKS: Containing—The Christmas Carol; The Cricket on the Hearth; The Chimes; The Battle of Life; The Haunted House. With all the original Illustrations. Cloth, 12*s.*

OLIVER TWIST AND TALE OF TWO CITIES. In one volume. Cloth, £1 1*s.*

OLIVER TWIST. Separately. With Twenty-four Illustrations by GEORGE CRUIKSHANK. Cloth, 11*s.*

A TALE OF TWO CITIES. Separately. With Sixteen Illustrations by PHIZ. Cloth, 9*s.*

*** *The remainder of Dickens's Works were not originally printed in demy 8vo.*

LIBRARY EDITION.

In post 8vo. With the Original Illustrations, 30 vols., cloth, £12.

	Illustrations.	Vols.	*s.*	*d.*
PICKWICK PAPERS	43	2	16	0
NICHOLAS NICKLEBY	39	2	16	0
MARTIN CHUZZLEWIT	40	2	16	0
OLD CURIOSITY SHOP AND REPRINTED PIECES	36	2	16	0
BARNABY RUDGE AND HARD TIMES	36	2	16	0
BLEAK HOUSE	40	2	16	0
LITTLE DORRIT	40	2	16	0
DOMBEY AND SON	38	2	16	0
DAVID COPPERFIELD	38	2	16	0
OUR MUTUAL FRIEND	40	2	16	0
SKETCHES BY "BOZ"	39	1	8	0
OLIVER TWIST	24	1	8	0
CHRISTMAS BOOKS	17	1	8	0
A TALE OF TWO CITIES	16	1	8	0
GREAT EXPECTATIONS	8	1	8	0
PICTURES FROM ITALY AND AMERICAN NOTES	8	1	8	0
UNCOMMERCIAL TRAVELLER	8	1	8	0
CHILD'S HISTORY OF ENGLAND	8	1	8	0
EDWIN DROOD AND MISCELLANIES	12	1	8	0
CHRISTMAS STORIES from "Household Words," &c.	14	1	8	0

Uniform with the above, 10*s.* 6*d.*

THE LIFE OF CHARLES DICKENS. By JOHN FORSTER. With Illustrations.

CHARLES DICKENS'S WORKS—*Continued.*

THE "CHARLES DICKENS" EDITION.

In crown 8vo. In 21 vols., cloth, with Illustrations, £3 16s.

	Illustrations.	*s.*	*d.*
PICKWICK PAPERS	8 ...	4	0
MARTIN CHUZZLEWIT	8 ...	4	0
DOMBEY AND SON	8 ...	4	0
NICHOLAS NICKLEBY	8 ...	4	0
DAVID COPPERFIELD	8 ...	4	0
BLEAK HOUSE...	8 ...	4	0
LITTLE DORRIT	8 ...	4	0
OUR MUTUAL FRIEND	8 ...	4	0
BARNABY RUDGE	8 ...	3	6
OLD CURIOSITY SHOP	8 ...	3	6
A CHILD'S HISTORY OF ENGLAND	4 ...	3	6
EDWIN DROOD AND OTHER STORIES	8 ...	3	6
CHRISTMAS STORIES from "Household Words" ...	8 ...	3	6
SKETCHES BY "BOZ"	8 ...	3	6
AMERICAN NOTES AND REPRINTED PIECES	8 ...	3	6
CHRISTMAS BOOKS	8 ...	3	6
OLIVER TWIST	8 ...	3	6
GREAT EXPECTATIONS	8 ...	3	6
TALE OF TWO CITIES	8 ...	3	0
HARD TIMES AND PICTURES FROM ITALY	8 ...	3	0
UNCOMMERCIAL TRAVELLER	4 ...	3	0

Uniform with the above.

THE LIFE OF CHARLES DICKENS. Numerous Illustrations.	2 vols.	7	0
THE LETTERS OF CHARLES DICKENS. 2 vols.		7	0

THE HALF-CROWN EDITION.

PRINTED FROM THE EDITION THAT WAS CAREFULLY CORRECTED BY THE AUTHOR, IN 1867 AND 1868.

Complete in 21 vols. Containing the whole of the original Illustrations.
Crown 8vo., 2s. 6d. each.

THE PICKWICK PAPERS. With 43 Illustrations by SEYMOUR and PHIZ.

BARNABY RUDGE: A Tale of the Riots of 'Eighty. With 76 Illustrations by GEORGE CATTERMOLE and H. K. BROWNE.

OLIVER TWIST. With 24 Illustrations by CRUIKSHANK.

THE OLD CURIOSITY SHOP. With 75 Illustrations by GEORGE CATTERMOLE and H. K. BROWNE.

DAVID COPPERFIELD. With 40 Illustrations by PHIZ.

NICHOLAS NICKLEBY. With 40 Illustrations by PHIZ.

MARTIN CHUZZLEWIT. With 40 Illustrations by PHIZ.

DOMBEY AND SON. With 40 Illustrations by PHIZ.

SKETCHES BY "BOZ." With 40 Illustrations by GEORGE CRUIKSHANK.

CHRISTMAS BOOKS. With 64 Illustrations by LANDSEER, DOYLE, MACLISE, LEECH, etc.

BLEAK HOUSE. With 40 Illustrations by PHIZ.

LITTLE DORRIT. With 40 Illustrations by PHIZ.

CHRISTMAS STORIES, from "Household Words." With 14 Illustrations by DALZIEL, GREEN, MAHONEY, etc.

AMERICAN NOTES and REPRINTED PIECES. With 8 Illustrations by MARCUS STONE and F. WALKER.

HARD TIMES and PICTURES FROM ITALY. With 8 Illustrations by F. WALKER and MARCUS STONE.

A CHILD'S HISTORY OF ENGLAND. With 8 Illustrations by MARCUS STONE.

GREAT EXPECTATIONS. With 8 Illustrations by MARCUS STONE.

TALE OF TWO CITIES. With 16 Illustrations by PHIZ.

UNCOMMERCIAL TRAVELLER. With 8 Illustrations by MARCUS STONE.

OUR MUTUAL FRIEND. With 40 Illustrations by MARCUS STONE.

EDWIN DROOD and OTHER STORIES. With 12 Illustrations by LUKE FILDES.

CHARLES DICKENS'S WORKS—*Continued.*

THE ILLUSTRATED LIBRARY EDITION.

Complete in 32 Volumes. Demy 8vo., 10s. each; or set, £16.

This Edition is printed on a finer paper and in a larger type than has been employed in any previous edition. The type has been cast especially for it, and the page is of a size to admit of the introduction of all the original illustrations.

No such attractive issue has been made of the writings of Mr. Dickens, which, various as have been the forms of publication adapted to the demands of an ever widely-increasing popularity, have never yet been worthily presented in a really handsome library form.

The collection comprises all the minor writings it was Mr. Dickens's wish to preserve.

SKETCHES BY "BOZ." With 40 Illustrations by GEORGE CRUIKSHANK.

PICKWICK PAPERS. 2 vols. With 42 Illustrations by PHIZ.

OLIVER TWIST. With 24 Illustrations by CRUIKSHANK.

NICHOLAS NICKLEBY. 2 vols. With 40 Illustrations by PHIZ.

OLD CURIOSITY SHOP AND REPRINTED PIECES. 2 vols. With Illustrations by CATTERMOLE, &c.

BARNABY RUDGE AND HARD TIMES. 2 vols. With Illustrations by CATTERMOLE, &c.

MARTIN CHUZZLEWIT. 2 vols. With 40 Illustrations by PHIZ.

AMERICAN NOTES AND PICTURES FROM ITALY. 1 vol. With 8 Illusts.

DOMBEY AND SON. 2 vols. With 40 Illustrations by PHIZ.

DAVID COPPERFIELD. 2 vols. With 40 Illustrations by PHIZ.

BLEAK HOUSE. 2 vols. With 40 Illustrations by PHIZ.

LITTLE DORRIT. 2 vols. With 40 Illustrations by PHIZ.

A TALE OF TWO CITIES. With 16 Illustrations by PHIZ.

THE UNCOMMERCIAL TRAVELLER. With 8 Illustrations by MARCUS STONE.

GREAT EXPECTATIONS. With 8 Illustrations by MARCUS STONE.

OUR MUTUAL FRIEND. 2 vols. With 40 Illustrations by MARCUS STONE.

CHRISTMAS BOOKS. With 17 Illustrations by Sir EDWIN LANDSEER, R.A., MACLISE, R.A., &c., &c.

HISTORY OF ENGLAND. With 8 Illustrations by MARCUS STONE.

CHRISTMAS STORIES. (From "Household Words" and "All the Year Round.") With 14 Illustrations.

EDWIN DROOD AND OTHER STORIES. With 12 Illustrations by S. L. FILDES.

Uniform with above.

LIFE OF CHARLES DICKENS. By JOHN FORSTER. With Portraits. 2 vols.

HOUSEHOLD EDITION.

(WITH LIFE.)

In 22 Volumes. Crown 4to., cloth, £4 8s. 6d.

MARTIN CHUZZLEWIT. With 59 Illustrations, 5s.

DAVID COPPERFIELD. With 60 Illustrations and a Portrait, 5s.

BLEAK HOUSE. With 61 Illustrations, 5s.

LITTLE DORRIT. With 58 Illus., 5s.

PICKWICK PAPERS. With 56 Illus., 5s.

OUR MUTUAL FRIEND. With 58 Illustrations, 5s.

NICHOLAS NICKLEBY. With 59 Illustrations, 5s.

DOMBEY AND SON. With 61 Illus., 5s.

EDWIN DROOD; REPRINTED PIECES; and other Stories, with 30 Illustrations, 5s.

THE LIFE OF DICKENS. By JOHN FORSTER. With 40 Illustrations, 5s.

BARNABY RUDGE. With 46 Illus., 4s.

OLD CURIOSITY SHOP. With 32 Illustrations, 4s.

CHRISTMAS STORIES. With 23 Illustrations, 4s.

OLIVER TWIST. With 28 Illus., 3s.

GREAT EXPECTATIONS. With 26 Illustrations, 3s.

SKETCHES BY "BOZ." With 36 Illus. 3s.

UNCOMMERCIAL TRAVELLER. With 26 Illustrations, 3s.

CHRISTMAS BOOKS. With 28 Illus., 3s.

THE HISTORY OF ENGLAND. With 15 Illustrations, 3s.

AMERICAN NOTES AND PICTURES FROM ITALY. With 18 Illus., 3s.

A TALE OF TWO CITIES. With 25 Illustrations, 3s.

HARD TIMES. With 20 Illus., 2s. 6d.

CHARLES DICKENS'S WORKS—*Continued.*

THE CROWN EDITION,

Complete in 17 vols. Containing all the Original Illustrations; and the Letterpress is printed from Type expressly cast for this Edition. Large Crown 8vo. Price Five Shillings each.

THE PICKWICK PAPERS. With Forty-three Illustrations by SEYMOUR and PHIZ.

NICHOLAS NICKLEBY. With Forty Illustrations by PHIZ.

DOMBEY AND SON. With Forty Illustrations by PHIZ.

DAVID COPPERFIELD. With Forty Illustrations by PHIZ.

SKETCHES BY "BOZ." With Forty Illustrations by GEO. CRUIKSHANK.

MARTIN CHUZZLEWIT. With Forty Illustrations by PHIZ.

THE OLD CURIOSITY SHOP. With Seventy-five Illustrations by GEORGE CATTERMOLE and H. K. BROWNE.

BARNABY RUDGE: a Tale of the Riots of 'Eighty. With Seventy-eight Illustrations by GEORGE CATTERMOLE and H. K. BROWNE.

OLIVER TWIST and A TALE OF TWO CITIES. With Twenty-four Illustrations by CRUIKSHANK and Sixteen by PHIZ.

BLEAK HOUSE. With Forty Illustrations by PHIZ.

LITTLE DORRIT. With Forty Illustrations by PHIZ.

OUR MUTUAL FRIEND. With Forty Illustrations by MARCUS STONE.

AMERICAN NOTES; PICTURES FROM ITALY; and A CHILD'S HISTORY OF ENGLAND. With Sixteen Illustrations by MARCUS STONE.

CHIRSTMAS BOOKS AND HARD TIMES. With Illustrations by LANDSEER, MACLISE, STANFIELD, LEECH, DOYLE, F. WALKER, etc.

CHRISTMAS STORIES AND OTHER STORIES, including HUMPHREY'S CLOCK. With Illustrations by DALZIEL, CHARLES GREEN, MAHONEY, PHIZ, CATTERMOLE, etc.

GREAT EXPECTATIONS. UNCOMMERCIAL TRAVELLER. With Sixteen Illustrations by MARCUS STONE.

EDWIN DROOD and REPRINTED PIECES. With Sixteen Illustrations by LUKE FILDES and F. WALKER.

Uniform with the above.

THE LIFE OF CHARLES DICKENS. By JOHN FORSTER. With Portraits and Illustrations. Will be added at the request of numerous Subscribers.

THE DICKENS DICTIONARY. A Key to the Characters and Principal Incidents in the Tales of Charles Dickens. By GILBERT PIERCE, with additions by WILLIAM A. WHEELER.

THE LAZY TOUR OF TWO IDLE APPRENTICES; NO THOROUGHFARE; THE PERILS OF CERTAIN ENGLISH PRISONERS. By CHARLES DICKENS and WILKIE COLLINS. With Illustrations. Crown 8vo., *5s.*

⁂ These Stories are now reprinted in complete form for the first time.

CHARLES DICKENS'S CHRISTMAS BOOKS.

REPRINTED FROM THE ORIGINAL PLATES.

Illustrated by JOHN LEECH, D. MACLISE, R.A., R. DOYLE, C. STANFIELD, R.A., *etc.*

Fcap. cloth, 1s. each. Complete in a case, 5s.

A CHRISTMAS CAROL IN PROSE.

THE CHIMES: A GOBLIN STORY.

THE CRICKET ON THE HEARTH: A FAIRY TALE OF HOME.

THE BATTLE OF LIFE. A LOVE STORY.

THE HAUNTED MAN AND THE GHOST'S STORY.

SIXPENNY REPRINTS of DICKENS'S WORKS.

OLIVER TWIST. With 28 Illustrations by J. MAHONEY. Medium 8vo.

READINGS FROM THE WORKS OF CHARLES DICKENS. As selected and read by himself, and now published for the first time. Illustrated.

A CHRISTMAS CAROL AND THE HAUNTED MAN. Illustrated.

THE CHIMES: A GOBLIN STORY, AND THE CRICKET ON THE HEARTH. Illustrated.

THE BATTLE OF LIFE: A LOVE STORY, HUNTED DOWN, AND A HOLIDAY ROMANCE. Illustrated.

CHARLES DICKENS'S WORKS—*Continued.*

THE CABINET EDITION.

In 32 vols., small fcap. 8vo., Marble Paper Sides, Cloth Backs, with uncut edges, price Eighteenpence each. Each Volume contains Eight Illustrations reproduced from the Originals. In Sets only, bound in blue and red cloth, with cut edges, £2 8s.

CHRISTMAS BOOKS.
MARTIN CHUZZLEWIT, 2 vols.
DAVID COPPERFIELD, 2 vols.
OLIVER TWIST.
GREAT EXPECTATIONS.
NICHOLAS NICKLEBY, 2 vols.
SKETCHES BY "BOZ."
CHRISTMAS STORIES.
THE PICKWICK PAPERS, 2 vols.
BARNABY RUDGE, 2 vols.
BLEAK HOUSE, 2 vols.
AMERICAN NOTES AND PICTURES FROM ITALY.
EDWIN DROOD; & OTHER STORIES.
THE OLD CURIOSITY SHOP, 2 vols.
A CHILD'S HISTORY OF ENGLAND.
DOMBEY AND SON, 2 vols.
A TALE OF TWO CITIES.
LITTLE DORRIT, 2 vols.
MUTUAL FRIEND, 2 vols.
HARD TIMES.
UNCOMMERCIAL TRAVELLER.
REPRINTED PIECES.

THE PICTORIAL EDITION.

CONTAINING UPWARDS OF NINE HUNDRED ENGRAVINGS.

Complete in 17 vols. Royal 8vo., 3s. 6d. each.

DOMBEY AND SON. With 62 Illustrations by F. BARNARD.

DAVID COPPERFIELD. With 61 Illustrations by F. BARNARD.

NICHOLAS NICKLEBY. With 59 Illustrations by F. BARNARD.

BARNABY RUDGE. With 46 Illustrations by F. BARNARD.

OLD CURIOSITY SHOP. With 39 Illustrations by CHARLES GREEN.

MARTIN CHUZZLEWIT. With 59 Illustrations by F. BARNARD.

OLIVER TWIST AND A TALE OF TWO CITIES. With 53 Illustrations by J. MAHONEY and F. BARNARD.

OUR MUTUAL FRIEND. With 58 Illustrations by J. MAHONEY.

BLEAK HOUSE. With 61 Illustrations by F. BARNARD.

PICKWICK PAPERS. With 57 Illustrations by PHIZ.

LITTLE DORRIT. With 58 Illustrations by J. MAHONEY.

GREAT EXPECTATIONS AND HARD TIMES. With 50 Illustrations by J. A. FRASER and H. FRENCH.

AMERICAN NOTES, PICTURES FROM ITALY, AND A CHILD'S HISTORY OF ENGLAND. With 33 Illustrations by FROST, GORDON, THOMSON, and RALSTON.

SKETCHES BY "BOZ" AND CHRISTMAS BOOKS. With 62 Illustrations by F. BARNARD.

CHRISTMAS STORIES AND UNCOMMERCIAL TRAVELLER. With 49 Illustrations by E. G. DALZIEL.

EDWIN DROOD, REPRINTED PIECES, AND OTHER STORIES. With 30 Illustrations by L. FILDES, E. G. DALZIEL, and F. BARNARD.

THE LIFE OF CHARLES DICKENS. By JOHN FORSTER. With 40 Illustrations by F. BARNARD and others.

THE TWO-SHILLING EDITION.

Each Volume contains a Frontispiece. Crown 8vo., 2s.

DOMBEY AND SON.
MARTIN CHUZZLEWIT.
THE PICKWICK PAPERS.
BLEAK HOUSE.
OLD CURIOSITY SHOP.
BARNABY RUDGE.
DAVID COPPERFIELD.
NICHOLAS NICKLEBY.
CHRISTMAS STORIES.
AMERICAN NOTES.
HARD TIMES AND PICTURES FROM ITALY.
GREAT EXPECTATIONS.
OUR MUTUAL FRIEND.
CHRISTMAS BOOKS.
OLIVER TWIST.
LITTLE DORRIT.
TALE OF TWO CITIES.
UNCOMMERCIAL TRAVELLER.
SKETCHES BY "BOZ."
A CHILD'S HISTORY OF ENGLAND.
EDWIN DROOD AND OTHER STORIES.